PUNJAB CRICKET ASSOCIATION
spice
spice

Cricket at Fever Pitch

Cricket
at Fever Pitch

KHALID A-H ANSARI
Edited by Clayton Murzello

Popular Prakashan
www.popularprakashan.com

POPULAR PRAKASHAN PVT. LTD.
35-C, Pandit Madan Mohan Malaviya Marg
Tardeo, Mumbai 400 034

ISBN 81-7991-257-4
(4005)

Edited: Clayton Murzello
Cover Photo: Suresh K.K.
Cover Design: Sushil Mhatre
Text seperator graphics: Niti Modi
Cartoons: Austin Coutinho and Satish Acharya

For enquiries: info@popularprakashan.com

Typeset by Vans Information Limited
35-C, Pandit Madan Mohan Malaviya Marg
Tardeo, Mumbai 400 034

Printed in India by Saurabh Printers Pvt. Ltd.,
Noida 201 301

Published by Ramdas Bhatkal for Popular Prakashan Pvt. Ltd.
35-C, Pandit Madan Mohan Malaviya Marg
Tardeo, Mumbai 400 034

FOREWORD BY SUNIL GAVASKAR

It's a real pleasure to write this though I am under no illusions that it will be even half as good as Khalid's writings have been over the years. Yes, over the years indeed, as I have known Khalid since the time he came over to my house to talk after the Indian team had returned from the triumphant tour of the West Indies in 1971.

That was my first interview after that memorable trip and I well remember Khalid coming in with Tariq and Sharique and how the two kids, after being shy at first, were running around the house and had virtually settled down and were still only when we were taking photographs before they left.

Khalid won me over as soon as he praised my mother's cooking for the snacks she had prepared and that was the beginning of a friendship which has seen both of us lose a fair bit of hair, though of course he hasn't ever bothered to colour his.

The other reason for the friendship is the trust that was built up when the interview appeared without a single extra word being put in my mouth and no fancy eye-catching and misleading headline either. While most people in public life love to see their names in print there's always the apprehension that an odd word here and there, if not more, will be added to make the story sound more interesting and that's why there's invariably a bit of reserve between the media and the public person. Often it isn't the fault of the one who has taken the interview for it may well be his boss, the editor or the night editor who may have given the mischievous headline, but of course, Khalid himself was the boss so there was never a worry of a headline or words being added for effect.

All the articles that Khalid has written over the years have one feature and that's integrity. When he takes a stand its because he has looked at all the angles and then taken a decision and once that's done then there's no budging from it, even if it means authority will be displeased. He has never been afraid to take on the establishment, especially when others are hesitant to do so and often has led the way. Be it simply politics or corporate politics or sport politics, he has never been afraid to take on the biggies if they are wrong.

His articles are clear, precise and come to the point without too much skirting around the main subject. There's thought in it, there's study in it, there's a vision in it and yes, often humour in it. That's what the readers will find in this book of compilation of the columns he has written over the years. It's not just good reading but also thought provoking and I am sure the book will be enjoyed by all those who get to read it.

As for me, I am sure that we will at a convivial evening in the none too distant future talk about the grammatical errors made by me in writing this foreword as he has done in the past regarding my columns and my pronunciation of certain words on TV, not that I have ever minded it because though Khalid doesn't realise it, for me it's free education in the English language.

All the best my friend and may you conquer more and more.

Sunil Gavaskar

ABOUT THE AUTHOR

Khalid A-H Ansari has a Bachelor's degree in Law (LL.B.), a Master's degree (M.A.) in Political Science from Bombay University and a Masters degree (A.M.) in Journalism and Mass Communication from Stanford University, U.S.A. Today he is the guiding force of Mid Day Multimedia Ltd., which publishes Asia's leading afternoon newspaper, MID DAY, in two languages from Mumbai and Pune, the INQUILAB Daily and other publications.

He is also chairman of M.C Media Ltd, whose activities include FM radio broadcasting and radio software and film production in Mumbai, New Delhi, Kolkata, Chennai, Bangalore, Ahmedabad, Pune and Goa.His biggest contribution to Indian sports, in the opinion of many, was his magazine SPORTSWEEK, which he started in 1968 and published until1989, when he took up an assignment abroad.

Here are some highlights of his professional career:

* Was a member of the official Indian delegation to the 46th session of the United Nations General Assembly in 1989.

* Started the Earth Times at the United Nations headquarters in New York and published the Earth Summit Times, the official newspaper for the Earth Summit in Rio de Janeiro in 1994.

* Was the Managing Director and Executive Editor of the Khaleej Times, Dubai and editor of the Asiad Chronicle, the official publication of the 1982 Asian Games in New Delhi.

* Was a member of the All India Council of Sports under Gen. K. Kumaramangalam and Field Marshal S.H.F.J. Maneckshaw.

* Covered the Kargil war in 1999 and the Fiji coup in 2000, the NAM conference in Harare and the CHOGM summit in the Bahamas.

* Covered the foreign visits of Presidents A.P.J. Abdul Kalam, Zail Singh and Fakhruddin Ali Ahmed, and Prime Ministers Rajiv Gandhi and Atal Behari Vajpayee.

* Is the Chairman Emeritus of the Squash Racquets Association of Maharashtra and a member of the Organising Committee of the New Delhi Commonwealth Games, 2010.

* Is a member of various government advisory committees and is associated with numerous charitable, social, cultural and sports organisations. The Abdul Hamid Ansari Charitable Trust, started by him in memory of his father, arranges free eye camps and computer study classes and sponsors vocational education for 500 girls per year from underprivileged sections of society.

* He is also a trustee of the CHAMPS Foundation, started by Sunil Gavaskar, which provides financial assistance to retired sportspersons in need.

* Son of renowned freedom fighter Abdul Hamid Ansari, he is the recipient of several honours and awards, including the Padmashri.

A NOTE FROM THE AUTHOR

From time to time, friends, publishers and readers of my column KHALIDOSCOPE in MID DAY and its predecessor HITTING OUT in SPORTSWEEK magazine have suggested that I publish a collection of my writings in book form.

"You owe it to posterity," has been the logic adduced most often to buttress their case, the sincerity of which I could never doubt, but the validity of which was, to my mind, debatable.

Besides, the passage of time in an age when microfilming was unheard of, ravage wrought by rain, termites and three moves of office premises over 40 years had played hell with the rudimentary files in which copies of SPORTSWEEK were bound and stored. The task of accessing the columns was, indeed, daunting.

The years rolled by, even as suggestions of a compendium of articles cropped up from time to time (notably from R.K Mehra of Rupa & Co. and Theo Braganza of Marine Sports), only to be put on the back burner, if not rejected outright.

Then, early last year, Dr. Rafiq Zakaria, distinguished lawyer, scholar and educationist who, for years, had been a close friend and associate of my late father, as also my mentor, broached the subject during one of our regular lunch meetings, at which we endeavoured to solve the world's problems.

Those who knew the late Dr. Z (as we affectionately called him) will vouch he was not one to be dissuaded easily, once he had arrived at a considered conclusion. In any event, polemics has never been one's strong suit.

"With your rich experience of covering sport the world over, you owe it to future generations," he decreed, brushing aside all objections.

It did not take long for the good doctor to get on the phone to Mr. Harsha Bhatkal of Popular Prakashan. A meeting was soon set up and ... no, the rest is not history, but thereby lies a tale.

"*Jab upar wala meherbaan to gadha pahelwaan*" (When The One Above smiles kindly, the donkey is wrestler") has been my *takia kalaam* in reference to my life and career.

It is my sincere belief that The One Above has always kept an (undeserved) benevolent eye on me in my years as pen pusher and *baraati* in the wondrous passing parade of life.

I can only hope and pray that the benediction will continue.

ACKNOWLEDGEMENTS

I am indebted to a number of people for their help in making this collection possible:

First of all my family for convincing me that this is, in their view, a book whose time has come.

I am grateful to cricket legend and former SPORTSWEEK editor Sunil Gavaskar, whose unobtrusive post-retirement deeds for good causes match his awesome accomplishments on the field, for his Foreword and to my good friend and hero Sir Vivian Richards, God-fearing human being, the likes of whom the Maker does not create too many, for his inspiration.

I am also thankful to his manager Melanie Etherington, publisher of The Antigua & Babuda Companion, for her gracious and unflagging assistance in keeping track of the peripatetic Sir Vivian and ensuring his Appreciation reached the publishers in good time before the deadline.

I would like to thank Zaheer Abbas, Bishan Singh Bedi, Inderjit Bindra, Roger Binny, Billy Bowden, Greg Chappell, Ian Chappell, Nari Contractor, Mike Coward, Jagmohan Dalmiya, Kapil Dev, Rahul Dravid, Raj Singh Dungarpur, Farokh Engineer, Ranjit Fernando, Karsan Ghavri, Michael Holding, HRH Tunku Imran, Imran Khan, Air Marshal (Retd.) Idris Latif, Field Marshal (Retd.) S.H.F.J. Maneckshaw, Bob Merriman, A C Muthiah, Bapu Nadkarni, K N Prabhu, Sir Vivian Richards, Dicky Rutnagur, Dilip Sardesai, David Shepherd, Rusi Surti, Sachin Tendulkar, Polly Umrigar, Goolam Vahanvati, Dilip Vengsarkar, Ajit Wadekar, John Wright for their very kind words about me. With all due respect, some of them sound like obituaries and, in all sincerity, I am not sure I deserve them.

Looking back, from time to time I have been strident in my criticism of some of them that stemmed out of exuberance and youthful earnestness evident in my earlier writings.

I assure them I did not intend being personal and hope they will understand that my humble endeavour, although seemingly obsessive, (if not pompous at times, as my friend the inimitable Bishan Singh Bedi would have me know), has been the glory of Indian sport.

It is a measure of their let-bygones-be-bygones magnanimity and indisputable love for cricket that they so readily acquiesced to the request of Clayton Murzello, editor of this collection, for an Appreciation, despite my published disapproval of some of their acts of omission and commission in the past.

I do not have adequate words to thank Clayton Murzello, journalist par excellence, true-blue professional and human being extraordinary, who worked round the clock into the wee hours after shift duties at MID-DAY and on his days off, to edit this book, even as he turned down numerous lucrative publishing assignments in favour of this one. The task of sifting thousands of articles, in particular, has been arduous.

I would also like to express my gratitude to Harsha Bhatkal of Popular Prakashan for his belief and encouragement and to Shivani Ganesh, senior editor at Popular Prakashan for her valuable suggestions and impressive efficiency.

My sincere thanks to Mattie Tomasevich of Sydney for her unbounded enthusiasm and inestimable inputs and Sanjeev Salian and Pradeep Pawaskar of MID DAY Multimedia for their resourcefulness in recovering, restoring and photocopying printed articles dating back 40 years.

I thank MID DAY graphic designer Sushil Mhatre for the cover design, senior staff photographer K. K. Suresh for the cover photographs and to Steffi D'Souza, my executive secretary, for her infinite patience and uncomplaining co-operation in attending to the multi-faceted nitty-gritty of book publishing.

Khalid A-H Ansari
Sydney (Australia),

February 2006.

TABLE OF CONTENTS

Issues

Events

Miscellaneous

“I have had a long association with Mr. Khalid A-H Ansari since the 1979 India-Pakistan series in Pakistan when we became great friends and have been in contact ever since.

He is a very humble, soft-spoken, knowledgeable and sensible person, somebody whom you would like to seek guidance from.

He is a master of journalism. His columns are interesting, insightful and knowledgeable. Above all, he is a man of class.”

ZAHEER ABBAS

BISHAN SINGH BEDI

“Khalid Ansari is a specimen of an aristocratic, social being—very upright and down to earth, who has forever cared for Indian sport.

He likes to be a bit pompous but I mean that in a positive sense. He is one of the best hosts in Bombay.

He is remarkably fit and quite a workaholic. A very restless individual, he is forever on the lookout for new ventures and avenues. All in all, a good friend and the kind of person you would like to meet in sporting circles.”

“What strikes me most about Khalid A-H Ansari is the facility with which he writes on varied subjects: be it politics, culture, business, social issues, even wars. And of course cricket. He is a true pro.

INDERJIT BINDRA

I have always read what he wrote with great interest and his insight into cricket is indeed comprehensive. To say he calls a spade a spade may sound too trite.

During his last visit to Mohali, his observations about media facilities made us sit up and have a fresh look. That is what good journalism is all about.

Khalid’s contribution to Mumbai sports and social issues has been immense. He has always backed causes not only dear to him but to the society at large.

As a cricket administrator I can say that his writings on sensitive issues have always been forthright and helped us in dealing with them.

Over the years quite a few recalcitrant officials were at the wrong end of his stick for right reasons. Even the people who have fallen foul of him cannot say his writings are born out of any malice.

Khalid is wherever sporting action takes place. His views are as refreshing and biting as they were when he was a young journo.

For him issues are more important than personalities and that’s why he is different from many of his ilk.”

ROGER BINNY

"I remember Khalid Ansari as a great personality. He had a passion for the game and supported it in his own way. He was very popular with all the cricketers and always had time for a word with each one."

"I first met Khalid Ansari in Bangladesh in April 2003 at the Pan Pacific Sonargeon Hotel.This was my first official appointment as an Elite Panel Umpire, following the World Cup in South Africa, a Tri Series between India/South Africa/Bangladesh.

BILLY BOWDEN

My first impressions of Khalid were that of a man that was honest, sincere and a professional journalist with a great love and passion for the game of cricket. Not only that, but he had plenty of knowledge and a great insight of cricket and what it stands for! I soon came to realise that Khalid is well respected not only in India but in all the cricket playing nations.

Recently I had the pleasure of joining Khalid on New Years Eve 2005 in Sydney, as he kindly invited both my family and I to join him to celebrate the New Year. I was reminded again what an honest and special person Khalid is and I can truly say there is no 3rd umpire needed on that decision!

GREG CHAPPELL

"I have known for some time that Khalid Ansari is one of India's leading cricket writers. I have had the pleasure of meeting Mr. Ansari on his various trips to Australia and have noticed that he has a special feel for the game. His interest in the game was developed during his playing years at college and I believe he still remains active on the squash court. Mr. Ansari has been highly critical of Team India when matters go out of hand but he is quick with his praise when his country's cricketers have made India proud."

"I first met Khalid Ansari in the early nineties when I started writing for his newspaper MID DAY. We often chatted about cricket and he always made me feel welcome as a contributor to the newspaper.

IAN CHAPPELL

In time we got to know each other better as we met in different parts of the world covering the game of cricket. I have come to appreciate his love for the game of cricket and his desire to contribute thought provoking pieces to a newspaper that prides itself on maintaining high standards.

In more recent times Khalid has become something of an honorary Australian spending more and more time in this country and especially in the beautiful harbour city of Sydney. I admire his choice of City as Sydney has one of the most beautiful outlooks in the world.

Mrs and Mr Ansari with cricket personalities during the 1974-75 India vs West Indies series.

Raising a toast along with Behram Contractor, Fredun de Vitre and Makarand Waingankar (left),

Bishan Singh Bedi speaking at a *Sportsweek* function

Khalid Ansari with
Field Marshal
Sam Maneckshaw

Posing for
Vogue Magazine

With Journalist
the late Berry Sarbadhidakary

With cricket administrator
S. K. Wankhede

The 'Noob' and
Sharmila Tagore

The author with the late PM Indira Gandhi

With Rajmata Gayatri Devi

Sunil Gavaskar, the editor of *Sportsweek* and *Lifestyle* with Mr. Ansari

Exchanging pleasantries with MAK Pataudi as Mrs. Ansari looks on.

Touring journalists at the Adelaide Oval during India's 1980-81 tour of Australia:
(from left) Dr Narottam Puri (AIR), Dicky Rutnagur (UK), Khalid Ansari (Mid Day), R. Mohan (The Hindu), Raj Singh Dungarpur (AIR),
K N Prabhu (Times of India), Jasdev Singh (AIR), Kishore Bhimani

With Bishan Bedi

Addressing a gathering at the United Nations.

With former President of India, Zail Singh

With England all-rounder Tony Greig on the 1972-73 tour of India

Khalid Ansari and Tariq Ansari meet former President of India Zail Singh at the Rashtrapati Bhavan

With Viv Richards

With a celebrity-studded rugby team at the Bombay Gymkhana - 2004

With Mumbai's celebrities at the Bombay Gymkhana

Bat autographed by Allan Border and Viv Richards

A ball autographed by Don Bradman

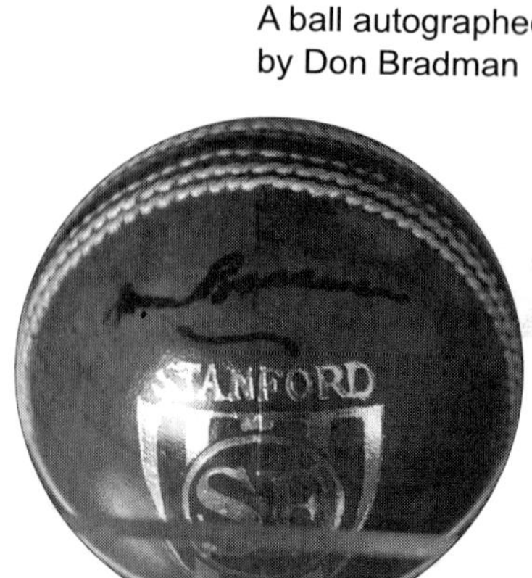

With John Major at a reception

With Vijaypat Singhania

With Jeff Dujon (left) and Michael Holding, both proud Jamaicans

With Sunil Gavaskar and Dilip Vengsarkar at the launch of *Sportsweek* and *Lifestyle*.

With HRH Tunku Imran

With Sunil Gavaskar and Field Marshal, Sam Manekshaw at the launch of *Sportsweek and Lifestyle*.

With CCI president Raj Singh Dungarpur and former India all-rounder Abid Ali (right)

Being awarded the Padmashri by former President of India K. R. Narayanan in 2001.

Acknowledging the cheers from a distinguished gathering after receiving the Padmashri.

With dignitaries and award winners after the Padmashri presentation at Rashtrapati Bhavan. Tennis stalwarts Leander Paes and Mahesh Bhupathi are on the left of the second row. Squash player Bhuvneshwari Kumari is sitting in the first row on the right.

Standing : Brijesh Patel, Gundappa Vishwanath, Sunil Gavaskar, Bishan Bedi, Anshuman Gaekwad, Khalid Ansari, Sitting : Mrs. Ansari, Mrs. Bedi, Mrs. Vishwanath, Mrs. Patel, Mrs. Gavaskar & Mrs Gaekwad.

Mr. and Mrs. Ansari with Eknath Solkar and S. V. Kadam (left), Mumbai Cricket's die-hard supporter

Mr and Mrs. Ansari with Vijay Merchant and S. K. Wankhede.

Because Khalid is spending more time in Sydney we have dined out together a few times and I really look forward to these occasions not only for the conversation but also because it makes me better acquainted with the best Indian restaurants in the City. For me Khalid has become a walking, talking Sydney restaurant guide.

I look forward to many more chats on cricket over stuffed kulcha and spicy kebabs. And I will also read with interest his published book of columns."

NARI CONTRACTOR

"My first recollection of Khalid Ansari is of a young, articulate man. From day one, I never felt that I was talking to a journalist when I spoke to Khalid. He was never trying to extract things out of you. Instead, his questions made for a nice conversation - question and counter question; question and counter question.

He never left you with that 'oh-what-have-I-said' feeling after an interview.

***Sports & Pastime* was the only magazine we had and when it closed down, Khalid started *Sportsweek*. He ensured we did not miss *Sports & Pastime* because *Sportsweek* was a good product. Khalid's rise has been gradual and good. And he has been decent all the way."**

"There is no greater challenge for a journalist and writer than to maintain a freshness of mind and thought over a long period.

MIKE COWARD

To this end Khalid Ansari has been most successful and, as a consequence, I suspect this splendid body of his work will be well received and resonate with readers for many years to come.

Too often, these days, the reader is given the bare minimum—a morsel for the moment. Khalid is of a very different school and one that should always be celebrated. He has served Indian journalism and sport with distinction by caring about his subjects and taking us into their lives with his clear and insightful writing. He has an eye for detail and takes the time to reflect, even contemplate.

These days Khalid spends some time in Sydney and his Australian colleagues and friends join me in wishing him great success with this fine collection of his work."

JAGMOHAN DALMIYA

"My association with Mr. Khalid Ansari goes back a long way. I had heard of him as the editor of an extremely popular sports magazine SPORTSWEEK that ruled India in the 1970s and the first part of the 1980s. When I came into cricket administration, I had the opportunity to meet the man.

As is reflected in his writings, Mr. Ansari is not only an erudite scholar, but also an extremely intelligent analyst of various sports disciplines, especially cricket. Even when the media has taken a contrary view on certain issues, Mr. Ansari has been bold enough to come out with facts in his articles.

The need of the day in the world of media is to have a few more personalities like Mr. Ansari who never hesitates to "call a spade a spade" irrespective of persons or issues. At a personal level, I have seen Mr. Ansari as a man of amiable disposition and a perfect gentleman."

"When I used to come to Bombay in the early 1970s, I read *Sportsweek* magazine which was brought out by Khalid Ansari. *Sportsweek* and *Sportstar* were very popular then. A few years later I came to know the man. What struck me was his great dress sense. Normally, people from the media don't like to dress well as they prefer casuals. But Khalid stood out.

He and his wife made a lovely couple and it was a pleasure to spend evenings with them. Khalid was not one of those who came into the box and rant away. We discussed things and those evenings were enjoyed and will be cherished."

KAPIL DEV

RAHUL DRAVID

"I've read Khalid Ansari even before I played for India. I first met him in 1996 and got to know him over the years. You can make out that he is a person who cares and has a balanced view on the game.

Khalid is a great supporter of Indian cricket, yet not sensationalistic in his writings. He's also taken up for Indian cricketers whenever they've been wronged. I've also got to know his son Tariq and it's always nice to have a chat with both whenever we meet."

"I have known Khalid Ansari since the late 1960s. I've also known him as a great sports lover whose contribution is huge. I respect him for what he has done for sports—encouraged and written about sports persons while he respects me for my love for sports.

When Hanumant Singh was dumped for the tour of Australia in 1967-68, I remember going over to Khalid's place to ask him to do something about it at the instance of skipper Mansur Ali Khan Pataudi, and he did take it up strongly.

Khalid is the only sportsman to become a scribe and does things with flair, be it writing or managing squash in the state.

RAJ SINGH DUNGARPUR

His idea of starting Mid Day was a great one and who can forget *Sportsweek*, the magazine that ran for 20 years? Khalid has been highly respected, forever dependable and someone who always has time for old sportsmen."

"I remember endorsing *Sportsweek*, the popular sports magazine which Khalid Ansari started in the late 1960s,when I used to be heard over Radio Ceylon saying: "I am Farokh Engineer. I read *Sportsweek*, do you? *Sportsweek*, the magazine that cares for Indian sport." It really caught on.

FAROKH ENGINEER

Khalid has been a friend and a good one. He did a lot for cricketers and did not expect anything in return. He has been straightforward and never afraid to speak his mind. If there is someone out of line you can be sure Khalid will put him in his place.

The launch of Khalid's *Cricket At Fever Pitch* in Mumbai promises to be a super occasion of a special book written by a truly special person whom I've had the pleasure and privilege of calling one of my dearest friends over the zillion years that we've known each other. I am sure the occasion and the book will be a thumping successes"

RANJIT FERNANDO

"I first came to know Khalid Ansari when I toured India with the Sri Lanka cricket team in the early 1970s, when we were not a fully-fledged Test cricket-playing nation. In those days, the contingent of cricket journalists wasn't anywhere near the numbers we see today, but were a very special breed and Khalid belonged to that era.

He always enjoyed your trust and had the knack of quoting accurately in interviews, without hurting anyone's feelings. He appealed to me straightaway since those days when he ran the leading sports journal, *Sportsweek*.

I have considered him to be a special, true friend. His honesty and high integrity has seen Khalid reach many milestones in the media world and the newspapers he heads now is a reflection of his own character—reliable and truthful. I have no doubt that he will achieve greater heights in the coming years since journalists of his calibre are timeless.

"I can never forget Khalid Ansari for many things. He was one of the first people who organised a modelling assignment for me. Not that it was lucrative in those days but it brought out the fact quite clearly that Khalidbhai always had the betterment of cricketers at heart. He is a good host too. Whenever we were in Dubai, a dinner at his home was a regular feature. He cares for sports and is a great human being"

KARSAN GHAVRI

"Mr Khalid Ansari is a gentleman I have seen and observed around the cricketing world for many years. The word "gentleman" in this case is not just used to describe a person of the male gender.

MICHAEL HOLDING

Since I have grown to know Khalid I can safely say the word is used in the true definition of the word. In my early days, I used to see my senior cricketers conversing with Khalid but never got involved due partly to my junior status as a cricketer but also due to my wariness of the press and their power of the pen.

It was my loss, as I later found out. Khalid has since, been a great friend, who I have spent memorable and pleasant hours with him away from the game and certainly look forward to many more such opportunities wherever we may meet around the cricketing globe."

"Khalid Ansari's contribution as a sports journalist and editor is well acknowledged, but his contribution to sports development has probably gone unnoticed. The Mid-Day/Petra Foundation programme of sponsoring the Malaysian Under 15 cricket team to Mumbai and the Maharashtra junior squash team to Kuala Lumpur is just one of the examples of his love and devotion to sport. Thank you Khalid for your contribution to sport at all levels."

- *HRH Tunku Imran, President of the Olympic Council of Malaysia, Patron of the World Squash Federation and President of the Malaysian Cricket Association*

"I have known Khalid Ansari since 1977, when I came to Bombay for the first time. I have always had great respect for him as a person and as a sports writer. What emerges from his writings is his passion for sports in general, and cricket in particular. I am sure when people read this compilation, they might not necessarily agree with him, but they will certainly feel his passion and enjoy the richness and variety of his experience."

IMRAN KHAN

AIR MARSHAL (RETD.)
IDRIS LATIF

"I will always remember Mr Khalid Ansari for his passion for sports. He is a genuine sports lover and nothing was for show.

He was always courteous, thoughtful and a great host. When we were in Bombay, we enjoyed MID DAY, the newspaper he started and through it we established contact with someone whom we truly liked."

"I have known Khalid Ansari for many years. A committed sports lover, he has contributed immensely to sport. I got to know him well when he worked with me in the All India Council of Sports (AICS), in which he was a great asset. We spent many a long and convivial hour discussing sport in different parts of the country where the AICS met."

FIELD MARSHAL (RETD.)
S.H.F.J. MANECKSHAW

"It is an honour to be asked to write an appreciation for the outstanding contribution that Khalid Ansari has made to sport, and in particular cricket.

BOB MERRIMAN,
Former President Cricket Australia and Current President, Cricket Victoria

"My first exposure to Mid Day was in August 1979 when I was fortunate enough to manage the Australian Cricket Team to India, under the leadership of Kim Hughes, for a three month tour. During this time I very much appreciated the frankness and friendship of Khalid Ansari during what was an enjoyable but demanding tour. I also came to respect the publication and its reporting on cricket and the excellent leadership that produced such an acceptable and enjoyable print outlet.

"Since 1979 Khalid and I have met on numerous occasions in many different locations, whether it was in the airport at Calcutta (where we were delayed some five hours and were able to exchange many and varied stories and experiences relating to the great game of cricket) or here in Australia or in London - again, his company has always been enjoyable and enlightening.

"Cricket is a great sport which attracts the opinion of many. These opinions vary in the extreme and this causes us to categorise the authority and quality of the information that we receive. I have been fortunate to have received much information on cricket and read many, many articles and books on the subject, and I rate Khalid Ansari amongst the leaders in communication and quality within the demands of our sport.

"I wish this book every success and I am confident that its readers will get total value and enjoyment from its publication.

Long live cricket."

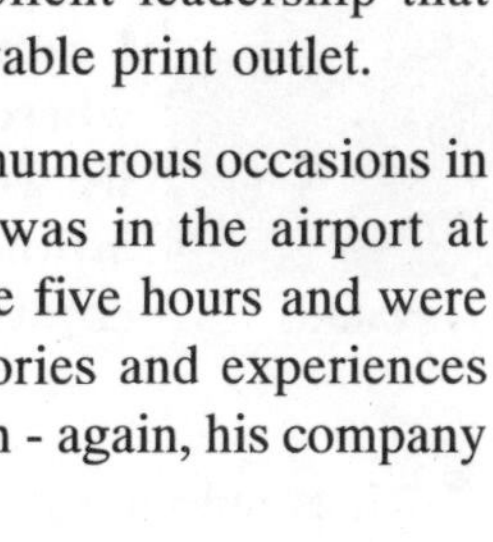

A C MUTHIAH

"I have known Khalid for the last 10 years or so. From the time I became President of BCCI, I came into close contact with him through my friends Raj Singh Dungarpur and Srikant Ruparel.

We often meet at the Cricket Club of India and quite often at Lord's. He is always impeccably dressed and has a good insight into cricket affairs. His approach to sports in general and cricket in particular is always constructive.

Although at times he is critical and frank in his writings on cricket, I have always found him to be constructive. I always enjoy my conversation with him, especially on cricket"

BAPU NADKARNI

"Khalid Ansari only compares with S K Gurunathan from Southern India where consistency in cricket writing is concerned.

As a journalist, he has been sharp, point-blank even to his friends but always very fair and that is why he has made a lot of friends off the field. I am not indulging in flattery when I say that he has always been very sincere and dedicated to his job and that always stood out."

K N PRABHU

"From Adelaide to Sialkot, Khalid Ansari and I have shared many moments at press boxes the world over. I first met him when he was in the advertising field and I never knew he would be one of us. He held his own and became a top professional.

I remember his dispassionate despatches from Pakistan (in 1978-79) where he brought to light the true strengths of the Pakistan team while we were looking at other factors like umpiring and so on. His cheerful attitude was a lesson to all of us and it showed in his writing that he enjoyed doing his job."

SIR VIVIAN RICHARDS

"It is indeed a privilege to be asked to write this for someone who I first met in India during 1974, whilst I was touring with the West Indies cricket team.

Having to interact with Khalid Ansari in his capacity as a press person, the first aspect which struck me about him was that he came across as very trustworthy, a quality which is very hard to find in such an environment.

Our association developed and it was Khalid who was solely responsible for giving me the opportunity to express my cricketing views through articles in his SPORTSWEEK publication."

Our friendship became even closer because, when dealing with the press in India, I've always looked at him as being 'The Godfather'. Not just because of his respected views, but I was always very impressed with his sense of attire!

I advise anyone who gets the opportunity to purchase '*Cricket at Fever Pitch*' by Khalid Ansari, to do so as quickly as possible. You are ensured of a most enjoyable read.

Happy reading!"

DICKY RUTNAGUR

"There are not many persons whom I have met or worked alongside who possess Khalid Ansari's reserves of energy. A touch of hair loss does provide a reminder that I have known the old boy for three decades and a half, but I have not observed the slightest drop of level in his reservoir of stamina.

There have not been many international sports events which Khalid, a very active sportsman for most of his life, has not covered, Olympic Games included. But the sport closest to his heart has been cricket. He has reported the game and written about its players with a recognisable affection. At the same time he has always been passionately fierce and justifiably when commenting on the machinations and intrigues that have, from time to time, plagued the sports controlling body.

Without doubt, Khalid Ansari will occupy a prominent niche in the colourful history of Indian newspapers"

DILIP SARDESAI

"I have known Khalid Ansari for several years and he has never stopped being forthright and fair in his writings on sport. Apart from writing with passion, he always gives his readers a fresh perspective and an in-depth view of things from wherever he is.

A likeable, polished human being, it has been a pleasure to know him and be a regular reader of the paper he started—*Mid-Day*, which is now an institution.

DAVID SHEPHERD

"It is always a pleasure to bump into Khalid Ansari on cricket tours. It's good to hear him talk passionately of the game, a trait among Indians. He's got vast knowledge and he's good company too."

RUSI SURTI

"I have known Khalid Ansari since I was a kid. And who can forget *Sportsweek*, which he first published in 1968.

I've been in Australia all these years and whenever I've come down to India I've made sure I caught up with Khalid just like I did when it came to men like Madhav Mantri, my mentor.

Khalid is a cricket fanatic and always called a spade a spade. He's been a good and fair sports journalists and the senior-most on the circuit. He's still at it and I enjoy his writing."

"Khalid A-H Ansari has been an alert eye to Indian sports ever since he started the popular magazine *Sportweek* which ran for two decades.

As a field journalist, his tremendious vision and commitments to sport have stood out. Having vision alone does not take you far. It's your ability to turn that vision into reality which counts in the end. Khalid Ansari has done that and that is why his contribution to sport is significant."

SACHIN TENDULKAR

POLLY UMRIGAR

"Khalid and I spent many hours on tour when I was the manager of the Indian cricket team in Australia. He was great company, good fun and a thorough professional.

There are no double standards with Khalid. He writes what he feels is interesting to his readers and there is nothing biased in his writings."

"We go back to Maulana Azad Road. It used to be called Ripon Road then. Khalid called me to his *Inquilab Daily* office one day.

He had started a wonderful weekly, *Sportsweek*. Cecil Hendricks used to write the racing column for him under the pseudonym 'Railbird.' He was the popular 'Pegasus' writing for the *Times of India* and the *Evening News*. When he stopped writing for *Sportsweek*, Khalid asked me to take over. I was in college those days and started a weekly column for him under the pseudonym 'Thoroughbred.'

It was good fun. Our relationship flourished even after Khalid moved out of the Bombay Central area. Some years later when he wanted to start an evening newspaper he called me for lunch to the Bombay Gym to discuss the new project. I had some trepidation since it meant taking on the redoubtable Times Group and the well established *Evening News of India*. However, Khalid loved challenges and the rest is history. *Mid-Day* was a success story and the *Evening News* closed down!

Khalid has been passionate about cricket. Two qualities about his writing stand out. The first is his ability and willingness to do some plain speaking. The second is his courage to stand up for what he believes is right. I am confident that the collection of his articles will be read with great interest by all cricket lovers and will read like a lively historical survey of cricket over the years."

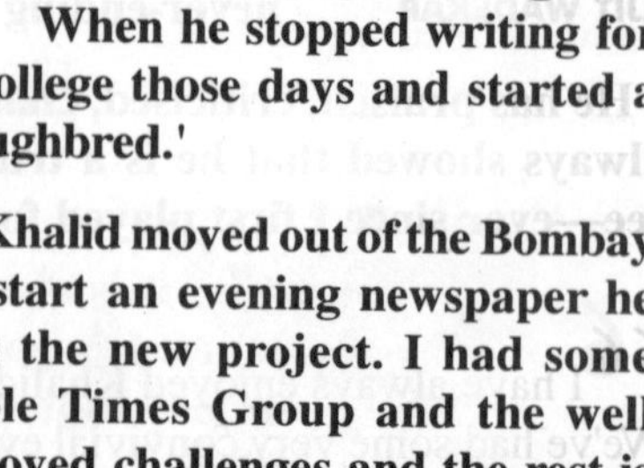

GOOLAM VAHANVATI,
Solicitor General of India

"It has been a pleasure knowing Khalid Ansari ever since I made an impression for Bombay in the early 1970s. But I read the byline long before that in Sportsweek, then India's most popular sports magazine, which was spearheaded by Khalid and ably supported by the late Sharad Kotnis, another great sports lover.

Khalid wrote and still does from his heart. If there's an issue which the public need an expert view about, you can be assured that it will not miss him. He has contributed immensely to sport through his writings which have been critical yet unbiased.

DILIP VENGSARKAR

He also guides the Squash Racquets Association of Maharashtra and continues to do his best for the sport he dearly loves. And yes, Khalid enjoys his squash as the beads of sweat would suggest in case you bump into him at one of the sports clubs in Mumbai."

AJIT WADEKAR

"Way back in 1971 when India triumphed in the West Indies, Indian cricket lovers had more than sketch images to admire, cherish and store away. For this we have to thank *Sportsweek*, the magazine which Khalid Ansari introduced to India's sporting world after the closure of *Sports and Pastime*.

Thirty five years later, Khalid is still at it—hitting his laptop keys from all across the globe. It shows his sporting knowledge, never-ending passion and most importantly, his love for sports.

He has praised, criticised, chastised through his writings but at the end of the day he always showed that he is a true sports lover and for a sportsman this was great to see—ever since I first played for India in 1966."

"I have always enjoyed Khalid Ansari's company and encouragement. We've had some very convivial evenings on tours. It was nice to get away, talk a little bit of cricket, have a nice meal and have a good laugh. I am looking forward to his publication and wish him all the best. And I will look forward to reading him."

JOHN WRIGHT

Personalities

With the Nawab at the Taj

SPORTSWEEK • ANNUAL 1969

The Place: The Taj Mahal Hotel, Bombay.

The Time: Lunch time, quite recently. Before the commencement of the Test series against the New Zealanders.

The Occasion: Lunch with India's cricket captain, the amazing Mohammed Mansur Ali Khan, Nawab of Pataudi.

M. A. K. Pataudi

Often criticized by the press as being too reserved and therefore inscrutable, Tiger Pataudi was in an affable mood as he submitted himself to a barrage of questions, both personal and impersonal, while revealing his culinary refinements and epicurean qualities.

It was obvious the problem of selecting India's team for the forthcoming series against the Kiwis and the Aussies had been weighing on his mind.

He seemed concerned about the absence from India at that time of Engineer, Surti and Prasanna. And with the dilemma of whether it would be prudent to 'blood' some of the promising youngsters now knocking at the door of Test cricket against the none-too-formidable New Zealanders or whether it would be wiser to weld into a seasoned combination more or less the same team that performed so creditably during the tour of New Zealand last year.

Speaking with obvious pride in this context, Pataudi referred to the tremendous team-spirit displayed by that team during the second-leg of its tour. And, of course, to the excellent fielding, pointing out that the tour was remarkable for the highest number of catches held by any Indian side during a four-Test series.

Also agitating his mind was the problem posed by the absence of pace bowlers in our country. He is of the opinion that it would be preferable to do without bowlers who have pretensions to be 'quick' and to have in their place specialist spin bowlers and (solid) batsmen who are also good fielders.

The 'Noob' repeatedly kept coming back to the subject of fielding, thus revealing the importance he attaches to this department of the game.

Whilst attributing the woeful absence of good pace bowlers in India to dietary and climatic factors, Mansur Ali strongly condemned the preparation of wickets in this country which were calculated to assist only spinners, in the process discouraging budding pace bowlers and robbing the game of all excitement.

To remedy this situation Pataudi recommends that we import expert groundsmen like Flack of Warwickshire, for advice and help in the preparation of lively wickets.

Sitting as I was on his right, I observed Pataudi had not twice noticed the cigarettes I had offered him.

This prompted me to ask the obvious question about his eye.

To which he replied that he had only 5 per cent vision in that eye.

To my query as to why he did not wear contact lenses he retorted that following the tragic car accident in Sussex on July 1, 1961, specialists had recommended contact lenses, but this would have meant a three-month layoff from cricket to enable his new eye to focus itself correctly.

And this the cricket-loving Pataudi was not willing to do.

So what did he do? Get out to the nets as soon as he could. And in the course of regular and arduous (as also agonizing) practice sessions, train himself to play with one eye.

Courage? Admirable enough to make the Gods weep. Grit and determination? Indeed! Of which great men are made.

Pataudi spoke of Nari Contractor in glowing terms, as a person as well as a cricketer and leader.

Reminiscing about the unfortunate incident when Contractor was cruelly struck on the head by a nasty run from Griffith, an accident that spelt 'finis' to Contractor's career and elevated himself to the position of captain at, the youngest-ever age of 21 years, 2 months and 18 days. 'Tiger' Pataudi expressed the opinion that 'Charlie did chuck' as "do some of our more ambitious trundlers at various levels of competitive play."

Mansur Ali spends most of his off-cricket hours managing his estates in Pataudi, which is almost a cricket-ball's throw from Delhi, and in Bhopal.

Future plans? Nothing is further from his thoughts than retirement. He would like to continue playing as long as he is fit and able.

English county cricket he would like to play again. But only for a short while. For, "it can be extremely taxing. And makes one stale. Look what's happening to poor Gary (Sobers)," he said.

Sobers, he considers the greatest all-rounder of recent times.

And of the cricketers he's either played against or watched in action, the following are the 'best' by his standards:

Indians: Vijay Manjrekar for batting and Subhash Gupte for bowling.

World: Peter May for batting and Alec Bedser for bowling.

Time alone will tell whether posterity will rate the Nawab of Pataudi among the batting and/or fielding greats...

At home with the Wadekars

SPORTSWEEK* • *September 12, 1971

Ajit Wadekar

THE days drag on interminably for an elderly couple at Shivaji Park, Bombay. For them 10 am. on Monday, September 13 seems so far, far away. For that's the day their worthy son will return home after his heroic exploits in a faraway land. And a young wife, their daughter-in-law, wishes the team were coming directly to Bombay instead of first stopping at Delhi even though she admits "it is no doubt a great honour for him and the team."

Wade is a sleepy little village near Thana in Maharashtra. Never in their wildest dreams could its inhabitants have dreamt that their name would one day be immortalized in the distant corners of the world, thanks to the ability, courage and determination of their descendant, appropriately named Ajit.

Nor did Laxman Bhaskar Wadekar, now 68, a retired clerk from the Railways Accounts Office and his wife Manorama ever dream that their third child, a son, born on April 1, 1941 would one day bring them and the nation such unbounded pride and joy.

The Wadekars are a modest, quiet-loving, God-fearing middle-class family, typical of those that reside in the Dadar-Shivaji Park area which can justifiably claim to be the nursery of Indian Test cricket.

Their home is almost literally a cricket-ball's throw from the Shivaji Park. Yet, despite all the efforts of his father, young Ajit could not be persuaded to take up cricket—or any other game for that matter—in high school. Introverted and of a serious bent of mind, Ajit was more interested in his books, often staying up until the early hours of the morning in preparation for his examinations.

The qualities of diligence, application and determination which he has so abundantly manifest on the cricket green were evident even in his school days. And nobody was surprised when Ajit passed the S.S.C. examination from the Chhabildas Lallubhai (C. L. Boys') School, Dadar with distinction (79%), scoring 100% in Algebra.

It was at Elphinstone College where he took up a course in science that Ajit was finally prevailed upon—under fortuitous circumstances—to take to cricket. During his first year the college team happened to find itself short of a player in an inter-collegiate match. And Ajit, who had never played with any other than a tennis ball in all his life was persuaded to take the field by former Bombay Ranji Trophy leg-spinner Baloo Gupte with, as his father puts it, "the tempting offer of a lunch allowance of Rs. 2.50."

Shifting allegiance to the Ramnivas Ruia College for reasons of convenience (the Elphinstone College was too far from home), Ajit was selected to represent his college and university in the very first year. And if further proof were needed of his talent, he savaged 324 off the Delhi University attack in the Inter-University Tournament finals the same year, a record which stood until last year when it was eclipsed by Sunil Gavaskar.

He joined the Shivaji Park Gymkhana the same year and represented Bombay in the Ranji Trophy against Madras at Madras. The rest is history. Some lunch allowance that!

Ajit Wadekar with junior

It was in college during an inter-collegiate cricket match that Ajit first set eyes on a pert fan called Rekha who admits it was love at first sight. And it was not long before the charming Rekha, said "yes," was prevailed upon to change her last name from Hazare to Wadekar. That was on May 13, 1965. And, insists Rekha, it was a marriage that brought Ajit luck. For the same year Ajit played his first Test.

A devoted wife, Rekha is to this day Ajit's most ardent fan. Among the first questions she put to me when I met her at Ajit's father's residence last Tuesday was: "Has he put on weight?" And "why haven't you been printing more pictures of him in action?" Employed, as her husband is, with a bank (the Dena Bank in her case), Rekha Wadekar confesses that "I just couldn't control myself when I heard over the radio that Abid Ali had scored the winning run . . . I almost danced with joy. I've never felt so proud in my life . . . and you should have seen the procession that came to our house that night : bursting crackers, singing, dancing, demanding *mithai*. It was a proud day. . . "

Talking animatedly of her husband, Mrs. Wadekar informed me for the many, many SPORTSWEEK readers who I know would be interested in these personal details, that Ajit is "also fond" of badminton and billiards, that he did his B.Sc. in mathematics ("got a second"), that he likes Western pop music, smokes occasionally, "is most definitely non-veg", "loves" Chinese food, "is just crazy about" comics and James Hadley Chase novels.

That he has two elder sisters, both married, and a younger brother Ashok, an engineer with Mahindra and Mahindra, who is an opening bowler and a good left-hand bat who has achieved the rare distinction of having captained the Shivaji Park Youngsters from the bottom ('G' Division) of the Kanga League to the 'A' Division. That Ajit is 'extremely attached' to his mother who interestingly enough "confidently predicted on the first day that we would win the third Test even though Ajit had lost the toss."

Such indeed is "mamta" and the power of a mother's prayer.

Good-bye, Skip

SPORTSWEEK* • *August 24, 1975

THE professional satisfaction that would have been normally derived from the "scooping" of the news of the retirement, from international cricket, of Mansur Ali Khan Pataudi is small compensation for SPORTSWEEK's disappointment at the decision itself.

If we are to accept "the Noob's" word for it, he is hanging up his boots to make room for younger cricketers. But, we're afraid, these words do not ring as true as they would have had the former India skipper retired at the height of glory. Pataudi is closer to the truth when he says that he's had enough and that his reflexes are not as sharp as they were, a bold admission indeed, which to a large extent explains Pataudi's lacklustre performances with the bat against Clive Lloyd's West Indians.

That there will be widespread disappointment among unbiased, discerning cricket lovers throughout the country cannot be doubted. We have been flooded with readers' letters asking Pataudi to, in effect, "reconsider his decision in the interest of Indian cricket," from the very day an enterprising UNI reporter flashed SPORTSWEEK's exclusive.

If one is to go strictly by cold statistics, Pataudi's achievements with the bat in first-class cricket are not particularly impressive, barring some memorable knocks. But if one considers the fact that it was Pataudi who brought into a rather listless, uninspired situation, a refreshing breath of positive, attacking cricket, despite a serious physical disability which would have broken the spirit of lesser mortals, his contribution to Indian cricket as astute captain, technically-equipped batsman and brilliant fielder are considerable. But for that unfortunate car accident, this natural athlete could have conceivably found a place in the hall of all-time cricketing greats.

And, it should not be forgotten that the players who quite recently brought unparalleled glory to Indian cricket were to a large extent nurtured and schooled under Pataudi. If a combination of factors conspired to deny Mansur Ali Khan a small share in the glory, the fault is not entirely his own.

Pataudi has often been misunderstood. Brought up in what were for long considered desirable westernised traditions, Pataudi's liberal education abroad fostered in him a spirit of independence which is rather alien to our psyche.

The thrusting upon him of the India's captaincy at the tender age of 21 under most unfortunate circumstances imposed upon him a burden for which he was unprepared and which he was rather immature to shoulder. In the brashness, impetuosity and exuberance of youth he did succeed in forming groups among fellow-cricketers, which could only have affected the cohesiveness of his team. His dry sense of humour was often misunderstood for haughtiness. A man of few words, his preference to keep to himself and to a chosen few was misinterpreted as 'segregation'. But nothing could have been farther from the truth, for beneath the cold even shy exterior, Pataudi is a warm, cultured, sincere person, true to his word.

This writer recalls his conversation with Tiger Pataudi during the Kanpur Test against Tony Lewis' team (1972-73). When asked about future plans, Pataudi replied emphatically "some people have suggested that I retire now that I have made what they call a successful comeback. But the thought of retirement has never entered my mind. I love the game and I shall keep playing as long as my country needs me and as long as I am able to..."

That's the man, Pataudi. At times cussed but always a true sportsman, in love not only with cricket but also with (and fairly proficient at) football, hockey, billiards, snooker and cycle-polo. One who has always played for the love of sports, he came back, a mature individual, because the country needed him and led the side admirably in India's tough series against the West Indies. He is stepping out because he is no longer able, by his own admission, to respond satisfactorily to the country's needs. While bidding good-bye to a great Indian cricketer, we wish him luck in his future endeavours.

To the extent that no one is indispensable, Pataudi's absence will not be felt for long. But the memory of his exploits will go down in the annals of Indian cricket.

No victimisation, please

SPORTSWEEK* • *September 28, 1975

Sunil Gavaskar

Among the items that may (at the discretion of the president) be considered at the annual general meeting of the Board of Control for Cricket in India at Jaipur on September 28 is the report of Gulabrai Ramchand, manager of the team, which participated in the Prudential World Cup.

There is a great deal of speculation as regards the contents of the report and all manner of wild rumours are now afloat in cricketing circles as to the possible 'disciplinary action' that may be taken against vice-captain Sunil Gavaskar.

All of this is, to our way of thinking, most unfortunate, since such situations can only be detrimental to the morale of any human being. Sunil Gavaskar is still young. He has a long way to go. He may not have quite justified the faith and high hopes reposed in him after his stupendous achievements in the Caribbean in 1971, but he is without a shadow of doubt, a batsman of tremendous potential which if fulfilled will surely mark him as among the greatest batsmen that this country has produced. His knock in the Bombay Test against the West Indies, earlier this year, had 'class' written all over it and was a resounding slap in the face of the critics who had written him off.

This writer was witness to Sunny Gavaskar's not-so-sunny run-crawl against England in the Prudential Cup last June. He was told by skipper Venkatraghavan and manager Ramchand in almost so many words that his innings was contrary to instructions which were unequivocally to the effect that he should either get on with the game and score as quickly as possible, and should that not be possible in view of the tight, restrictive bowling and defensive, field placement (reasons which Gavaskar has himself adduced), to throw away his wicket.

If this were indeed the case, the tour selection committee of which Gavaskar too was member (the other two were the captain and manager) should have taken IMMEDIATE disciplinary action against the errant batsman by dropping him for the inconsequential cake walk of a match against East Africa which followed. Or better still, Gavaskar should have, as suggested by this writer at that time, stood down from that match as a self-disciplinary measure, which while setting a splendid example would have raised his stock immensely. This would also have spelt 'finis' once and for all to the unpleasant episode.

But that was not to be and the witch-hunt continues, all of which must be a terrible ordeal for the Bombay opener.

Disciplinary action, if it is to be effective, must be immediate. Over three months have elapsed since the incident occurred. The tension and agony should have been punishment enough for Gavaskar.

We therefore submit that if the manager's report in fact faults 'Gavvy' for what is tantamount to insubordination and playing in a manner which was detrimental to his team's interest, Gavaskar should be severely reprimanded and warned. Stronger action, which might have been justified at an early stage, would at this juncture be harsh and raise suspicions of victimisation as was the case with Bishen Singh Bedi last year. Most importantly, it could adversely affect the career of this most talented cricketer.

It will be recalled the Board was hell-bent-on-leather as regards 'disciplining' Bedi last year because some of the pooh-bahs were personally involved.

The 64-rupee question now is: will the president place the report for consideration at the AGM? For, what's sauce for the goose is not always sauce for the gander where our cricket bigwigs are concerned.

I'm not nasty, says Greig

SPORTSWEEK

Tony Greig

Institute an award for the Most Popular Man of the Series, put it to a popular vote (what else!), the winner - by a mile - will be a 6 ft. 7 in. blonde giant with the handsome looks of a Greek god, a puckish bloke named Anthony Greig.

The 'natives' (to quote a visiting journalist) adore him—the fact that he's half-South African notwithstanding. And as this living proof of the thesis that sport is a builder of bridges among men himself admits in a heavily Afrikaans-accented bass voice. "I'm just crazy about them too, believe you me."

Greig (pronounced Greg) was "a little bit worried" when he first arrived in India. "I didn't want anything to go wrong," says he. Nothing has - barring that unfortunate episode at Madras in which emotion got the better of reason. And Greig is certainly the wiser for it.

Make no mistake about it. Beneath the façade of clown is a sober, dedicated, thinking cricketer blessed with an alert mind which is as capable of getting agitated over international relations as it is of cogitating dispassionately about the subject closest to his heart—cricket. The appointment of this shrewd cricketing brain as skipper of Sussex therefore appears to make a lot of sense. And there are many among the knowledgeable who mark him out as a future England captain.

FAILING

The discerning here couldn't but have been impressed with his clever, clever bowling spell at Eden Gardens when he claimed five wickets, by the manner in which he exploited the weakness of our senior batsmen against the away going ball and the general failing of the tail-enders against the yorker.

And one may now confess that the confident manner in which he faced our spinners at Delhi, adapting his stance to Chandra's bowling, caused many (this writer included) more than one sleepless night wondering about how we could penetrate his seemingly impregnable defence twice in order to win.

Fortunately for India the form displayed by Greig in the early stages of the tour, the class demonstrated in Australia, which made him "the most exciting discovery" of the World XI series, has not been much in evidence after the Calcutta Test. But a player of Greig's class can as the pundits say, strike form at any time. If that were to happen even the most partisan in the packed stands would find difficulty concealing their delight, so popular is this cricketer.

The son of a Scottish RAF squadron leader who trained pilots in South Africa at the end of the last War and a "oh so sweet South African mother", Tony Greig learnt his first lessons in cricket at the age of six from a female, yes female, kindergarten teacher in Queenstown, South Africa.

TRADITION

The sporting traditions of the Greig family (which had a lucrative department store business near Edinburgh, Scotland) sustained young Tony's interest in the game, which developed into a near-passion at the age of 10 when he was chosen for coaching by Sussex professionals.

A strong believer in the value of coaching at an early age ("ideally from the age of six - more to fire off a love for the game than to teach them the cover drive"), Greig attributes the high standard of South African cricket, despite the fact that their cricket engagements are restricted due to reasons political, to a vast, efficiently-run coaching scheme at the schools level.

There are 30 county cricketers coaching schoolboys right now in South Africa. Basil D'Oliviera's out there too coaching non-European schools.

Would he consider an offer to coach in India? "Sure, provided the money's right."

"Today's youngsters get up to too much mischief," feels Greig who always wanted to be a teacher. "Unfortunately teachers today are not encouraging sport sufficiently. Sport should be part of one's education," says he.

As a schoolboy, Greig also played rugby and tennis. Now a spot of squash and golf… "there's no time really. On rest days I like to just lie around."

Hobbies? "Main hobby: my wife, easily the best in the world. We got married two years ago, are expecting our first child around the first of May…"

NEVER

"The love for cricket in India is absolutely unbelievable," says Greig, "I've never seen anything like it. The people are so friendly… I have yet to meet a person on this tour who has mentioned South Africa to me. This is because they love sport, which over-rides all barriers. I'm convinced if sportsmen were running the situation the world would be a much better place to live in. Take the World XI series last year. Our team had players of different races, religions, nationalities, what-have-you, but there were no problems at all. In fact we got along marvellously…

"It's a tragedy your cricket-crazy crowds cannot see the South Africans in action. They've seen everyone else and I'm sure it would be an incredible experience for them to witness players of the calibre of Mike Proctor, the Pollock brothers and Barry Richards who I consider the best batsmen in the world today. And I'm sure the sort of people that they are the Springboks too would give anything to play in India. If that were to happen, so many problems would be solved."

That's the man, Greig: "I love cricket. And I want anybody who loves the game to be happy."

About this tour, "It's been absolutely wonderful. To me there cannot be a better Test ground in the world than Eden Gardens. Everybody there was so terribly involved in every ball that was bowled. It was an unforgettable experience. I think it was the greatest sight I've ever seen: the lush outfield, all the colours in the world in the overflowing stand…

"If I were asked to choose one ground in the world to play on, I'd plump for Eden Gardens. At first I was a bit apprehensive of the crowd but soon realised that they loved cricket so much it would be the greatest tragedy in the world for them to burn the stands… I made the mistake of asking for one orange. I got fifty…

"I tell you, I really enjoyed myself playing in Cal. How do you keep a straight face on a ground like that? The blokes in the stands were understandably one-sided, but they were also knowledgeable. And well-behaved. There was this guy up in the stands sounding his gong. When I went down on my knees and asked him to stop, the people in the stands asked him to stand. I thought that was grand…"

The present Indian team, according to Greig, is good, but it would be going too far to call it great. Any Test side to be considered great must be well-balanced, it must have two fast bowlers. And I think your batting must improve. The potential is there but it is yet to be realised…. some of your batsmen seem too tense. The Gavaskar we see here is not the one I saw during the World XI series. He doesn't look as relaxed and assured as he did in Australia.

"You have undoubtedly a great spin attack and in Solkar the best close-to-the-wicket in the game today. But there must be two fast bowlers somewhere among your 550 million people. I can't believe there aren't. All this talk about physical limitations is a lot of nonsense. What you need is proper coaching… and this brings me back to the importance of coaching at an early age…"

"In my book," says Greig, "cricket's such a great game because it is a leveller. This is one of the first lessons I learnt. When I hit up 156 on my debut for Sussex (vs. Lancs) the papers were full of me. I started to believe I was the greatest thing that happened to cricket. But I had my middle-stump knocked back first ball in the very next match. I then realised in the dressing-room that anything can happen in this game…

"And," says Greig, who has come in for a great deal of criticism for playing his cricket perhaps just a little too hard, "as far as I'm concerned there is nothing better than real, hard, competitive cricket. I know I've been called names for my comments on the field, for showing emotion. But I tend to get involved in the game. And I feel that if my comments can get a batsman it's just too bad for him. But the great thing about this game is that after knocking a batsman's head with bouncers all day one can split a beer with him later. I know some chaps don't like doing it, but I'm not nasty…"

Agree.

Berry Sarbadhikary —RIP

SPORTSWEEK • December 26, 1976

Berry Sarbadhikary

THE tragic passing away of Berry Sarbadhikary has deprived Indian sport and sports journalism and broadcasting of a veritable doyen, a pioneer, a trailblazer who brought dignity to his profession and honour to his country.

The widely-travelled 'Berryda', as all of us at SPORTSWEEK affectionately and respectfully knew him, was a true ambassador of the country. His gentle, affable nature (he had an infinite capacity for 'empathy'), his polished demeanour which reflected his genteel upbringing and his sympathetic disposition endeared him to all those who had the pleasure of knowing him at home and abroad.

The list of 'firsts' chalked up by Berryda over a long and successful career spanning 72 years during which he covered 104 Tests is most impressive indeed. His book *Indian Cricket Uncovered* remains a classic and *My World of Cricket* went out of print almost as soon as it was released.

A household name in India, Berryda was loved, respected, revered in the West Indies. The late Sir Frank Worrell and his wife Velda were dear friends of his.

Proof of the love and admiration which the West Indies had for Berryda was provided by Clive Lloyd's 1974-'75 touring team which presented him a handsome purse at the conclusion of the Bush Trophy matches in Bombay, as did the Rotary Club of Bombay Mid-town and a host of friends after his retirement as cricket commentator.

Blessed with the ability to laugh at himself, Berryda believed in the adage that money should be 'current', not hoarded. Born in a distinguished Calcutta family and brought up in affluence, he counted among his intimate friends innumerable Maharajahs, Nawabs as also the hoi-polloi.

His earnings as author, journalist and broadcaster were considerable, but large-hearted friend and good host that he was, accustomed to the good things of life, Berryda did not have much to show for his efforts when he retired from All India Radio in 1972.

Berry Sarbadhikary was a true 'pro'. I had the pleasure and privilege of having him as house guest during Tony Lewis' team's tour and, therefore, had the opportunity of seeing for myself the tremendous stamina and capacity for hard work which he possessed.

Mild-mannered and soft-spoken, Berryda could be critical but never scathing, trenchant but never abrasive. He did not dip his pen in arsenic. Above all, he was always constructive and responsible.

Berryda's neat exterior mirrored an orderly mind. He always dotted his 'i's and crossed his 't's. He never missed a deadline and one could almost set one's watch by the arrival of his column in the office on Friday morning, the envelope neatly addressed in his elegant handwriting. Propriety was another trait, which characterised his personality. He was always punctilious in the matter of correctly addressing people and personalities.

Sarbadhikary engaged in serious discussion during a Test match with Ted Dexter
(Courtesy : Sen-Raleigh Ltd., Calcutta-1)

Around the time of his death, the Rotary Club of Bombay Midtown, of which I have the honour of being a member, was considering appointing Berryda editor of its Bulletin, a part-time assignment which would have fetched him substantial income for fairly easy work for a man of his professional abilities. Berryda was himself in the process of completing the work of updating his 'India-West Indies' souvenir, which could have been a money-spinner.

His desire, therefore, to take his life and his three-page letter to the police in which he attributes his decision to 'financial difficulties' is most bewildering. Besides, he had far too many friends, admirers and well-wishers who would have gladly helped, if called upon to do so. And, when you consider the fact that Berryda reportedly had a bank balance of Rs. 70,000 and a regular income, the fatal decision appears to be most bewildering, with more to it than meets the eye.

When Bishen Bedi most thoughtfully phoned early on the morning of the rest day to convey the news, my first reaction was that of disbelief. And one still finds it difficult to believe that the fun-loving Berry Sarbadhikary, with his joie de vivre, should decide to opt out for the reasons stated.

Berryda belonged to a fast vanishing species. He personified the very best aspects of old-world charm and grace. The Maker does not cast His children in the same mould any longer. RIP.

Gavaskar denies 'fatigue'

SPORTSWEEK • January 18, 1981

"I really don't know how to react. Perhaps they mean well, on the other hand the suggestion may be a tongue-in-cheek one," said India cricket captain Sunil Gavaskar to SPORTSWEEK when asked to comment on a suggestion made in certain quarters to the effect that he is a drained hero, sorely in need of a break.

A school of thought exists at the moment that Gavaskar, apart from trying to shoulder the considerable burden of captaincy, has been bearing the brunt of India's batting on his shoulders without a break in a time and age when the emphasis is on unremitting pace bowling.

Critics, well-meaning and otherwise maintain that for 10 long years Gavaskar, now aged 31, has been the kingpin of the Indian batting at a time when there has been a dramatic increase in the number of matches all countries play.

A former England Test opener once described the role of the opening batsman as the most nerve-wracking job of all.

Gavaskar said it was like being at the receiving end of a coconut shy, especially for batsmen whose game is based on unwavering concentration as in the case of Gavaskar as also Geoff Boycott, Glenn Turner, Bill Lawry, Conrad Hunte and Trevor Goddard of South Africa.

Critics point out that in 1974 after 10 years of opening England's innings, Geoff Boycott pulled out of Test cricket saying he could no longer maintain concentration and did not make himself available again until 1977.

The opinion is also expressed that he had opted out because he was afraid to face fast bowling.

But in the past two years at the age of 38 and 39 Boycott has effectively answered his critics by staging a magnificent comeback.

He is now poised to tour the West Indies, the happy hunting ground of pace bowlers from the Caribbean.

Mention is also made of New Zealand's stalwart Glenn Turner who opened the New Zealand innings with distinction for nine long years since 1968 and decided that enough was enough to escape from the pressures of Test cricket, particularly the role of opening batsman.

It is being suggested that Sunil Gavaskar has not had a real break from the game ever since he started playing for his country and that perhaps a two-year break would do his game a world of good.

"I'm not sure about that," says Gavaskar of the suggestion, "for one thing staging a comeback after a long layoff may not be all that simple a matter. Besides I'm enjoying playing cricket although I must confess I do not particularly look forward to the small matches."

How about his zest for the game and appetite for runs?

"I think I still have a great deal of zest left. As far as the appetite goes, I shall leave it to others to evaluate in terms of performance hereafter."

Prophetic words? An indication of the shape of things to come from the "Little Master" who says he never plays for records but who is only six centuries short of the world record of 29 Test centuries scored by the legendary Don Bradman.

Lloyd toasts Indians

SPORTSWEEK • March 9, 1983

The West Indies cricket captain Clive Lloyd raised his glass of champagne to propose a toast soon after Air Jamaica flight 609 had taken off from the Norman Manley airport and winged its way to Trinidad over Port of Spain, called the wickedest city in the world in the 17th century because it was the port of call of pirates and buccaneers.

"Here's to the Indians," he told SPORTSWEEK, "for a great match, for their sportsmanship and the manner in which they fought. May the other Tests be as exciting."

Lloyd was on his way to his hometown, Georgetown in Guyana. Travelling with him were former West Indian Test batsman Basil Butcher and wicketkeeper Jackie Hendricks and Sportsweek correspondent Tony Cozier.

Lloyd described his team's victory, as one of the closest Test matches of recent times, one which had spectators sit on the edge of their seats as seldom before, as truly 'magnificent'.

He said the Test was the first the West Indians were playing in a year and it was good for them to get mentally attuned to conditions.

Lavishing praise on Andy Roberts who took 5 for 39 in the second innings to lay the foundation for victory (he had match figures of 9 for 100) and Smokin' Joe Viv Richards, Lloyd said he knew his team could achieve the victory target despite limitations of time.

"The instructions were to go hell bent for leather and how splendidly the boys responded," he exclaimed.

Lloyd opined that he expected the touring Indian side to improve as the series progresses. "After all they have not been in the Caribbean for very long so far."

He told this writer who was travelling with Lloyd and companions from Jamaica (Xaymaca as the Arawak Indians, the earliest settlers from South America in A.D. 1000, called it) to Trinidad ahead of the Indian team which was to travel later in the day.

"Sharma has looked very good so far, so has Mohinder but the Indian batsmen seem to be getting out in their thirties and forties for some reason.

"I expect 'Sonny' Gavaskar to come good any time now. Hope that happens soon from the spectators' point of view. He and Vengsarkar are the batsmen we respect most. And we have a lot of respect for Madan Lal. He will make a lot of difference whenever he returns to the side," said Lloyd.

We are being victimized —Bandula Warnapura

SPORTSWEEK* • *May 18, 1983

Reproduced here in Warnapura's own words are extracts of a wide-ranging discussion: -

Bandula Warnapura

"We are being victimised. Extreme pressure is being brought on us. Our point of view has been blacked out. Not a word of what we have to say is being published in any newspaper in Sri Lanka after only two installments of an interview with tour manager Tony Opatha were published. We have been banned for 25 years, can you imagine? We are contemplating going to court against the ban.

"Only one out of the 14 who toured has been able to get his job back. Some of us, who were coaching school and college students free are now prevented from so. The severity of the ban indicates that those who run the sport in the island are scared that we might take over control, that their people may be ousted.

"I wish to make it clear that we are totally opposed to apartheid. And our tour, in no way, should be taken to mean that we support the South African Government's racial policy. But we are protesting against the double standards of our cricket board, payment-wise and treatment-wise.

"We had a dispute with our board over the fact that D.S. D'Silva was offered Rs.1 lakh (Sri Lankan) as against only Rs. 30,000 offered to the others including the captain. We protested against this discrimination. All 35 players in the pool for the national side protested against this discrimination, against the board's arbitrary and unfair selection policy. But the board didn't like the unity of the players. It considered the move a union of sorts and tried its level best to break it.

"We are totally against apartheid but decided to tour South Africa because we wanted to hit back at the people who hurt us. We came up against a wall and had to climb it. Besides you cannot leave the financial side out in today's context. As national players we have to maintain a certain level of living. We cannot, for example, go to the market and ask for lower vegetable prices or whatever just because our board does not pay us well enough.

"Yes, we were well paid for the South African tour. The range was between Rs. Seven to 15 lakhs Sri Lankan (the current rate of exchange is approximately two Sri Lankan rupees to the Indian).

"Public reaction? I would say that in Sri Lanka it is 90% in our favour. I have yet to meet a person here who understands the situation and is yet against the tour. In South Africa the reaction was mixed. The Asians or coloureds didn't like us playing there. I would say the blacks were not really interested although a few did come to watch us play.

"Eight of our players coached black schoolboys in Soweto and there was no reaction against us. We hope that one day coloureds and blacks will represent South Africa in sport. Why did Ian Botham and Viv Richards refuse lucrative offers to play in South Africa? I don't know. Maybe because they are not in the same situation as us. It is difficult to say whether or not we will go to South Africa again, given the chance. Under the present ban, with no chance to explain to the board or to the people through the mass media, what option do we have?"

Warnapura, 30 and married, is the father of a one year and an eight-month-old girl. He lives in Colombo and until the fateful South African tour was employed as assistant factory personnel manager with the Ceylon Tobacco Co. (A subsidiary of the Dutch American Tobacco Co.).

Said he in parting, "I shall never forgive myself for letting down my club team by leaving midway through a two-day match". The whole deal (meaning the South African tour) was worked in Holland by Tony Opatha and here in Colombo by Duleep Mendis"

With Opatha now in Holland again on a coaching assignment and with no early prospect of the ban on the Sri Lanka 'rebels' being lifted, there is every possibility of Sri Lankans forming part of an Asian touring team to South Africa consisting also of Indian and Pakistani players.

Are you tuned in, Board of Control for Cricket in India?

Good to be back—Clive Lloyd

SPORTSWEEK • September 28, 1983

Back in Bombay after eight years is West Indies Test captain Clive Lloyd and Kapil and his sorely tried "devils" had better watch out.

"Good to be back. I have fond memories of your city and your people," he told me over lunch at the Bombay Gymkhana.

Good reason, too. For it was here in Bombay at the Brabourne Stadium that Lloyd made a memorable Test in 1966 scoring 78 and 82 not out.

As captain of the West Indies side of 1974-75, he hit a brilliant 242 in the first test ever to be played at the Wankhede Stadium.

The West Indies skipper was in the city with Michael Holding and Jeff Dujon, who missed the three-day match now being played against the West Zone in Kanpur.

"I feel real good," said Lloyd after a squash match against Dujon at the Gymkhana's courts, "we are all fit and well and looking forward to the match." Dujon, former Indian stumper Farokh Engineer and Nirlon joint managing director Virenchee Sagar were also present. Lloyd expressed the view that his team was hoping for a sporting wicket at the Wankhede Stadium.

"Unfortunately," said he, "the wickets we encountered on this trip have been far from satisfactory. It is imperative that sporting wickets be prepared which will last at least three days."

Going by that criterion, Lloyd opined that of the three Tests played so far, only the wicket at Delhi may be said to have been of international standard. He was amazed that a Test should have been played at the Gujarat Stadium in Ahmedabad without a single match ever being played on it earlier on.

Amiable, soft-spoken Lloyd who not long ago was awarded an honorary doctorate by Manchester University spoke at length about the standard of cricketing in this country.

"It is not my intention to complain or whine and I hope I won't be misunderstood when I say this but it is my considered opinion that the umpiring in the Tests so far has been incompetent." (He singled out Swaroop Kishen as being the exception).

He made particular mention of the fact that the umpires in Ahmedabad refused to show him the ball after it had been replaced for getting out of shape.

"And", said he, "we were aghast that the Indian team was allowed to take the ball into the dressing-room during the lunch and tea breaks.

"Mind you, we are not saying anything irregular was done by the Indian team but the rules are specific in so far as they stipulate that the balls will be in the custody of the umpires during all breaks. To that extent, the umpires were ignorant of the rules," said he.

The West Indies skipper also expressed the point of view that the umpires in both the New Delhi and Ahmedabad Tests had wrongly interpreted the rule as regards deliberate padding. He commiserated with Dujon who, Lloyd felt, would have completed his century at Ahmedabad but for the fact that the umpire disallowed what was clearly a neat, deliberate deflection off the bat for four to fine leg.

Stressing the fact that he was in no way implying that the umpires were biased, Lloyd also referred to the fact that a substitute fielder had been wrongly allowed for Anshuman Gaekwad in the second innings at Ahmedabad,

"It was no secret that Gaekwad was at nets that (fourth) morning. The fact of the matter is that he batted quite comfortably and confidently, so there should have been no question of a substitute fielder for him earlier on," said he. "The relevant point is whether he was injured before or during the match."

"Talking of injuries," continued Lloyd, "we should be grateful there were no serious injuries on that Ahmedabad wicket. Somebody could have been very seriously injured the way the ball kept flying from just short of the good length spot. It was reported that wicket would take turn from the second day onwards. From what we saw, the ball started turning viciously from almost the second delivery".

Clive Lloyd (whose wife Waveney and two and a half year old son Jason arrived in Bombay from Manchester on Tuesday along with Farokh Engineer's wife Sherry) was "horrified" at the behaviour of the crowd in Ahmedabad.

"It was absolutely mystifying, the manner in which even batsmen, who scored 60 runs were booed by the crowd. I have yet to witness such curious behaviour in any part of the world," said he.

'Budhi' back for 'benefit'

SPORTSWEEK • October 5, 1983

REMEMBER Budhisagar Krishnappa (B.K) Kunderan, the former Test wicketkeeper-batsman who thrilled cricket *deewane* with his dashing exploits in the '60's?

Kunderan with wife Linda

'Budhi' is back in Bombay preparing for his 'benefit' which has been sanctioned by the Bombay Cricket Association (B.C.A.) and which will be played at the Wankhede Stadium in the form of the Ranji Trophy fixture between Bombay and Saurashtra on January 6, 7 and 8. 1984.

The product of the Board of Control for Cricket in India's mass coaching scheme, Kunderan played 18 Tests for India in which he scored 981 runs for an average of 32.70. He has two centuries and 30 Test dismissals (23 catches, seven stumpings) to his credit.

Kunderan toured the West Indies in 1961-62 and England in 1967. He represented his country at home against Australia in 1959-60, Pakistan in 1960-61, England in 1961-62 and '63--64, New Zealand in 1964-65 and West Indies in 1966-67.

Kunderan struck a purple patch in the 1963-64 series against England scoring 523 runs for an average of 52.50 which was the highest on both sides.

Brought in as a last-minute replacement for the injured Farokh Engineer, 'Budhi', the Man of the Match, blended savage aggression with remarkable patience to score 192 in six hours and 50 minutes. This is still the second highest score in Test cricket by a wicketkeeper, the highest being 209 by Imtiaz Ahmed of Pakistan. In the Ranji Trophy, Kunderan aggregated 2,637 runs at an average of 48.83.

The superbly fit Kunderan who is now 44 years old has been playing as a highly successful and popular professional first in the North Lancashire and then in the Scottish league (for Drumpellier in the latter) ever since he migrated to England in 1969.

Budhi and his English wife Linda have two children, Dhillon 14 and Kiran 10.

Captaincy taxing: Zed

MID-DAY* • *October 12, 1983

PAKISTAN cricket captain Zaheer Abbas returns home to Karachi today a contented man.

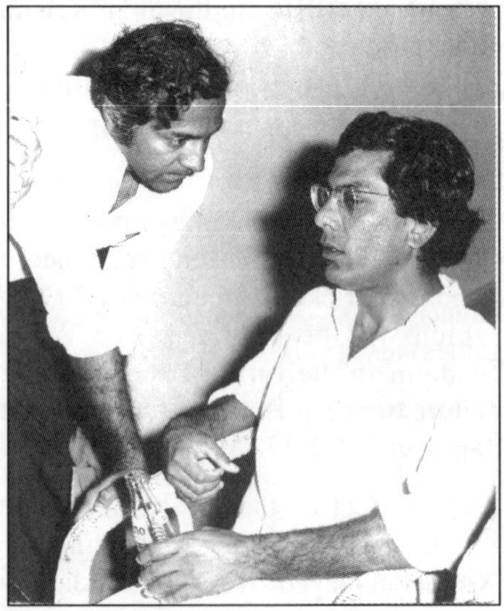

Khalid Ansari with Zaheer Abbas on his 1979-80 tour of India

"Despite the inclement weather, it's been a significant and satisfying tour for us," Zaheer (Zed) told MID-DAY last night.

"When we left home we were written off as a second-rate team which did not have a ghost of a chance, by our press and people.

"And everybody here in India expected us to be pushovers since we were without Imran Khan, Sarfaraz Nawaz and Abdul Qadir," said Zaheer.

"But we have more than proved to all detractors that our young team was more than a match for World Cup champions, India," said he. "Had we been favoured with better weather, I have no doubt that we would have turned the tables I would not go to the extent of saying that the umpiring has been biased, but it's pretty apparent many of your umpires are ignorant about the rules of the game."

Zaheer pooh-poohed the charge that he, as captain, had adopted negative or defensive tactics during the Test series.

"On the contrary, I would say it was India which failed to go all out for a win. Why argue about it? Let's just see the figures, compare the number of runs which the two teams scored on the average and the overs bowled per hour or day and you will get the answer yourself."

Referring to Sunil Gavaskar's column in MID-DAY ("Test Special"), Zaheer said, "it's surprising that he should criticise us for negative tactics. One only needs to take a look at his own performance as captain during the last series here in India against us to see matters in the right perspective," he added.

Zaheer stated that whereas India is capable of beating the West Indies during the forthcoming Test series, he added, "you will certainly have to do something about your attack." He opined that India had only one world-class bowler in Kapil Dev.

"The other Indian bowlers are just mediocre," he stated, "They may be capable of keeping, the runs down as they did during the World Cup, but they are not what I would call match-winning bowlers. I do not see them being able to bowl the opposition out twice, especially on the docile wickets in our part of the world, unless the other team bats really badly."

The Pakistan skipper hinted that Imran Khan is still not fully fit to bowl and that the disability may affect his team's chances during the forthcoming tour of Australia.

Zaheer confessed that the cares of captaincy had affected his performance as batsman. "So often during this series I found myself awake at four in the morning worrying about what to do on the field the next day. No, being captain, especially on a tour of India which presents its own special kind of problems and pressures, is no fun at all." said the holder of no less than five world batting records.

The Pakistan selection committee will announce the team for Australia today and it does seem as though Zaheer will be more than relieved to be a member of the touring party under the stewardship of Imran Khan, despite the praise showered upon his leadership qualities during the tour just concluded by team manager Intikhab Alam and selection committee chairman Haseeb Ahsan.

Zaheer's decision to go to Australia just in time for the Tests (he will miss the one-day games) also indicates that he will not be captain on the tour.

Zaheer singled out Azeem Hafeez as the find of the tour and paid fulsome tribute to Wasim Raja's brilliant innings in Jalandhar as the highlight of the tour from his team's point of view. He had no doubt that Sunil Gavaskar would achieve the distinction of bettering Sir Don Bradman's Test record of 29 centuries "in the very near future".

"Gavaskar still has a lot of cricket left in him and there is no reason why he should not notch up many more hundreds," said he.

"On the whole," concluded Zaheer, "it's been an enjoyable tour. The people have been wonderfully hospitable everywhere and I'm sure most, if not all, members of my team will want to return to India. Only, I wish the timing of the tour will be better and that we will be favoured with better weather the next time."

"And oh yes," said 'Zed', "please thank all your readers on our behalf for their warmth and kindness. They have been marvellous."

We proved far superior—Kapil

SPORTSWEEK* • *January 15, 1986* • *Sydney

Indian cricket Test captain Kapil Dev is extremely disappointed that his team did not win the Test series against Australia.

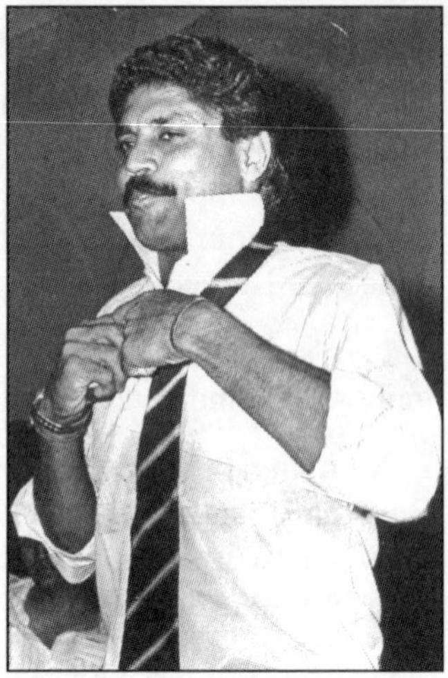

Kapil Dev

He told SPORTSWEEK at the end of the third Test at the Sydney Cricket Ground yesterday, that he was sorry for his players who had worked "so hard and with so much devotion".

"We proved that we are definitely the better side and we proved we can win Test matches."

When asked if he was enjoying the job of captaincy, Kapil replied that he was absolutely prepared to give up the job if the selectors felt he was not the right man for it.

"Although I personally feel that results are not everything, if the selectors are not happy with my performance, they can take the captaincy away". He stated the important thing in his opinion was for the captain—as indeed for every player—to "give 100 percent". He felt he was giving the job all that he was capable of.

The captain stated that the senior members of his side, namely Sunil Gavaskar, Mohinder Amarnath and Syed Kirmani had been extremely helpful as regards imparting their experience to the junior members of the team and to him personally.

"We are like a family. If they feel they can give me friendly advice they come to me themselves. Similarly, if I feel they can advise, I do not hesitate to consult them". But the skipper did concede the fact that he likes "to be in the front seat all the time."

Kapil made special mention of Ravi Shastri who he felt had improved tremendously and of Shiv Lal Yadav. "Spinners take time to settle down," he said but he was disappointed with Sivaramakrishnan's performance.

"But he is still young and I am sure he will come to terms with himself," said he, adding that the spinners have to learn to take punishment from the batsmen.

Kapil Dev declined to comment on the umpiring saying that it up to the Press to come out and point out substandard umpiring "I will make my own report if required but that is essentially the job of the manager—and of the Press which can be more effective.

"It is not good for players to criticise the poor umpires every time. After all they have a job to do. I am not saying anything about the umpiring in this Test except that it is essential to have umpiring of quality".

The Indian captain was confident that his team would put in an impressive showing in the limited-over tournament.

“I have no doubt we will live up to our reputation as world champions,” he said.

When asked about the relations between the two teams in the just-concluded series he stated “incidents will always occur in international cricket”.

Team manager S. Venkatraghavan opined that India were unfortunate not to win the series comfortably. He declined to comment on the umpiring but said rain had robbed India of a well-deserved win in Melbourne and Sydney.

He felt India were the superior side in all departments of the game.

“It is sad we did not win. Winning makes all the difference”.

Gavaskar realises ambition

MID-DAY • August 23, 1987 • London

"Little Master" Sunil Manohar Gavaskar demonstrated to the world at large on the third day of the MCC bicentenary match at Lord's on Saturday that he is second to none as a batsman on this planet as he helped the Rest of the World XI score 421 for 7 at close of play on the rain-affected third day.

No prizes need be awarded for explaining why the former India captain has never been given the credit due to him for his mind-boggling, leviathan efforts as a record-shattering batsman.

In fact, Gavaskar must have wondered often what it would take on his part to make the insular British press and the blinkered cricketing fraternity at Lord's and elsewhere in the British isles take note of his exploits.

The answer must have dawned upon Gavaskar at an early enough stage of this match which has been imbued with all the attributes and aura of a historic event of international dimensions.

And how characteristically did he seize the opportunity to proclaim to his detractors and to those who begrudge his heroic deeds that his records and accomplishments have been well-deserved, the result of blood, tears and sweat in the best traditions of Winston Churchill himself!

Gavaskar's epic innings which lasted 12 minutes under seven hours against the likes of Marshall, Hadlee, Rice, Shastri and Emburey who are considered the finest exponents of bowling in the world, shall linger forever in the memory of those who were fortunate to witness it.

Here was vintage Gavaskar, the supreme artiste who was always in authority, who had an answer to all the subtleties and subterfuges, not to mention the fire and hostility of the MCC bowlers.

Thanks to Gavaskar's 188 and his fruitful association with Pakistan captain Imran Khan who scored 82 runs which bespoke his pedigree as among the world's outstanding all-rounders, the Rest came within an ace of bettering the MCC first innings total of 455 for 5 declared.

Persistent showers overnight and a heavy downpour yesterday morning delayed the remorseless and inevitable crossing of the Rubicon by Gavaskar who achieved what was perhaps the last of his personal ambitions—that of scoring a hundred at Lord's—by about 45 minutes.

Gavaskar flicked the first ball of the day faced by him, off Marshall who was bowling with the same fire and hostility that he had done on the previous day, for three. An exquisite cover drive and a crisp square cut off Clive Rice took his score to 92. Followed a nudge to square leg for two and two more off a dainty glance to fine leg to take the Bombay opener to 96.

One was now witness to the curious spectacle of seeing Gavaskar nervous on the threshold of a century—his 82nd in first-class cricket.

But SMG was not to be denied. Following a few attempts to steal a single with help from ever-willing partner Imran (he came in ahead of Miandad who was nursing a bruised back), Gavaskar turned Shastri to short fine leg for a single and was home.

The century was given a standing ovation by the large crowd. Ravi Shastri was the first to congratulate Gavaskar and all members of the MCC team gave the "Little Master" a warm and prolonged ovation.

Azhar should step down as captain

MID-DAY • April 13, 1999 • Sharjah

AJAY Jadeja's captaincy in the last two Coca Cola Cup triangular series matches here has been truly inspirational.

Mohd. Azharuddin

Standing in as skipper in place of the injured Mohammed Azharuddin for part of the first clash against England, he motivated his depleted side to a sensational heart-stopping win last Friday, claiming three crucial wickets in the only over he bowled in international cricket in two-and-a-half years.

Then, on Sunday in the important return tie against England, Jadeja again led from the front with an aggressive yet not overly adventurous unbeaten knock of 74 to end the desert adventure for all practical purposes of next month's World Cup hosts England.

Apart from Jadeja's personal contribution, what has impressed most has been the manner in which he has boosted morale, inculcated team spirit, spurred his weary, battle-scarred troops after repeated defeats against Pakistan to two consecutive victories over a determined and thoroughly professional opposition for whom Sharjah has been a happy hunting ground.

This has been in sharp contrast to the laid-back, uninspiring, Nawabi demeanour of Azharuddin who has shown an increasing propensity to let matters drift, a reluctance to strike and seize the initiative at the opportune moment, an inability to arouse and inspire his embattled warriors to great deeds, unlike his Pakistan counterpart Wasim Akram.

It is no secret that the present Indian side is in disarray following its recent string of uninspiring performances. It is palpably dejected, dispirited, demoralised on the eve of the World Cup.

For this state of affairs, the national selection committee's well-intentioned but unwise policy of unbridled experimentation and asinine chop-and-change is to blame.

Equally at fault is Azharuddin's self-righteous aloofness and inability to inculcate in his team a positive mindset and a fierce determination to win.

Jadeja has breathed a refreshing new spirit of camaraderie among his mates, helped restore confidence and self-belief, the smiles have returned, foreheads appear less creased, shoulders don't droop as much.

Many considered Jadeja frivolous and too easygoing to be trusted with the burden of captaincy. He has proved them wrong. He has shown he possesses a shrewd cricketing brain, flair, inventiveness and courage under pressure.

Howsoever impressive his track record as captain in terms of statistics and heroic accomplishments the world over with an elegant bat, Azhar seems to be past his prime, alas.

At a pinch, he deserves a place in the World Cup 11 but certainly not as captain.

In the national interest, Azhar should step down even at this late stage in favour of Jadeja.

Anil Kumble's good deed

MID-DAY • January 8, 2000 • Sydney

HE may not have done his reputation as a joint world record-breaking bowler much good during the recently concluded Test cricket series against Australia.

Anil Kumble

But Anil Kumble has certainly demonstrated that he has the milk of human kindness flowing through his veins in abundant measure.

With the third Test here ending after only three days, the Indian cricketers had time on their hands to indulge their fancies before their departure for Brisbane yesterday morning.

And what did the engineer by profession do with his time?

A Good Samaritan act, which brought unalloyed joy to a heart patient at St. Vincent Hospital in Mosman.

Informed by a friend that 28-year-old Falgun Jariwala was awaiting a heart transplant, Kumble decided to bring cheer to the patient by visiting him in hospital.

Nurses monitoring Falgun's heartbeat and blood pressure noted immediate changes in his condition while Kumble posed for a photograph and wrote a message of good wishes before leaving Falgun.

Meanwhile, the controversy regarding racism in Australian cricket continues to rage.

The tone of some of the letters written to newspapers is remarkably strident but others are comparatively prudent in their assessment.

One such letter which appeared yesterday in a Sydney daily says: "While, I certainly feel a great deal of indignation about the racism encountered by Indian cricket fans at the SCG (Sydney Cricket Ground), I can't help but reflect on a recent trip around India.

"I encountered several female travellers who had attended the cricket in Delhi and been subjected to relentless verbal and physical sexual harassment by Indian cricket fans. Something about stones, glass houses and clearing up one's own backyard springs to mind."

I'm innocent: Gibbs

MID-DAY • April 16, 2000 • Johannesburg

AFTER a tumultuous week in South African cricket, Herschelle Gibbs has denied his involvement in match-fixing or spread-betting allegations involving disgraced former captain Hansie Cronje.

Herschelle Gibbs

On the eve of the decisive Herschelle match in the three-match Standard Bank one-day series to be played at the Wanderers Stadium here on Saturday, Gibbs said he was stunned when he was implicated in the Indian betting scandal.

"I felt bad but I knew I was innocent. Nothing would ever make me do something so irresponsible."

"I think somebody who would become involved in something like this would have let their country down, and themselves and the team, and it is terribly unprofessional."

Apart from Cronje and Gibbs, the players implicated are Pieter Strydom and Nicky Boje.

Gibbs said, "Nobody approached us. When we were told about it we thought it was a joke."

In the transcript of the taped cellphone conversation between Cronje and London-based bookmaker Sanjiv, alias Sanjay Chawla released by the New Delhi police, Chawla is alleged to ask, "and how many runs for Gibbs?" to which Cronje replies, "less than 20".

Gibbs scored 19 in the one-day international against India at Faridabad the next day.

In an obvious reference to this, Gibbs said, "there is simply no guarantee you are going to score more than five runs every time you play. Anybody with insight into the game would know that. It doesn't bother me."

Saying he felt sorry for Cronje, Gibbs added, "he is a great man and one of the greatest captains who has ever played the game."

"I've known him for a good few years and I've still got the utmost respect for him. He will always be a great friend of mine."

MORE SHOCKS LOOM

ACCORDING to Saturday Argus of Cape Town, New Delhi police have released new transcripts of alleged conversations between Cronje and an illegal bookmaker that they claim further implicate Cronje in match-fixing practices which he has been denying.

The latest transcripts allegedly refer to the last of the five-match series in Nagpur. In the transcripts Cronje indicates to the bookmaker, Sanjiv Chawla, that off-spinner Derek Crookes will open the bowling, that other "non-regular" bowlers will bowl and that India will make at least 250 runs.

All this came to pass the following day.

The transcript reads:

Chawla: "Who will bowl the first over?"

Cronje: "Crookes and (Henry) Williams."

Elsewhere in the conversation, Cronje informs Chawla that Lance Klusener will be the first change bowler, a "prediction" borne out in the match.

He tells Chawla not to worry. "We will be bowling our non-regular bowlers."

Pieter Strydom, not a regular bowler, bowled his full quota of 10 overs.

DAWOOD IBRAHIM CONNECTION

NEWSPAPERS here have published reports alleging that the kingpin behind the illegal betting syndicate has been identified by Indian intelligence sources as Dawood Ibrahim.

According to The Argus of Cape Town, "allegations made against him (Ibrahim) relate to terrorism, drug-running, arms dealing and now cricket match-fixing."

Apart from the criminal investigation in India and a soon-to-be instituted judicial inquiry in South Africa, Hansie Cronje could also face criminal charges here relating to his possession of $8,200 in apparent contravention of exchange control regulations.

Cronje's lawyer handed the money to the Reserve Bank, money Cronje has admitted receiving from a bookmaker during the recent tri-nation series involving South Africa, Zimbabwe and England.

It is illegal for South Africans to posses foreign currency unless they are on the verge of travelling or have returned recently.

"F*** HANSIE AND ALL WHO SAIL WITH HIM"

ROBERT Kirby of the *Johannesburg Mail and Guardian*, in a strongly worded article entitled, "F*** Hansie And All Who Sail With Him" writes, "people are actually saying that he (Cronje) has been brave and that he deserves admiration for having single-handedly assumed the moral responsibility of exposing the rackets. . .

"In fact Hansie Cronje is an unscrupulous liar and the thief of far more than money. His greatest iniquity is that he has stolen trust and faith from the young, that he has crudely eroded the happy optimisms (sic) of children."

In an editorial, the *Saturday Star* says, "in the midst of the angst, Shaun Pollock led his team to an unexpected, but richly deserved, victory on Wednesday night.

'It was all down to Cronje, the new captain said after the match.' The past, present and future of the squad was all due to him. Fine words, Shaun. But let's not kid ourselves.

"Whatever happens to Cronje, the future belongs to you and your boys. Don't let us down. Please."

Spectators at the second one-day match at Cape Town's Newlands stadium displayed a poster featuring a photograph of Cronje on a United States dollar bill instead of that of George Washington.

POSTSCRIPT: According to Reuters news agency, South African president Thabo Mbeki who is attending the Group of 77 summit in Cuba was asked to comment on the Hansie Cronje scandal.

He replied laughingly "save me from that... it's too embarrassing... too bad."

Get off your high horse, Dalmiya

MID-DAY* • *November 29, 2001

Perhaps the best news to come at the end of disastrous South African cricket safari is that our pride and joy, Sachin Tendulkar, is after all, not guilty of "ball tampering".

Jagmohan Dalmiya

This column has been advocating from Day 1 that, instead of engaging in an egoistic battle with the International Cricket Council (ICC) over relatively unimportant issues, Board of Control for Cricket in India (BCCI) president Jagmohan Dalmiya should have been concerned with the damage that match referee Mike Denness' high-handed rulings had caused to the *izzat* of our nation, Tendulkar, captain Sourav Ganguly and four of their teammates.

Posterity will now record that today's world's best batsman was guilty, not of cheating, but a minor technical impropriety. Also, that the punishment handed down to him was way out of proportion to the offence.

Whereas it cannot be denied that Tendulkar was guilty under the laws of the game for not "calling upon an umpire to supervise his attempts to clean the ball", as Denness' terms it, his resort to the age-old device of blaming the media for the avoidable furore that he caused is laughable.

Dalmiya should now step off his high horse and adopt a conciliatory position in his dealings with the world body to ensure that the present series against England is not jeopardised.

The long term interest of the game demands it.

A tale of two captains

SUNDAY MID-DAY • *December 25, 2001*

Nasser Hussain

The game of cricket could have done without England cricket captain Nasser Hussain's shenanigans in the current Bangalore Test which, if not in breach of its laws, undeniably contravened its spirit. Its image already grievously scarred by a series of body blows stemming from the betting and match-fixing scandals and the recent Mike Denness controversy, the unsporting ultra-defensive tactics of the England captain do not do its image any good. And the paying public is justified in feeling that such tactics result in their being short-changed.

The unfortunate happenings in the Test were surreal, as though evil genius Douglas Jardine had been reincarnated, reviving memories of the former England captain's infamous Bodyline series of 1932 which led to his being condemned to damnation and hellfire in the then civilised game. Interesting similarities exist between Jardine and Hussain and their deeds:

For one, the two England captains share a common Indian heritage. Jardine was born in our very own Bombay, *aamchi* Mumbai, and Hussain's father in Madras, *nammude* Chennai.

For another, both acted within the existing framework of the laws of the game, although interpretations of the law concerning wide balls differ.

Brilliant leaders and tacticians, both were driven by a fierce desire to win for England - at all cost.

Finally, there was the 'other' factor—in the case of Jardine, the great and dreaded Don Bradman, in that of Hussain, Sachin Tendulkar—both the scourge, thorns in the side of the opposition. A careful scrutiny of Law 25.1(a) defining what constitutes a wide, read in conjunction with Test Match Playing Conditions reveals that Nasser Hussain ensured that Ashley Giles and Andrew Flintoff bowled on the stumps from time to time. To that extent he cannot be accused of resorting altogether to negative tactics.

But an unreasonably excessive number of the left arm spinner's deliveries, bowled from over the wicket in the rough outside the line of leg stump were wide and the burly pace bowler repeatedly kept digging the ball short. Umpires Jayaprakash and De Silva would have been perfectly justified in calling many of Giles' and Flintoff's deliveries no-balls but they failed to do, thereby making a mockery of the proceedings. Seven consecutive maiden overs were bowled by the two in what, initially on the second afternoon, was a fascinating battle of attrition but a big y-a-w-n subsequently.

The ploy continued well into the third day when Giles finally wore down Tendulkar's Job-like patience to have him stumped for the first time in the 143 innings that he has played. However, one cannot resist the question whether Hussain's tactics were merely defensive (in keeping with his mantra that defence is the best form of offence) which would have been perfectly legit, or negative, which revised ICC rules seek to discourage to prevent a mass exodus of spectators away from the five-day game. Test Match Playing Conditions stipulate that Law 25.1, mentioned above, will apply, but in addition:

For bowlers attempting to utilise the rough outside a batsman's leg stump, not necessarily as a negative tactic, the strict limited over wide interpretation shall be applied.

For bowlers whom umpires consider to be bowling down the leg side as a negative tactic, the strict limited over interpretation shall be applied. It must be said to their credit that Flintoff and Giles executed Hussain's crafty gambit to perfection, cleverly mixing deliveries on the stumps with negative ones. His natural free stroking style shackled, the normally unflappable Tendulkar (his knock in this Test must rank among his best) was palpably discomfited.

Denied any joy from his complaint to the umpires on the score of negative bowling, he got embroiled in an uncharacteristic verbal exchange with Hussain. The umpires' tactful handling prevented the situation from getting out of hand. But correct and strict application of the laws concerning negative cricket could have prevented it in the first place.

Can we expect sporting behaviour today, Mr Hussain?

MID-DAY* • *February 3, 2002

Nasser Hussain

There is no denying the fact that the unprecedented demand for tickets for today's one-day cricket international at the Wankhede Stadium is a barometer of the absorbing clashes thus far in the series.

Equally, it cannot be denied that the general behaviour of the England team, and its captain in particular, have left a great dial to be desired.

Given Nasser Hussain's shenanigans, starting from his controversial and unsporting resort in the Test series to leg theory reminiscent of the one indulged in by the notorious Douglas Jardine, the Test and one-day series have, fortunately, not taken an ugly turn.

This has been only because of our peoples' traditional passivity, tolerance, even a misplaced notion of hospitality that is often mistaken for wimpishness.

It is sincerely hoped that, in today's crunch encounter, the deportment of the visitors, in whose off-field professions of good relations and sportsmanship, and actual on-field demeanour one has witnessed a vast chasm, will be bereft of the unsporting deeds of which Hussain and Co. have been culpable.

Mumbai's cricket deewane are known to be knowledgeable and sporting in the extreme in their appreciation of the game.

But they also perspicaciously comprehend the fine delineation between playing hard to win—and unsporting bending of the laws of the game.

On many occasions, they have also shown undisguised disdain for petulant and churlish behaviour. To that extent, Hussain and Co. should be forewarned.

Mid-Day's cricket correspondent Ehtesham Hasan has zealously exposed some unsavoury acts of omission and commission of the touring team during the one-day games in Kanpur and Delhi.

Hasan has pointed to repeated instances of excessive appealing, showing dissent over umpiring decisions, unconscionable sledging and use of their favourite four-letter word, impudently questioning the umpire's authority (as in the Jeremy Snape sunglasses standoff and the incident in which Hussain threw the ball at Sourav Ganguly and appealed for obstruction).

Ehtesham Hasan has also referred to the visitors' 'whining'.

Naughty, naughty Sourav

MID-DAY* • *May 7, 2002

Even though embers of the Gujarat inferno continue to glow flambently after over two months of the tragic Godhra holocaust, it's time for this column to move on to matters of lesser gravitas, without pangs of guilt for demonstrating Nero-like insouciance.

Saurav Ganguly

While the despicable elements responsible for the senseless misdeeds in Gujarat were busy revealing the most heinous aspects of human nature, elsewhere life has gone on in all its glory, such being the nature of human existence.

Amidst the grim political scenario, Indian foreign exchange reserves completed a four-week surge of $1.6 billion over the past two days even as South African space tourist Mark Shuttleworth returned to earth. In Myanmar, the military junta released 56-year old Nobel Peace laureate and pro-democracy leader Aung San Suu Kyi after 19 months of house arrest.

And, as reported in yesterday's *Mid Day*, French bigot Jean-Marie le Pen was shamed in the French presidential poll and British racist MP Ann Winterton was kicked out of the Tory party.

Glad tidings from the world of sport, almost as though to distract attention from the sordid happenings in the state of the Mahatma, has come in the form of Vishwanathan Anand being crowned champion in the prestigious Eurotel Chess Championship and the now-on, now-off tennis duo of Leander Paes and Mahesh Bhupathi winning the ATP Mallorca Open title in Spain last Sunday.

Sing Hallelujah, in the interim period, India won a cricket Test in the West Indies after 26 long years.

But, given the never-never-change habits of our pampered cricketers, it has taken less than a fortnight for the delirium following the Second Port of Spain Test victory to give way to dark despair following the 10-wicket shellacking at Bridgetown.

In the cacophonous post mortems and 'expert' opinions now being expressed ad nauseam, a seemingly trivial, but important, incident seems to have escaped attention.

According to the cricket correspondent of the Times of India, now touring the Caribbean with the team, umpire Asoka de Silva had a "little word" with skipper Sourav Ganguly for employing alleged negative tactics during the final session of the second day of the third Test.

As is well known, at 161 for four, in reply to India's paltry 102, and with only the tailenders to follow, West Indies captain Carl Hooper and Shivnarine Chanderpaul were turning the tide with some innovative batting while going for quick runs against India's feeble and now tiring spin attack.

At this stage, the Indian bowlers allegedly bowled "wide outside Chanderpaul's leg-stump" to a packed on-side field with only two fielders on the off, thereby damming the flow of runs.

The correspondent says that Harbhajan "continued with this tactic for a couple of overs" before umpire Asoka de Silva "stepped in". The umpire reportedly spoke to the off-spinner and captain Ganguly and "soon they had to discard the tactic".

Asked whether or not he had warned the captain, De Silva is quoted as saying, "I just had a little word with him. Yes, it was about the bowling."

Although KHALIDOSCOPE was not witness to the happening on television, there is no reason for this column to doubt the veracity of the *Times*' report.

That being the case, one has to take cudgels with Sourav Ganguly over the incident which, although it did not attract a warning in accordance with the new International Cricket Council (ICC) rules, was certainly contrary to the spirit of the game similar to the notorious leg theory contrived by Douglas Jardine and perfected, it would appear, by his successor Nasser Hussain, both of whom incidentally, were born in India.

Howsoever admirable his aggressive attitude and hunger for victory, the tactics employed by the Indian captain at Bridgetown were a condemnable display of bad sportsmanship. But for deft handling by the umpire, the incident could have taken an ugly turn.

Earning respect, the Viv Richards way!

MID-DAY • November 2, 2002 • Kolkata

Sir Isaac Vivian ('Viv') Alexander Richards was distraught as we discussed, into the early hours of Friday, the whys and wherefore of the decline of West Indies cricket from Olympian heights to Stygian depths.

Viv lamented the lack of discipline and application in the present squad.

Viv Richards with Carl Hooper on the 2002 tour of India

"What the lads need to do is earn respect," he told me.

Respect is precisely what the West Indies batsmen played for yesterday.

And earned abundantly, one might add.

On Thursday night, West Indies players, including Shivnarine Chanderpaul and Marlon Samuels, had attended a fund raising dinner organised by the resuscitated Indian Cricket Players' Association.

But from the manner in which they batted yesterday while pursuing their score of 446 for five - for a lead of 88 - they demonstrated that they were certainly in no mood to dole out any largesse - or mercy, for that matter - to their Indian counterparts.

Before commencement of this Test, Chanderpaul, who had taken diksha (spiritual initiation) from Swami Vidyananda in Guyana, prayed at the Bharat Sevashram here and offered floral tributes to Swami Pranabananda.

It seems Swamiji's blessings were showered upon the diminutive Guyanan, who ground the Indian attack into the dust while helping put his side within sight of a possible victory.

Chanderpaul has been the scourge of Indian bowlers. Yesterday's was his fifth century against India (sixth overall) and his first abroad. His average against India is a near Bradmanesque 81.42. It is obvious Chanderpaul has no respect for the pretensions of bowlers - slow or pace - from the land which his ancestors left by sea some 150 years ago as indentured labourers.

Nevertheless, the left-hander is refreshingly aware of his roots, as was evidenced when he kissed the turf at the Gardens after completing an exceedingly well-deserved century.

Chanderpaul's unbeaten 136 runs, in a knock of true character, have come from 255 deliveries, mostly on the leg side. Statistics from Wisden's 20-20 television programme indicate that approximately 70 per cent of his scoring strokes were on the leg - and 30 on the off-side.

Chanderpaul is far from being a purist's delight. Nor is he an aesthete's dream-come-true. Gifted with the ability to play late, he is a superlative player of spin bowling. His patience is comparable to that of the Biblical Job, his pugnacity akin to that of legendary pugilist Muhammad Ali.

In his face-saving endeavours, Chanderpaul was gallantly assisted in a sixth-wicket partnership of 191 by Marlon Samuels, who has made a comeback to the West Indies side after a spell in the Styx. His silken touch, as revealed in his unbeaten 89 yesterday, had class emblazoned across it. His exclusion from recent Windies sides is, therefore, incomprehensible.

The Indian pace attack looked ragged in the absence of Zaheer Khan.Unfortunately, Ashish Nehra is yet to establish his credentials to take over from Javagal Srinath the mantle of spearhead of the Indian bowling.

Well as they toiled on an unresponsive track. Anil Kumble (one for 150) and Harbhajan Singh (three for 101) may have benefited had they flighted the ball for variation and turn.

On a day in the sun in which Indian fieldsmen did little of note, wicketkeeper Parthiv Patel's performance was outstanding. The diving catch he held to dismiss Carl Hooper would have done credit to the very best in the business. It can now be said that the cherubic 17-year old 'keeper-batsman has arrived.

Wavell Hinds, centurion in this Test, and Chris Gayle, who missed his 100 by 12 runs, have revealed tremendous potential.

After the return to the side of injured Brian Lara, captain Carl Hooper, along with Chanderpaul, Samuels and Ramnaresh Sarwan would make for a formidable batting line-up.

In the bowling department, Mervyn Dillon is improving with experience.

Hopefully the lessons learnt during this tour should stand promising pace bowlers Jermaine Lawson and David Powell in good stead.

This is predicated on many ifs and buts, but, other things being equal, this cricketing bunch from the Caribbean may, yet, earn the kind of respect that Viv Richards, their legendary chief of selectors, expects of them

BRIEF SCORES:

India 358 all out (S Bangar 77, VVS Laxman 48, P Patel 47, J Srinath 46) and 471 all out (S Tendulkar 176, VVS Laxman 154) drew with West Indies 497 all out (C Gayle 98, W Hinds 100, S Chanderpaul 104; Harbhajan 5-115)

Dalmiya is caught in a dilemma

***MID-DAY* • December 24, 2002 • Sydney**

Jagmohan Dalmiya

With the standoff between the Board of Control for Cricket in India (BCCI) and seven of its players over participation in the February-March '03 World Cup in southern Africa continuing to defy solution, the Indian Board has come in for trenchant criticism from the Australian press.

In a hard-hitting article in yesterday's *The Australian* newspaper, Mike Coward, has accused the BCCI of holding the "international cricket community to ransom".

Writes Coward, Australia's most respected cricket writer, "In their latest affront to the International Cricket Council, they have withdrawn the names of the 30 cricketers they belatedly submitted for participation in the World Cup in southern Africa starting in 47 days.

"The names, which should have been lodged by December 1, were withdrawn last Thursday just 24 hours after they had been tendered," says Coward, an occasional contributor to *Mid-Day*.

According to Coward, "the ICC hierarchy is seething at what they believe to be a bloody minded campaign by the BCCI and its recalcitrant and provocative chief Jagmohan Dalmiya, to undermine the World Cup.

"The game's governors everywhere are aghast at the arrogance of the BCCI, which continues to flout the participating nations' agreement it signed on March 13 this year.

"Its failure to negotiate sponsorship concessions from the players has left at least seven players in direct conflict with the World Cup sponsors and, unless it has an immediate change of heart, the BCCI is facing large damage claims."

The columnist does not name the players but it is no secret that Sachin Tendulkar, Sourav Ganguly, Rahul Dravid, Anil Kumble, Virender Sehwag, Javagal Srinath and Harbhajan Singh have huge financial stakes in the imbroglio between the BCCI and the recently-formed Indian Cricket Players' Association.

Six of the present Indian players are under contract with Samsung, which is a competitor of LG. Other players under contract to Fiat, to which Tendulkar is also contracted, have a conflict of interest with Honda, another World Cup sponsor.

If Tendulkar and his affected teammates are unable to sign the ICC contract in its current form, they would be ineligible to play in any ICC event, including the next two World Cups in southern Africa and the West Indies in 2007.

Should Tendulkar or any of his teammates fail to play in the World Cup, it will be an automatic breach of contract with the Global Cricket Corp. (GCC), the tournament's marketers and broadcasters, who have signed an Australian $1 billion (approximately Rs 27 billion) deal with the ICC.

The GCC is wholly owned by Rupert Murdoch's The News Corporation. The ICC, on its part, has guaranteed to GCC that all nations will send their strongest teams to the World Cups. It will, therefore, be liable for damages in the event of India not being able to send its best players.

Dalmiya has called a special meeting of the BCCI tomorrow. He has reportedly been told in no uncertain terms that ICC will make no further concessions.

India is the only country that has not been able to resolve the differences between the parent body, the BCCI and the Test players association. Coward attributes this failure to the "poor relationship" between the BCCI and its players.

Coward also writes, "although it is well known the BCCI is the richest Board in the world, it continues to pay its players abysmally, as compared with the situation in Australia."

However, the writer does not mention the astronomical amounts of endorsement contract money which Indian players make and Australian cricketers do not. Ironically, the biggest beneficiary of advertising contracts is Test captain Steve Waugh, who earns a large percentage of his endorsement money from Indian advertisers.

According to ICC president Malcolm Gray, India could face large compensation claims should the BCCI fail to honour the agreement.

"It is impossible to quantify the level of claims before the event", Gray is quoted as saying, "but it is clear that if the BCCI does not meet its obligations and there are damages made as a result, the BCCI faces the potential of these claims being made against it for non delivering on its contract".

Jagmohan Dalmiya, it appears, is caught between a rock and a hard place: between the ICC, run from London by two Australian Malcolms—Gray and Speed, the former being president and the latter chief executive—and the Indian cricketers.

Due allowance should, therefore, be made for the points of view of Mike Coward and other Australian journalists.

Interestingly, the fact that Jagmohan Dalmiya, a former ICC president, is among seven members of the ICC's World Cup contracts committee, responsible for ensuring that the ICC honours its agreements, makes for a rather piquant situation for the wily businessman, the *ustaadon ka ustad*, who could teach his peers much more than a trick or two in the cut and thrust of sports politics.

McGrath's praise for India is left-handed

MID-DAY* • *January 13, 2004* • *Sydney

One cannot help feeling that Australian pace spearhead Glenn McGrath's praise for India's widely acknowledged remarkable showing in the recent Test series is grudging and—forgive the pun—left-handed.

Glenn McGrath

What he gives with one hand, he hurriedly retracts with the other. In his newspaper column in a Sydney newspaper McGrath writes, "The focus on us not winning the series we were expected to win easily is understandable but let's give credit to India. It is a case of India being on the rise than us being on the wane."

Saying that South Africa are highly rated, McGrath believes Australia and India are the top two teams in Test cricket.

"This series saw two very good teams play on very good batting wickets and India were up to the task," McGrath writes.

But the veteran strike bowler of the Australian attack quickly adds that the nature of the wickets has been overlooked in all the opinions expressed about the series.

"The two things India never like when they come to Australia are bounce and seam, and all our wickets didn't offer that", McGrath says in a seeming case of sour grapes.

"I'm sure when we next tour India they will produce slow, turning wickets which will perfectly suit their bowlers," he writes.

Referring to Australia's narrow win over India in the first one-day match last Friday, McGrath writes, "Our win did not surprise me because we definitely have the wood over them in limited-overs cricket.

"We showed we had their measure in the World Cup final and also in a later one-day series in India."

McGrath insists that his team is not in decline and that it can still dominate world cricket.

Reverting to his thesis about Ricky Ponting team's being able to dominate world cricket McGrath says, "Good teams learn from their experiences and we will learn from this drawn series."

He singles out Simon Katich for special mention saying the New South Welshman was one of the few batsmen to look comfortable against Anil Kumble.

Ganguly could have done better

MID-DAY • February 7, 2004

Sourav Ganguly

His expression said it all. At the Melbourne Cricket Ground (MCG) yesterday, the sands of time were running out on Sourav Ganguly's relentless passion to achieve unprecedented cricketing glory in Australia.

All his efforts to curb counterpart Ricky Ponting's unremitting drive towards victory were proving to be of no avail.

Ponting's unconcealed annoyance at failing to personally lead his team to victory, when he fell at 88, 13 short of his team's victory target, was an essay in contrast.

To a large degree, apart from his own - repeated - batting failure, Ganguly is to blame for the manner in which he handled his bowling attack and, straightaway, irrevocably surrendered the initiative.

Although India would have probably lost anyway, given their paltry score of 222 to defend, the moment was lost with an inexplicable decision on the captain's part.

With Irfan Pathan, the find of the tour who has the likes of Richie Benaud, Ian Chappell, Mark Taylor and Ian Healy singing his praises, available, Ganguly's decision to toss the new ball to Laxmipathy Balaji with a palpably inadequate score to defend, was mystifying.

As it turned out, whatever initiative Ganguly tried—to be fair, he was not wanting in that regard - failed to materialise on the day.

But, Ponting's did!

The coming of the winning runs from a Yuvraj Singh overthrow, with not a single fielder backing up, would have been comical had it not been reflective of the mental aspects that decided the thoroughly deserving home team win.

At the end, one had to conclude that Team India will need a superlative effort in Sunday's second final in Sydney to live up to the skipper's claim that his team is at par with, if not superior to, the world champions.

For the information of followers of the game back home who might wonder what—really—went wrong in yesterday's final of the tri-series: quite simply, India were outplayed by a mentally and technically tougher and better organised team.

After Sourav Ganguly won the toss for the sixth (!) time in this series by calling "heads" and decided to bat, he stated that past performances did not count for much as far as he was concerned.

Ricky Ponting, on the other hand, said, "no matter what they (India) might say, their past (and recent) record would be at the back of their heads".

The timorous manner in which India's vaunted batsmen faced up to the "chin music" orchestrated by Brett Lee, Jason Gillespie and Brad Williams on a wicket that was conducive to stroke-production soon put Ganguly's and Ponting's diametrically opposite views in perspective.

The suspicion that the demons of Perth continue to stalk the shell-shocked Indian batsmen was soon confirmed. They appeared to be doppelgangers of the hitherto vaunted maestros whose pyrotechnics have lit up this Australian summer.

India's travails were as much self-inflicted as they were the result of Australia's superior pre-match strategising and brilliant tactical captaincy, in the form of astute bowling changes and field placements.

The gambit to bowl shorter-around eight metres from the stumps—and aim the deliveries at the body rather than on and outside the off-stump had the batsmen in all kinds of strife.

Lee and Gillespie bowled with admirable discipline and pace, Lee clocking a fastest delivery of 151 km/ph.

Lucky to survive when attempting to cut Brett Lee to fine leg where he perished twice—against Australia and Zimbabwe at Perth—Sehwag was bowled off his gloves in awkwardly fending off a rising delivery from Jason Gillespie.

The Najafgarh dasher just refuses to learn from his mistakes. Rahul Dravid's misery continues apace ever since the unfortunate ball-tampering episode. In every match since, the elegant vice-captain has perished after showing promise of a big score.

VVS Laxman, who was out to a good low catch by Andrew Symonds at deep gully, was the only top order batsman to take the battle to the opposition, despite being struck on the helmet, until Ajit Agarkar and Hemang Badani confirmed that there was neither devil in the wicket nor any inordinate terror in the attack.

With the top six batsmen back in the pavilion for an embarrassing 75, Agarkar and Badani threw their bats around and, thanks to dropped catches and missed run out opportunities, helped post a fighting score with a courageous record partnership of 102 off 119 balls.

For all his prodigious talent as all-rounder, Agarkar remains an enigma. The 26-year old Mumbaikar's fabled consecutive ducks are inexplicable when you consider his match-winning Test century in England and his valuable contributions with the bat on this tour.

No praise can be too high for the unflappable Badani who, despite a nasty blow on his helmet once again as in the last game against Zimbabwe, remained unbeaten and helped India attain a modicum of respectability.

Pathan impressed again with the bat, strengthening his credentials as budding all-rounder, but his run out, along with that of Anil Kumble cost the side dear.

After the match, Ganguly said, "We will have a good game in Sydney if we can get runs." As it turns out, the buck stops with the skipper and his eminently capable batsmen.

Why blame the poor, inexperienced bowlers?

If anybody is whingeing, it's Adam Gilchrist

***MID-DAY* • February 11, 2004**

Adam Gilchrist

Australian cricket vice-captain Adam Gilchrist has accused Indian skipper Sourav Ganguly of "squealing" in the second final of the tri-series last Sunday. Ganguly complained to Australian skipper Ricky Ponting that Brad Williams had "sledged" him all the way from "the Sydney gate to the wicket" when he came out to bat, but did not want to make an issue of it.

One does not know the reason for the captain's reluctance but one wonders if it was driven by the fact that the match was all but lost and that pushing it would only have made him and the team look like bad losers—which, in fact, Gilchrist has now insinuated.

"I believe there was a bit of verbal jousting going on, but from what I believe it was very minor and he (Ganguly) was very quick to run squealing to the umpire and the captain (Ricky Ponting) and everyone.

"All I can say about that is whenever the word sledging comes up, we seem to be thrown in as the bully boys, but I can promise you it ain't the case."

Gilchrist's deviousness and self-righteousness are incredible.

For one thing, millions of viewers can vouch for the fact that Ganguly "was not very quick to run squealing to the umpire and the captain and everyone."

The only person he spoke to was Ponting, as he ought to have done, apart from the umpires.

Ganguly's decision to treat the incident as an aberration and not bring it to the attention of the umpires was, if anything, a sporting gesture, whatever the state of the match.

Moreover, teams the world over know only too well the Australian team's boorish behaviour, which has given the game a bad name and prompted Cricket Australia to devise a code of conduct for its players.

If anybody is whingeing, it is Gilchrist. Besides, he should have had the guts to express himself when Ganguly was still in Australia, not after he and his team have returned home.

Not only is this an instance of the pot calling the kettle black, it is a case of being blatantly and deplorably economical with the truth.

The pointless Tendulkar puzzle

MID-DAY* • *October 23, 2004* • *Sydney

The transparency as regards Australian cricket captain Ricky Ponting's thumb injury, treatment, recovery and precautionary measures is in stark contrast to the totally unnecessary and counterproductive secrecy surrounding Sachin Tendulkar's tennis elbow problem.

Sachin Tendulkar

The hold-your-cards-close-to-your-chest policy is of a piece with the Board of Control for Cricket in India's overall cloak-and-dagger mentality in all such matters and betrays a siege mindset.

Ponting left home yesterday to join his team in Nagpur today as they prepare for the third India-Australia Test starting on Tuesday.

The 29-year old told the media here yesterday that he should be 100 per cent by early next week although he will not play at Nagpur and focus on being fully fit for the Mumbai Test commencing on Nov. 3.

"The first couple of days when I get there I'll go pretty easy with catching and fielding drills," Ponting told the press

"I just really want to get used to the feel of having the ball back in my hands again and take it pretty slowly. I have had some protective guards made to field in if I'm not overly confident. I think I'll have a pretty good idea the first few days after I arrive."

Tendulkar, himself a man of few words, and BCCI officials have shed very little light on the champion batsman's true condition.

While Tendulkar's chances of playing at Nagpur remain shrouded in secrecy and double-speak in turn, Ponting is delighted that everything has progressed "very quickly". He says there is a lot more calcification on his thumb now and that it has healed a lot faster than expected.

However, the tourists' team management will handle the skipper's injury with kid gloves to ensure that he is not only fully fit to give the best of himself in the possibly decisive Mumbai Test but also shipshape for the Australians' crowded itinerary thereafter.

Even as Sachin Tendulkar races against the clock to be similarly ready for the tough battles ahead, Australian assistant coach Tim Nielsen said Ponting's task is not easy as he has played no first-class cricket since September 21 when he broke his thumb.

Nielsen said, "It takes a bit of time to adjust to conditions but it will be more his ability to bat for long periods.

"That will be the big thing. That's something he will have to get used to, the physical stress of playing over here as much as the conditions.

Ponting is reportedly carrying several specially designed protective braces to wear. If found fit to play, he will avoid his customary second slip fielding position but he is not certain if he will wear the thumb guard while fielding in the cover or mid-wicket region.

"I have had some protective guards made to field in if I'm not very confident. But I've still got another two weeks until that fourth Test and by then I should be confident with it, taking into account the training I will have done," Ponting said.

However, by contrast, there was very little forthcoming along similar lines about the Indian legend–and seemingly very little concern that rushing Tendulkar into the Nagpur Test would not be in the interest of the team nor the star player himself.

All that Board of Control for Cricket in India (BCCI) doctor Anant Joshi says is that Tendulkar is "making good progress".

"I checked Sachin and found he has improved. It is up to him to decide his return. It is a question of him feeling comfortable about playing again," Joshi said. One would have thought the doctor knows best!

The Mumbai maestro will undergo a fitness test tomorrow to assess his recovery. It will be a wonder if we are informed about the true state of affairs.

That's being unsporting, Mr Ponting

MID-DAY* • *November 9, 2004

Since he is no man's fool, Ricky Ponting must have an exceedingly low opinion of Rahul Dravid's intelligence as also a vainglorious estimation of his own powers of persuasion. How else can one explain the Aussie captain's reported suggestion to the India stand-in captain to join him in a formal protest over the Wankhede Stadium wicket, which the tourists querulously blame for their defeat in last week's Mumbai Test?

Ricky Ponting

Upon his return to Sydney on Sunday, Ponting, in an outburst of injured self-righteousness, said he would register his dissatisfaction with the wicket in his official captain's match report to the International Cricket Council (ICC)

And, believe it or not, Ponting actually believes that he can "enlist the support of Dravid to impress on the need to have more genuine Test pitches."

"Genuine" Test pitches? Please enlighten us, skipper: what is a "genuine" Test pitch as against a counterfeit one?

Mr Ponting: Is a "genuine" wicket one on which the ball rears menacingly at head and torso, terrifyingly whistling past the chins and ears of hapless batsmen, unaccustomed to fiery pace and pronounced lift as at Perth or in New Zealand, making a mockery of the sporting concept of a level playing field?

For a long time now, batsmen from around the world, unaccustomed to playing on such minefields, have been easy meat for Australia's gleeful lethal fast bowlers, who have terrorized them on home turf to set the stage for victory

The strange aspect is that Ricky Ponting cannot possibly have forgotten the shellacking received at the hands of the New Zealand pace bowlers on hazardous wickets during the drawn series in that country in 2001–02.

Nor, indeed, have the Indians completely overcome the nightmare of the 2002–03 tour of NZ, and South Africa of the 2003–04 series there. Sourav Ganguly's side took the "substandard" wickets in their stride without whingeing. And, if memory serves one right, so did the Aussies. So why the whining now?

Perhaps because they were denied the desperately wanted 3–0 victory? Perhaps because this would have enabled the captain himself to claim credit for a Test win in the series?

If Ponting had his way, he would have all Indian wickets similar to the vexed one at Nagpur, which, resembled the green tops in Australia, thanks to the illogical obduracy of Nagpur officials and groundsman Kishor Pradhan, who had no compunction in cutting their noses to spite their faces

Ponting has the temerity to pontificate gratuitously that "India's cricket would be better served with wickets such as the seamer-friendly one at Nagpur", which, we may add, caused Messrs McGrath, Gillespie and Kasprowicz to rub their eyes in disbelief and salivate in anticipation, upon first setting eyes upon it.

The Aussie pacemen capitalised gleefully upon the manna from heaven offered by India's feuding officials and sent the Indian batsmen to the cleaners to carve out an emphatic, impressive win that enabled their team to breach what Steve Waugh termed the Final Frontier.

It is very possible that—the groundsman's gift apart—but for rain and the benevolence of wicket-keeper Parthiv Patel, the series could have been drawn 2–2, enabling India to retain the Border-Gavaskar Trophy. But, then, this is in the realm of "If my aunt had been a man, she would have been my uncle," ifs and buts.

One would have thought that Ponting, with his 80-Test experience would have fathomed by now that any home team in the pantheon of international cricket, from almost the advent of the game of cricket, has had the acknowledged right to prepare wickets to suit its own bowlers.

Thus it has been and so it shall remain, unless the ICC decrees otherwise.

For Ponting to attribute his team's 13-run defeat solely to a wicket he describes as "substandard", without regard for his team's remarkable gutless capitulation in the second innings is unsporting, in poor taste and smacks of sour grapes

After all, it is not as though two separate wickets—one for the Aussies and one for the home side—were prepared for the Test.

The assured manner in which Sachin Tendulkar and VVS Laxman batted on the third (and last morning) of the Test while putting on 91 runs in 119 minutes in positive fashion to lay the foundation for a shock victory, expose Ponting's diatribe for what it is.

Australia's batsmen were the victims of their own incompetence against top-class spin bowling brought on by needless, self-induced panic through sheer fear of what the Indian spinners would do on a crumbling wicket, after the unexpected success of part-time spin bowler Michael Clarke (six wickets for nine runs), caused, again, by some inept batting on the part of India's lower-order batsmen.

Former Test captain, Polly Umrigar, who supervised the preparation of the controversial wicket, has stated that "Ponting dug his own grave" in that the exaggerated turn which the wicket produced in the fourth innings was the result—or folly—of the Aussie skipper who should have known, as even Mumbai maidan captains do, that the use of the half-tonne heavy roller by him twice would break up the hard wicket.

There were simply no ghouls in the wicket. All the kerfuffle is nothing but what we were taught at school about a bad workman blaming his tools or *naach na jaane aangan tedha* (the bad dancer blames the dance floor).

Ponting is reported as saying, "It's the sort of wicket where you're always in two minds about what to do".

He goes on to add, "If you try to stand there and defend, you're eventually going to get out. If you try to play a shot here and there you're a good chance of getting out as well. You can't fault any of the guys. We tried our hardest and we ended up getting close."

How's that for tautology?

But then, Mr Ponting, doesn't unpredictability of wickets make cricket the gloriously uncertain game it is renowned to be? Surely, you don't expect the rest of the world to tailor-make green-top wickets for your bowlers and batsmen to perpetuate your status as world champions?

Mr Ponting, you are the leader of an awesome team that is, undeniably, in a class of its own. Your demeanour should, therefore, be in keeping with your mighty deeds on the field.

We are tempted to believe that Adam Gilchrist, your deputy who so ably led your team to victory, could never be guilty of the kind of churlishness and indiscretion that you have shown.

Don't look for scapegoats in the wicket, Mr Ponting. Your batsmen were gauche last Friday. And, with death staring them in the face, the Indian spinners bowled superbly. It's as simple as that.

Johnnie Wright is hurting

***MID-DAY* • November 17, 2004**

His countenance and body language bespeak the gentle coach's anguish at the steep decline in his wards' performance after the halcyon tours of Australia and Pakistan.

John Wright

I have never seen him as disconsolate as last Saturday after India lost to Pakistan at the Eden Gardens. He locked himself in his room immediately after the game and failed to appear for breakfast the following morning in the hotel's coffee shop, as is his wont.

"John Wright from the Indian cricket team", as the unassuming Indophile likes to describe himself, told MID-DAY's Clayton Murzello in Jaipur on Monday that he wants more "hunger to win" from his players to get back to the levels we had achieved on the two tours.

Wright said he would like to see a change in attitude towards winning and greater discipline and determination.

"I aimed to lift things by 10 per cent after the Australia and Pakistan tours. I am very disappointed personally that we have not achieved that. We have LOST 10 per cent and may be more.

"I want to get that 10 per cent," he said determinedly, adding, perhaps ominously, "If I cannot get that, then someone else deserves a turn."

Straight-from-the-heart talk from a dedicated, hard working professional, who helped his Indian team earn respect the world over, only to see it slide again into the Slough of Despond.

The self-effacing, soft-spoken former New Zealand captain makes no bones about his disenchantment with his team's carelessness and lack of effort on and off the field.

Although noncommittal on the subject of the players' distraction as a result of endorsements and seeming obsession with commercialism, Wright believes the time has come for non-performers to be discarded.

"Success can be viewed as an enemy. It is one of the challenges of being an Indian cricketer. The hype, fame and love is here but it must not detract from your hunger or give you a comfort zone," Wright told MID-DAY.

"Anything that gets in the way of putting in everything that is required to perform at your best—whoever it is, me or whoever—you need to have a good look at yourself. It's all about performing for your team to win on behalf of the fans you play for."

Wise words, earnestly expressed!

For quite some time now, our national selectors have persevered with many underachievers, who have done the team a great disservice.

The fact of the matter is that many of the selectors are in awe of some of the superstars in the team and just do not have the balls either to drop them or even ask them to shape up or ship out.

This has led to the formation of a cabal in the side and the breeding of an undesirable sense of security and complacency.

I have nothing against commercialism, nor the astronomical sums of money the players now make during what is, essentially, a limited career span. If sponsors are prepared to fall over themselves in wanting to sign up the prima donnas, good luck to them both.

Moreover, cricketers (in fact most sportsmen in our country) are not all well-educated or professionally qualified do anything else after their playing days are over, as we have seen in so many sad cases.

That said, commercial considerations must never be allowed to come in the way of players giving their best at ALL times.

As things stand, its time the non-performing prima donnas were brought down a few notches.

The only way to re-induce in them the "hunger" that Wright speaks of, is to deprive them of the opportunity of making undeserved big bucks, by dropping them from the side.

Their exclusion from the national side will ipso facto drive away present and potential commercial suitors. As simple as that!

There is tremendous talent in our country waiting to be tapped. The time has come to stop the free ride these Goliaths with feet of clay have been enjoying.

There's no reason why we shouldn't follow the Australian Way: Only the fittest and most deserving must wear the country's cap. Lack of form or performance?—Out you go to make way for someone more deserving.

(The last Australian tour of India saw even Darren Lehmann and Brett Lee carry drinks).

The time to make a beginning, to experiment, without waiting for the series against the never-ever-learn Bangladeshis, is NOW that the substandard South Africans are touring our country.

And, talking of 'hunger' and 'changing attitudes' brings me back to my pet subject: How about appointing a full-time motivator (as, indeed, also a professional media manager), as many of the top teams are now doing?

It is no mere coincidence that India's impressive performances in the last World Cup and in Australia and Pakistan came during and immediately after the time sports psychologist Sandy Gordon was associated with the team.

But, then, that's a topic for another day, to be dealt with exclusively and in some detail.

POSTSCRIPT: "Heard the latest? The ICC wants its 'elite' umpires to go back to school—to learn geometry."

— Former Test skipper Nari Contractor's take on the parent body's ruling on what constitutes a legal bowling delivery

Warne's 'cheap' thrills

MID-DAY • April 17, 2005 • Sydney

Trouble is no stranger to Shane Warne, whose photograph, with his pants around his thighs and a cigarette hanging out of his mouth, was published in last Tuesday's SUN newspaper of London and reproduced in Mid-Day the same day.

Shane Warne

The world's highest wicket-taker with 583 wickets, Warne has a knack of getting into hot water.

Just a few weeks before last Tuesday's shenanigan at his home ground in Hampshire, Warne was in the middle of a storm in New Zealand over an allegation that he asked an Auckland (New Zealand)-based newspaper not to publish an allegation that he sent an explicit text to a New Zealand woman.

This latest texting allegation was revealed when the Sunday News claimed to have been approached by an unnamed person seeking Aus $27,800 (approximately. Rs 2 lakhs) to reveal a story about Warne.

But the paper claims that before it began investigating, it was contacted by a former New Zealand Test cricketer who said Warne would be available for an exclusive interview if it dropped the story.

Warne asked the newspaper, through his lawyer, not to publish the allegation—his request only confirming the story and prompting the paper to reveal it.

Shane Warne's brother and manager Jason, immediately described the report as "not a story".

Cricket Australia, the Australian cricket board, after speaking to the champion bowler distanced itself from the affair, only issuing a statement that said,

"It is very clear that this is s private life matter for Shane Warne".

The matter has been dropped and Warne lives another day to carry on his nefarious obscene SMS activities with impunity.

If Warnie is around, excitement cannot be too far behind.

Not too long ago—in 2000, in fact—Warne bombarded English nurse Donna Wright with text messages, followed by similar objectionable communications to Helen Cohen Alon, a South African mother of three, who accused the cricketer of fathering her child.

Then there was the Melbourne strip tease dancer, with whom Warne is alleged to have had an affair. On and on, ad nauseam.

So incensed was a female columnist of a Sydney-based newspaper, that she addressed Shane Warne: "Warnie, come on text me. You know you want to".

"I'm beginning to think I'm the only woman in the world you haven't. I'm offended. As my friends will vouch, I love nothing better than sending the odd text or 200 on a night out. So we have that in common for a start.. I know you'll come around and text me—you can't help yourself."

It's still early days, but it is not yet known if Warnie rose to the challenge. The great leg-spinner, who was banned from the World Cup in Africa for taking a diuretic, for which he blamed his mother, is now in England, captaining Hampshire in the county championships first division on a two-year contract, with an option for a further two.

How come Kaps fits in here?

MID-DAY • May 8, 2005

Believe it or not, but Kapil Dev, India's greatest and, arguably, most athletic and fittest cricketer in his heyday, has been nominated for a team of the World's Portliest XI, being chosen by an Australian website.

Dev is said to have "grown quite soft around the middle" during his playing days.

Erapalli Prasanna and Bishan Singh Bedi have also been nominated by visitors to the interactive site.

Not intended to be taken seriously, the Australian Broadcasting Corporation (ABC) Website Forum has invited fans to send in their nominations of "portly" Test players.

Names in the post-1970 team include Pakistani skipper Inzamam-ul-Haq (pre-diet), former Australian skipper Mark Taylor, former Sri Lanka captains Arjuna Ranatunga and Duleep Mendes, Australians Shane Warne, Darren "Boof" Lehmann, Merv Hughes, Rodney Marsh, David Boon, Gary Gilmour, Keith Stackpole (nicknamed "Billy Bunter"), England captains Ian ("Beefy") Botham and Mike Gatting, as also Colin Cowdrey, Robert ("Blobert") Keys, Colin ("Hambone") Milburn, Eddie Hemmings and, surprisingly, Tom Graveney and Fred Titmus.

Dalmiya's services still vital

MID-DAY* • *December 1, 2005

Jagmohan Dalmiya

Despite its strong disapproval of the involvement of politicians in our sport, KHALIDOSCOPE welcomes the election of Sharad Pawar as BCCI president.

In any event, the previous dispensation of Ranbir Singh Mahendra, himself a career politician with strings craftily pulled by the wily Jagmohan Dalmiya from behind the scenes, was political to the core, ingenious manipulation and horse trading being its strong suit.

I am delighted at the news that Pawar met his nemesis Dalmiya yesterday to "ask him for his cooperation."

The gesture, apart from being in the highest traditions of sportsmanship, augurs well for the future of the game.

Dalmiya's response is not known as yet, but knowing him as I do, I am confident Dalmiya will not deny Pawar—and Indian cricket in general—the benefit of his awesome business acumen, impressive administrative abilities and powers of persuasion.

During the India-Pakistan Test in Chandigarh in 2005 (MID DAY, dated March 15), I had written that it would be wonderful, indeed, for Indian cricket if the impressive financial and administrative qualities of Dalmiya and former Board president Inderjit Singh Bindra could be married.

If Sharad Pawar can harness the impressive leadership and business credentials of former presidents Dalmiya, Bindra and A.C. Muttiah to the passion and sincerity of purpose of Raj Singh Dungarpur, Indian cricket would have an embarrassment of financial managerial riches at its disposal.

There is no denying Dalmiya's dictatorial style of functioning, his dependence on a coterie of handpicked parasitic, inept *ji-huzoors*, his abrasiveness towards ICC functionaries that incurred their wrath and boomeranged in the form of Indian players being singled out for unjust and unwarranted action.

Also well known is his ham-handed handling of the television rights issue in 2004 that led to huge financial loss for the BCCI.

On the other hand, to Marwari Kolkatan Jagmohan Dalmiya must go a large amount of credit for the robust financial health of the BCCI and for spreading the gospel of cricket in Asian nations.

By espousing the cause of subcontinental nations through the ICC and the Asian Cricket Council, Dalmiya broke the stranglehold of entrenched first-world-nations who treated the game as their fiefdom.

No less impressive was the spirited manner in which he stood up for the honour and dignity of Indian players when disenchanted elements in the ICC—at times, because of Dalmiya's intransigence and arrogance, in the first place—sought to punish them wrongfully.

No offence is intended when I say that Jagmohan Dalmiya's reign as czar of Indian cricket—both de jure and de facto—had extended much longer than was good for the game, nor is pun is intended when I use the well-worn expression about power and corruption, namely: Power corrupts and absolute power corrupts absolutely.

Change is the essence of life. Dalmiya and his coterie had well passed their use-by date. The time had come for blowing away of cobwebs by winds of change, for sweeping changes in the upper echelons of Indian cricket.

Some old names figure in the new hierarchy, which is not altogether undesirable, since experience has its own considerable merits. However, the induction of new faces at different levels of the BCCI will, hopefully, inject fresh ideas in the running of a religion, which goes by the name of cricket in our country.

Given his well-known ambition, resourcefulness, resilience and survival instinct, it would be foolish in the extreme to write off Jagmohan Dalmiya for all time to come.

Be that as it may, one hopes the outstanding abilities of the administrator par excellence and financial genius will not be lost to Indian cricket to which, to be fair, he has made a huge contribution.

The heartwarming performances of the national team should not be allowed to cloud the gargantuan problems that face Indian cricket.

The new set-up would do well to professionalise its working and to make it accountable. To this end, the appointment of a chief executive should be its top priority.

Also, if I as a media person may add, the creation of the post of a permanent media manager with well-defined functions.

Waugh and the art of sledging

***MID-DAY* • October 24, 2005 • Sydney**

In his autobiography, "Steve Waugh: Out Of My Comfort Zone" former Australian captain Steve Waugh has revealed details of his heated exchange with Brian Lara and his most famous sledging incident with West Indies fast bowler Curtly Ambrose in Trinidad in 1995.

Waugh writes about how he almost exchanged blows with Brian Lara during a heated exchange. The pair stood toe to toe and Lara said: "C'mon let's go. Let's get it on right now".

Waugh says: "I'm no boxer and players should never forget the eyes of the sporting world are on them. The umpire gave us a stern warning and we got on with the game."

Then there was the run-in with West Indian Curtly Ambrose.

According to Waugh, Ambrose repeatedly stared him down during a furious spell of quick bowling, prompting the Aussie captain to ask "What the****are you looking at?"

Waugh writes that Ambrose was stunned because "No one had ever been stupid enough to speak to him like that".

Ambrose is said to have replied: "Don't cuss me, man".

Writes Waugh: "Unfortunately nothing inventive or witty came to mind, rather another piece of personal abuse, "Why don't you go and...."

PS: On the subject of sledging and colourful vocabulary, former Australian captain Bobby Simpson has denied charismatic England all-rounder Andy Flintoff's recent charge that he was rather indiscreet in his choice of words when speaking to him.

Flintoff was referring to the "magic moment" his career turned around, when his county coach Simpson had a couple of well-chosen words for him after he had wasted his early potential by overindulging and letting his weight to balloon to an extent that he lost his place in the England Test side.

Said Flintoff: "He called me a c..., 'Freddie, you're a c..." He was talking about the way I was playing. I just sat there and listened".

As an Australian columnist said: "Makes one wonder what all the fuss over the word 'carrot' is all about!"

Flint-off Hollywood

MID-DAY • August 16, 2005 • Manchester

Andrew Flintoff

Even as Pakistani fast bowler Shoaib Akhtar is busy using his superstar status to counsel Pakistani youth in the British Midlands about the real meaning of Islam at a time of racial and religious strife, Andrew "Freddie" Flintoff is all set to say: "Yabba Dabba Doo" in a Hollywood film.

Andrew "Freddie" Flintoff has become England's newest sporting hero following his brave exploits in the Edgbaston Test. Flintoff, nicknamed "Freddie" after the TV 'toon character Fred Flintstone, is now all set to take his fame across the Atlantic.

The star is expected to pull in £20 million through mega-money sponsorships deals from blue chip companies, advertising contracts and promotional work. Cricket fans may even release a chart-topping record praising his superstar status.

Hollywood powerbrokers are gushing: "He's got bags of presence and popularity and he's named after Flintstone. That's great," one is reported to have enthused.

A small role is also expected to come his way shortly in a new movie about Fred and Wilma's adventures in prehistoric Bedrock.

It has now come to light that Flintoff has been boosting his fitness by a gruelling fitness regimen at a boxing gym, where British Olympic medallist Amir Khan also trains.

Newly crowned British light-middleweight champion Jamie Moore says of Flintoff: "He is a phenomenal trainer. He does everything that we do and boxers have to train exceptionally hard. He never shirks anything. He's amazing.

"He does a real boxer's skip with the rope, does circuits involving the bag and jumping over a bar and even punches away at someone wearing a body bag."

"Boxing has a lot to do with balance. If you can get better balance, it improves your cricket game as well and that has clearly happened with him."

"He would be there at 10 in the morning with the rest of us and right through until noon every day for three months."

"Freddie initially started coming to the gym just to lose weight and build up a little bit of stamina but he just got hooked on it."

"He's such a lovely, down-to-earth guy. I know he's a superstar but there are no airs and graces about him. He is just one of the lads when he is in there. He is not a big time Charlie."

Deserving man got the nod

MID-DAY • May 22, 2005 • New Delhi

Greg Chappell

Reports about the confabulations at the momentous meeting here last Friday, that saw Greg Chappell anointed coach of Team India coach, vary. Some versions would have us believe that Sunil Gavaskar made an eloquent, if dissenting, case for Mohinder Amarnath, our own homegrown Punjab *da puttar* stalwart.

But my role in the selection process informs me that there were no two opinions about the crisp, superbly crafted presentation by Aussie legend Chappell, who finally—and, in my opinion, deservedly—got the nod.

What impressed the five-man selection committee, most of all, was the former Aussie captain's vision and the role his philosophy can play in putting in place a long-term structure for Indian cricket, starting at the grassroots level.

Chappell's stress on stated intention of familiarising himself with the activities and talent at the National Cricket Academy and 'fringe payers' in the India "A" and Under-17 teams is particularly gratifying.

Although I would have liked nothing better than to see good friend Amarnath or any other Indian coach given the assignment, their unfortunate—comparative—lack of expertise and experience in modern coaching methods has worked to their disadvantage. As is well known, Mohinder's claim to fame begins and ends with coaching Morocco and Bangladesh.

Moreover chances are, a foreign, self-respecting coach of the stature of Chappell will be far better able to stand up to the politics and machinations that have been the curse of Indian cricket and, in fact, all Indian sport.

KHALIDOSCOPE, which has been consistently stressing the critical importance of mental aspects in sport, is delighted to learn that the new coach will take the help of sports psychologist Sandy Gordon to improve the mental strength of our players.

About his younger brother's appointment, the no-nonsense Ian Chappell, says, "Despite my oft-expressed failure to understand the need for coaches at the international level, we argue very little about the concept.

"Greg takes a holistic approach to the job and is constantly on the lookout for long-term improvements rather than any quick fix. However, one thing the BCCI should understand: he is well aware of his worth and will never undersell himself."

In a recent article, Greg Chappell, a respected thinker on the game, writes, "Cricket will have to get a lot smarter and begin to understand that the coach is but one small cog in the overall development process and that the coach is only as good as the players that come through.

"Without a recognisable and well-structured development process, the biggest part of which is first-class cricket, the system will fail to deliver players properly prepared for Test cricket".

Chappell, whom I have had the good fortune of knowing for many years, goes on to write, "However well-credentialed, the coach cannot teach people how to play."

Citing the success of Australian coach John Buchanan, the new Indian team guru opines, "John has not taught any of the Australian players how to play but he has helped them to develop as individuals and he has played a big part in development of the group.

"A coach is and should be, foremost, a man manager who can help the player with technique, mental and personal problems. He should be someone who organises the team preparation and who can work with the captain on planning and tactical issues."

Chappell feels cricket needs to change the coaching model. "It needs to change from relying on one person to become a package, including other coaches and experts from a variety of fields, that can put in place a long-term structure that will also serve the short term needs better than any one person can do.

"This may be a radical departure from what cricket around the world is doing but it is the way of the future because the correct system misses the point of how the game of cricket is unique", he wrote in a syndicated column.

Outlining his long-term plan, Chappell wrote, "There is a limit to the number of people who have the necessary qualifications to do the job. So the idea of a group of people who manage the process on an ongoing basis to keep the whole thing fresh makes sense. It will take some lateral thinking to get around to this creative and exciting way of thinking that will allow India to lead the world on and off the field."

Greg Chappell, who played 87 Tests, led Australia to eight series wins (as against three defeats) and scored 7110 Test runs, inclusive of 24 centuries, displays sharp business acumen.

He says, "From a financial point of view this model will be more costly than the current model, but the BCCI needs to look at a financial structure that sees the national team with its own business plan and budget to make the right mix of experts and technology available to provide leading-edge information to the team. If the team goes backwards the long-term cost will be substantially more than a well-funded model would be now.

"This model or something like it will need to be in place for India to become world champions."

To a large extent, it was Greg Chappell's unique and impressive vision that helped tilt the balance in his favour, ahead of Tom Moody, Mohinder Amarnath and Desmond Haynes.

That being the case, it now becomes incumbent on BCCI to provide the celebrated new coach the wherewithal, infrastructure and backup support to enable him to lead Indian cricket, now stuck in the quagmire, to a brave new tomorrow.

Up close with Viv Richards

MID-DAY • 2000

It's been eight years since he retired from first-class cricket. Nevertheless, Isaac Vivian Alexander Richards' zest for the game remains undiminished.

"Cricket is no longer what it used to be. Today it's all about sledging, mental pressure, one-upmanship. The Aussies are ruling the roost today largely because they have developed pressure tactics into a winning art," the Master Blaster told Khalidoscope on a flight on Saturday.

Viv Richards

His eyes incandescent, Richards stated there is no dearth of talent in the present Indian side. "What your guys lack is mental toughness," he assured.

"I'd be more than happy to help mentally toughen your lads," said Richards whose contribution in instilling self-belief and fierce pride in the West Indies side that he led with distinction is second to none.

His eyes incandescent, his demeanour cocky as ever, Viv Richards reminisced about his run-ins with Dennis Lillee and Craig McDermott.

"I'm not advocating foul language but it's important to give as good as you get out there in the middle. Fast bowlers, in particular, tend to be bullies when they have the ball in their hands. They have to be put in their place. Body language counts for a lot.

"I remember the treatment we gave Craig McDermott when he came out to bat after being particularly obnoxious when bowling. He trembled like a leaf when I asked Amby (Curtley Ambrose) aloud to bowl around his rib-cage," Richards said with a guffaw.

"I'll never forget watching Javagal Srinath on television apologising to Ricky Ponting in the Sydney Test earlier this year for having struck him on the arm and the batsman's sharp response that made poor Srinath cringe.

"That one incident knocked the stuffing out of Srinath and Ponting went on to a big score.

"Take Kiwis Chris Cairns and Dion Nash, for instance. Their vocabulary on the field is enough to rattle the best of batsmen. Here's where mental strength comes in. Sunil Gavaskar had it in abundance or he would never have scored 34 Test centuries in the face of intimidation by the world's fastest bowlers."

The former West Indies skipper, who is on private visit to Mumbai, confessed to SUNDAY MID-DAY that he is some what bewildered with all the allegations of bribery and match-fixing that are flying thick and fast.

"During my playing days, we were never approached. We had too much national pride, I guess, although some shady guys were around a lot of the time when we toured India."

Keen to be au fait with the latest scandals concerning Indian cricketers, Richards expressed the point of view, "I may be rather naïve but in my book all this is tantamount to treason."

An International Cricket Council (ICC) ambassador and tourism envoy for Antigua, Richards is disillusioned with the state of West Indies cricket.

"Unfortunately, the wrong sort of people are now running the game in the Windies. It's sad to see the sacrifice of our principled cricketers, who resisted lucrative 'blood money' offers to play in South Africa, come to nought."

He bemoaned the fact that today's West Indian cricketers are in too much of a hurry to hit the big time, primarily for commercial gain.

"There are no short cuts to success. One needs discipline and hard work, qualities that are at a discount back home," he said adding that he expects a close series between the West Indies and Pakistan.

"Both sides seem to be struggling with their batting. They make scoring even 150 runs seem like 500. The West Indies are sadly missing the genius of Brian Lara."

Stating that he would like to get involved with coaching of youngsters back home, Richards added, "Don't believe the rubbish about our youth preferring basketball and soccer to cricket. Our youngsters have always played more than just one game. The problem with our cricket is lack of infrastructure and facilities," said Richards who has also represented his island at international soccer.

"Our administrators lack commitment, our selectors are out of touch with the modern game. It was a pity to see a person of the standing and caliber of Clive Lloyd ousted as coach unceremoniously."

Be that as it may, the Board of Control for Cricket in India (BCCI) would do well to give Vivian Richards' offer the consideration it deserves, especially since he has made Mumbai his second home.

Issues

Stop intimidation before it's too late

***SPORTSWEEK* • 1975**

The near-fatal injury to New Zealand cricketer Ewan Chatfield prompts the question: when does the bouncer, a pace bowler's legitimate weapon, transcend the bounds of legitimacy?

That the 5 1/2 oz. cricket spheroid, hurtling through the air at speeds up to 90 miles per hour can be a deadly weapon cannot be denied, witness the casualties and fatalities at club level in different parts of the cricket-playing world. In fact, injuries to first-class cricketers from the rising delivery pitched short of a good length, date as far back as the days of W. G. Grace. For us in India, the serious skull injury to former skipper Nari Contractor in the 1962 Bridgetown Test was a horrendous reminder of the deadly abilities of uncompromising bowlers whose all-consuming desire can be to get a batsman 'out'—literally and figuratively—at times through means contemptible.

The game of cricket has come a long, long way from the days when it was a gentleman's pastime on the village green. As played at the international level it is today characterised by qualities not far removed from jingoism and fierce, fanatical national pride. Insofar as winning, oftentimes at all cost, has come to be the paramount 'virtue', the old-world graces and refinements have inevitably gone by the board. Besides, as in other walks of life, Mammon has stormed the scene, in its wake placing success at an absurd premium in battles between the cricketing Joneses. Sad to say, this is particularly true of the Battle for the Ashes and was distressingly so in the one just concluded.

When one considers the reluctance of umpires around the world to strictly enforce the provisions of Law 46 regarding persistent short-pitched bowling, the number of casualties is mercifully—and, surprisingly—small.

That this should be the case—and here we confine ourselves to first-class cricket—due, not so much to concern and commiseration on the part of the speed-merchants as to the fact that batsmen (other than tailenders) have been, by and large, technically equipped to withstand the onslaughts of the 'typhoons,' the 'hurricanes' and the 'tornados.'

But now in India, as elsewhere, one witnesses the sad spectacle of persistent bouncers being hurled at tail-enders who by the very fact of being so are technically incompetent to protect life and limb. The most recent instance for this was during the last series against the West Indies, when the hapless Prasanna—no Don Bradman when it comes to wielding the willow—was at the receiving end of a barrage of bouncers, as was Bedi during the 1974 series against England in that country.

The reluctance of international umpires to give effect to Law 46 in the 40 years since it has been in existence defies logic the more so in the face of the increasing tendency towards intimidatory bowling. In fact, the shortcomings of the umpires in this regard has encouraged bowlers to contravene the provisions of this Law with impunity.

We could not agree more with Mike Denness when he stated at the conclusion of the recent series Down Under that legislation is called for to, in effect, prevent death on the cricket field. Of the many theories—sensible, stupid, 'sick'—expounded towards that end, the one concerning the line drawn short of the good length spot to be supervised by the square-leg umpire, would appear to suffer from the disability of being not quite feasible.

The proposal, advocated by Arvind Lavakare in a recent issue of SPORTSWEEK, which places a restriction on the number of bouncers which a bowler may send down per over and which a team may bowl in an innings, is easier of application but suffers from the handicap of providing a pace bowler the temptation to send down two bouncers per over, even though they may not be quite necessary. Nor does it make provision for adequate safeguards for tailenders against the thunder and fury of fast bowlers, if not 'body-line' exponents and chuckers.

The sooner the ICC addresses itself to the pressing task of clearly defining intimidatory bowling, amending the law if need be to facilitate its implementation, the sooner it lays down clear-cut norms for its effective application and ENSURES application, the safer will the game be.

If the ICC wishes to make sure that the game of cricket remains a 'gentleman's game' even in this materialistic day and age it is imperative that it form an international panel of umpires, which would be subject to periodic review and scrutiny in the matter of application of all Laws (including that concerning intimidatory bowling) as is the case with hockey and football.

This proposal will, in all probability, provoke a storm of protest from the purists who see red at the mere mention of neutral umpires or an international panel of umpires to do duty in countries other than their own. The raison d'etre for an international panel it must be emphasised is not so much the ensuring of impartiality and uniformity in umpiring decisions (umpires are after all, mere mortals with feet of clay) as an attempt at ensuring that the laws of cricket are applied effectively.

We have no quarrel with those who strive might and main for the preservation of tradition. But very often the demands of changing times make some departure from hallowed traditions unavoidable, in fact essential. We sincerely hope a human life will not have to be sacrificed to drive home this point.

Cricket selectors: Does your heart ever cry for India?

MID-DAY • August 28, 1997

So the Indian cricket team is back from Sri Lanka—bruised, battered, badly beaten.

Jagmohan Dalmiya and Chairman of Selectors Ramakant Desai

What is new, one may well ask.

Ignominious defeats have become par for the course for our much-vaunted cricketers.

Defeats, alas, are more the norm than wins. Snatching defeat from the jaws of victory is increasingly a matter of habit while a cricket-crazy nation, disillusioned, disenchanted and hungry for distinction, bears it with characteristic stoicism.

But the seemingly calm forbearance masks a raging, seething anger against those who are responsible for the embarrassing performances at the international level.

Losing is as much a part of sport as winning, one might well argue.

But for a team to lose with such monotonous regularity when it has the potential to win against all comers is frustrating in the extreme.

For it to repeatedly turn in below-par performances because of the selfishness, insouciance and devil-may-care attitude of a bunch of so-called "experts" in the form of selectors who are out of sync with today's cricket is infuriating.

The good news is that the term of the present selection committee expires tomorrow.

The bad news is that they will sit on judgement as to which players should do duty for the nation against Pakistan in the forthcoming Sahara Cup in Toronto.

Judging by the results they have produced, the selectors should resign en masse today itself, owning responsibility for the team's abysmal performances since they took on the role of inquisitors.

But then, is that not asking for the moon in a nation in which accountability is an alien concept?

Or is it? Perhaps Messrs. Ramakant Desai et al can prove to a distraught nation that it is not.

And, the venerable gentlemen of the Board of Control for Cricket in India (BCCI) can demonstrate that they are capable of mature, constructive foresight by breaking away from the shackles of rusty, cobwebbed thinking and appointing only three selectors—irrespective of zonal consideration—who understand the nuances and complexities of modern cricket, who are committed to the national interest and who can rise above petty regional, personal and sectarian considerations. If the articles of the cricket control board have to be revised to enable this, so be it.

And surely, the board can demonstrate that it is contemporary, nay, forward-thinking, by appointing a physiotherapist who knows his onions.

The days of quacks and charlatans who masquerade as medical specialists are long past, as demonstrated by the Sri Lankans and Pakistanis who have not let false national pride come in the way of appointing foreign nationals to this crucial post. And the results are there for all to see.

Talking of national pride, given the fact that our homegrown coaches have not been able to deliver the goods, would there be any loss of national prestige if we were to avail of the services of a certain gentleman called Bobby Simpson who served his country with distinction as player, captain (during the tumultuous Kerry Packer era) and later as coach, as our part-time advisor/coach?

We hear from the grapevine that he would be only too happy to be involved on a specific, limited (not full-time) assignment.

A certain Sunil Gavaskar could help in this regard.

But then the gentlemen who govern our cricket destiny have no time—and scant regard—for the likes of Sunil Gavaskar, Kapil Dev, Dilip Vengsarkar and Ravi Shastri.

Thereby hangs a tale.

Link cricketers' pay to performance

MID-DAY • February 29, 2000

B*irds do it, Bees do it,*

Even Eskimos do it...," sang Frank Sinatra. With apologies to the memory of the legend, one is tempted to take the liberty of altering the words of the old favourite (in the cricket context) to: "Aussies do it, Proteas do it, Even Poms do it...,"

The allegorical reference is to the announcement by the England and Wales Cricket Board (ECB) last week that, commencing tomorrow, England's leading players will receive performance-related payment, a practice adopted by Australia and South Africa with impressive success.

According to ECB chief executive Tim Lamb, the overhaul of the salary structure is aimed at "improving the results of the national team that has slid to the bottom of the unofficial World Test rankings."

Given India's recent dismal performances in Australia and the four-wicket defeat at the hands of South Africa in under three days last week, the moment is at hand for the Board of Control for Cricket in India (BCCI) to devise a similar wage structure for India's glorified cricketers whose ranking in World Test cricket is marginally higher than that of England-but only just.

The earnings of the Indian demigods are unreal in the context of prevailing Indian salaries and wages—and with no co-relation to performance, at that!

Add to that the fortunes that cricketers' commercial contracts attract and you have a situation that cries for immediate redress.

For too long now have the pampered, worshipped cricket superstars performed in a manner that has embarrassed, frustrated, nay angered, millions of their idolaters in the length and breadth of the country.

KHALIDOSCOPE has been arguing for quite some time now that the situation demands drastic chemotherapy that will strike at the root of the cancer.

Since the disease is mired in crass commercialism, the prognosis calls, among other things, for a shake-up of the pay structure of Indian cricketers along the lines successfully adopted by the all conquering Australians, South Africa and now England.

The ECB move is in response to demands by English critics who have faulted their players for operating in a 'comfort zone' with no extra incentive to perform consistently at a high level.

Since India's spoilt cricket super-brats operate in a similar 'comfort zone', it's time they, too, were made to really and truly earn their fat-cat wages.

Under the plan envisaged by ECB, 16 players will sign new six month contracts (one-year in the case of senior players) similar to those adopted by Australia and South Africa.

According to Lamb, "If the England team is winning, then the players that make up that team will receive higher rewards."

Within the remuneration package for those contracted to England, a significant proportion will be performance-related pay.

In addition to a basic salary, there is quite an attractive additional amount of money that is available to recognise success. On top of it there are win bonuses that have been provided by sponsors in the past.

Importantly, the performance-related pay would be based entirely on results achieved by the team as a whole and will not be awarded on an individual basis.

ECB has budgeted an extra 750,000 pounds for player remuneration this year, a practice the BCCI can quite easily match, if not better, given its robust state of financial health.

Australia does it. South Africa does it. Even England does it.

It's time the Indian Board, too, did it.

Moment of reckoning, this, for Board president Dr. A.C. Muthiah, coinciding with the Union Budget.

Probe cricket I-T disclosures

MID-DAY* • *March 3, 2000

The bombshell dropped by Additional Commissioner of Income-Tax Vishwa Bandhu Gupta, by revealing that the Rs 16 crore disclosure by a former India Test cricket captain under the Voluntary Disclosure of Income Scheme (VDIS) in 1997 might be "match-fixing" money has added fuel to an already burning subject.

Coming at a time when Indian cricket is at its nadir, the disclosure has assumed the form of a conflagration.

The national interest demands that the Board of Control for Cricket in India institute a fresh inquiry to unearth the truth behind this putrefying cancer.

The additional commissioner's refusal to name the captain in his exclusive interview to Narendra Kaushik (MID-DAY, February 29) has opened yet another Pandora's Box at a time when dark, cloak-and-dagger deeds, unfortunately, seem to be the order of the day in Indian cricket.

Gupta, who had earlier created a controversy by alleging that BJP leader Sushma Swaraj was closely associated with underworld don Dawood Ibrahim's front man Romesh Sharma, has called for "comprehensive confessions" saying it would be unfair to name just this one individual. According to him, "There may be some more cricketers who declared their black money under the scheme."

Vishwa Bandhu Gupta has stated that he will write to the Chief Justice in the hope that the Supreme Court will treat his letter as a public interest litigation.

Gupta is of the view that the government can take back its promise to keep names of declarants under the scheme confidential.

"The promise was not part of the original scheme," he says, adding that it was "made possible through an administrative circular". He calls for the officials who issued it to be "hauled up".

Whatever the moral and ethical aspects, the fact of the matter is that cricket-wise, the shocking allegations buttress the arguments of those who are convinced, despite the clean chit given by the Justice Y Y Chandrachud Commission, that some of our senior cricketers have been involved in large-scale match-fixing.

They may also unravel, to some extent, the mystery concerning what has now come to be generally acknowledged as the uncanny ability of the Indian team to "snatch defeat from the jaws of victory".

Although last week's four-wicket defeat at the hands of South Africa cannot be ascribed to non-cricketing reasons, some recent performances of the Indian team warrant close scrutiny:

* India's defeat at the hands of the West Indies at Bridgetown in 1996-97 by the narrow margin of 38 runs while chasing an eminently attainable target of just 122 runs.
* Defeat against lowly Zimbabwe at Harare in 1998-99 by 61 runs in a match in which India was bowled out for a meagre 173.
* Defeat by a mere 12 runs in the epic encounter against Pakistan at Chennai in 1998-99.
* Defeat, again, by 46 runs at the hands of Pakistan in the crucial and controversy-ridden opening match in the three-nation Asian Test Championships in Calcutta in 1998-99.
* It does not call for the investigative skills of a Sherlock Holmes, Perry Mason, Hercule Poirot, even Inspector Eagle or Inspector Ghote to smell that '*daal mein kuch kaala ho sakta tha*', even though a malfeasance (nay, crime) such as match-fixing is not easy to prove.

Although sensational, Mr. Gupta's revelations cannot be dismissed lightly, nor should his motives be questioned.

Concurrently, the Board of Control for Cricket in India (BCCI) should shed its shibboleth and avail of the services of a psychologist to provide an alternate to tainted money as a motivation for the Indian cricketers.

The legendary Vince Lombard of the Green Bay Packers in the USA and Ron Borassi of the Victorian Australian Rules Football team are prime examples of motivators who inspired their mediocre teams to great heights.

And, tennis legend-in-his-lifetime Andre Agassi is known to travel on the circuit with a retinue of almost 10 consisting of a motivator, psychotherapist, physiotherapist, tennis coach, fitness specialist, dietician, physician, bodyguard et al.

There's no reason for the BCCI not to discard its antediluvian approach and move abreast of the times. It certainly has the wherewithal for it.

Since the paramount problem of the present Indian cricket team lies not so much in technical as in mental aspects, a start should be made post haste by acquiring the services of a professional psychotherapist who could address himself in all earnestness to the player's lack of confidence and low self-esteem.

Along with linking players' wages to performance, the sooner this is done the better.

'Hang' the guilty, But...

MID-DAY • May 31, 2000

Manoj Prabhakar

In all the utterly maddening and confusing cacophony engendered by the release of the videotapes by the James Bond-like Manoj Prabhakar over the past weekend, the words of Indian captain Sourav Ganguly—"I don't believe these allegations"— make the most sense.

"Allegations without the support of adequate proof are simply valueless," Ganguly said to MID-DAY correspondent Debasish Datta in Dhaka on Monday.

That Prabhakar's professional undercover camera work—aided and abetted by a website reporter—should create a *tehelka* (sensation) is hardly surprising given the obsessive following of the game in the country. Equally unsurprising is the fact that an overwhelmingly large majority of people in our country, irrespective of their level of interest in the game, seem convinced that the tapes conclusively prove that Kapil Dev Nikhanj et al should be summarily hanged.

Accustomed to almost a daily diet of wrongdoing in our public life, starting at the very top among politicians, our populace has reached a stage where it is prepared to believe the worst about one and all—and to hell with the truth.

"If there's smoke, there must be fire" has become the national syndrome.

However, this column takes a contrary view and submits that the tapes, although potentially invaluable in aiding the ultimate judicial process, do not prove anything substantial conclusively by themselves as regards the match-fixing allegations.

All that they demonstrate, without doubt, is that some former players and past and present officials were informed by Manoj Prabhakar that Kapil Dev had approached him (Prabhakar) in the Singer Trophy match in Colombo with a blandishment to under-perform.

But they do not—repeat do NOT—conclusively PROVE the fact that an offer was actually made in the presence, or otherwise, of witnesses. Nor did any money change hands.

In fact, a close examination of the transcripts highlight the fact that, despite his best efforts to get his close friend and hotel roommate Navjot Singh Sidhu and Nayan Mongia and Prashant Vaidya to confirm that they had heard Kapil Dev make his offer, they did not do so.

Our cricketers at all levels, as indeed people from different walks of life, are not particularly averse to making wild, sweeping allegations against others for motives which only they understand.

We, in the business of purveying news, come across innumerable professedly well-intentioned 'informers' who, upon investigation, are found to have an axe to grind. If we were to rush to print with all that we are made privy to by 'reliable' sources, we could have written tomes by now.

Or be behind bars, singing the '*Jailhouse Rock*'.

In this instance, allegations of bribery and match-fixing have been flying thick and fast for many years now. Cricket correspondents, including we at Mid-Day, have become weary of baseless, unsubstantiated allegations which spare nobody, not even Sachin Tendulkar.

To their credit, Indian sports writers have, on the whole, exercised commendable restraint and have not rushed to print since, in most cases, they were mere second, if not fourth-hand, hearsay without a shred of proof.

This is no brief for the people concerned, but if, therefore, the likes of Sunil Gavaskar and Ravi Shastri took whatever Manoj Prabhakar told them with a pinch of salt, since they were unsubstantiated and did not rush to print or merely field their counsel, they ought to be commended, not condemned.

Kahuna fair hai?

***MID-DAY* • April 25, 2005 • Sydney**

Although Australian captain Ricky Ponting has dismissed England's demand for a ban on his new carbon graphite bat as much ado about nothing, the Kookaburra blade may still be banned.

Ricky Ponting

Saying, "I don't care too much", Ponting maintains he has been using the bat for five to six years 0now and that the only purpose is to "make the bat look more appealing."

However, a Sydney newspaper has, in its possession, a copy of a catalogue, available in Australia and England, which says that the Kahuna is "*Improved for 2005 with graphite power matrix reinforcement for increased durability and enhanced power.*"

The game's laws are explicit in that they categorically state that added material on bats is only allowed to strengthen or reinforce the willow, not increase the power.

Ponting claimed last week that the graphite on his bat is "almost like a sticker on the back of the bat. That's all there is to it."

Although only 50 per cent of the back of a bat is allowed for advertising, the graphite and sticker on the back of Ponting's bat cover the entire back of the bat.

The MCC believes the bright fluorescent green sticker flouts the spirit of the game.

Former Australia captain Ian Chappell told KHALIDOSCOPE last week, "The bat could pose a bit of a problem. The game's governing body would be well advised to stick only to wood".

Ian Chappell's brother, Greg, another former Aussie skipper, while saying that the Poms are "getting a little paranoid" suggests, tongue-in-cheek, that "they should check Ponting's wrists and go into his genetic background to discover where he is getting his advantage from".

ICC chief executive Malcolm Speed has denied reports that the bat, dubbed the Kahuna (meaning 'important person' in Hawaiian), has already been cleared although he said he could use it for the time being.

The International Cricket Council (ICC), the cricket world governing body, has maintained that the bat will be reviewed by the Marylebone Cricket Club (MCC), the supreme lawmaking authority, and the ICC cricket committee, of which Sunil Gavaskar is chairman.

Speed has reiterated that the practice of “corking” a bat, whereby a bat is hollowed and filled with cork is illegal and becoming a big concern.

He said yesterday, “During the Cricket World Cup 2003 there were a number of oversized bats detected and manufacturers were put on notice that it was expected that they would produce bats that comply with the laws at all times.”

New Zealand manufacturers are said to have started the practice of “corking”, a practice Ponting admits to being aware of.

“Corking” of baseball bats has been standard practice for some time to enable faster swing and time to see the ball.

The Australian captain and Kookaburra managing director Bob Elliot maintain that the graphite does not provide extra power. Elliot attributes this MCC move as an attempt to “destabilise” the Aussies ahead of the Ashes series starting next July.

Score-books show that Ricky Ponting has been in superb touch since using the bat.

The ICC will discuss the bat as part of its overall review of bats at its next meeting in May.

PS: Former Australia skipper Allan Border believes England’s bowlers are capable of taking 20 wickets in a match to win a Test but is convinced the Australian batsmen have too much class to let that happen.

Shabash, Selectors

MID-DAY • March 22, 2002

On a day on which the POTO (Prevention of Terrorism Ordinance) met with disapproval in the Rajya Sabha, the Indian cricket board selectors' choice of players yesterday for the West Indies tour will, in all probability, meet with general approval from the cricket-crazy millions in the country.

To be fair, the cricket selectors' job is a thankless one in a nation in which passionate opinions equal, if not exceed, the number of fans.

Nevertheless, cynical, dyed-in-the-wool critics apart, dispassionate aficionados will agree that Messrs Chandu Borde et al have displayed an admirable degree of integrity and concern for the national interest.

Whereas the majority of players selected were obvious choices, there is bound to be some debate over the retention of VVS Laxman and the recall of Wasim Jaffer.

Given his abundant batting skills, Laxman's continuing inconsistency has been frustrating, if not infuriating.

Nevertheless, his 167 in Sydney in January 2000 and his epic match-winning 281 in Kolkata, both against the hitherto all-conquering Australians, are still the talking point among players and media Down Under, as being among the more memorable knocks in recent times.

Inconsistency notwithstanding, awesome talent such as this surely needs to be persevered with.

The toss-up between the swashbuckling Yuvraj Singh and Wasim Jaffer must have engaged a lot of the selectors' time at yesterday's meeting.

Jaffer's two centuries in recent Duleep Trophy matches, and the fact that he is a specialist opening batsman, probably won him the nod for a recall to the Test squad after his disappointing debut against South Africa in 2000 even though Deep Dasgupta has also been accommodated as batsman-wicketkeeper in preference to the experienced Nayan Mongia.

An element of parochialism here? Your guess is as good as ours, dear reader.

Hopefully, our maverick selectors will not overlook the explosive batting skills of Yuvraj Singh, against whom gross injustice has been done for some time now purportedly for reasons of lack of fitness and alleged 'swollen headedness,' for the one-day series commencing on May 25.

The selectors' wisdom in including four 'fast' bowlers (in addition to all-rounder Sanjay Bangar), in view of the wickets in the Caribbean, and only two spinners is debatable.

Whereas Sairaj Bahutule was considered, off-spinner Sarandeep Singh and left-arm spinner Murali Kartik did not figure at all in the selectors' deliberations.

The return to the squad of Sachin Tendulkar, Anil Kumble, Javagal Srinath and Ashish Nehra can only spell bad news for the hapless West Indies, who have sadly plumbed the depths from their pristine days in the sun.

Without in any way scoffing at the widespread euphoria over India's hard-fought victory over Zimbabwe in the series just concluded, this column would like to recall, for the benefit of our perennial optimists (bless their souls), that our gurus had similarly written off Nasser Hussain's England team as 'second rate.'

They would do well to remember India's pathetic record abroad.

Finally, as argued repeatedly in this column, the services of a sports psychologist would have been invaluable during the arduous tour. But, then, the Board of Control for Cricket in India always claims to know best.

Here's wishing Sourav Ganguly and his lads the very best.

Time for some action, gentlemen

MID-DAY • August 7, 2002 • London

It's been almost two weeks since the breach of security incident concerning Sachin Tendulkar at Lord's and the one in which television commentator Harsha Bhogle and his colleague Gautam Bhimani were allegedly humiliated and manhandled by an insolent, inebriated steward at the ground.

Harsha Bhogle

The Board of Control for Cricket in India (BCCI) promptly took up the serious issue of security of Indian cricketers during the current tour but the England Cricket Board seems to be dragging its feet.

Had the incident occurred in India, the English establishment and 'gentlemen' of the press would have been up in arms, shouting blue murder and, possibly, even threatening to call off the tour.

Obviously due to professional reasons, Bhogle and Bhimani chose not to report the incident (which occurred in the course of their professional work) with the police, preferring, instead, to complain to the concerned cricket authorities.

They were assured that an inquiry would be conducted and appropriate action taken against the guilty, if proved.

As of today, there is no sign of any action having been taken to vindicate the honour of the two aggrieved mediamen who happen to be among the most gentlemanly professionals around.

This appears to be yet another instance of the arrogant, high-and-mighty, supercilious attitude of the powers-that-be at the so-called Mecca of cricket against people of dark pigmentation.

It is here that Indian legend Sunil Gavaskar was insulted some years ago, which prompted him to turn down MCC honorary membership at that time.

There have been numerous other instances of non-white players and mediapersons being subjected to similar humiliation, especially at Lord's, the latest being former Test captain Bishan Singh Bedi during the India-England Test a fortnight ago.

Only recently, the great Tiger Woods was insulted while entering the golf course at Muirfield.

These incidents certainly do no credit to sports administrators of a country which claims to cherish sporting values.

A sign at the W. G. Grace Gate at Lord's states: *Play hard, but play fair*.

The behaviour of the security staff at the gate is, by no stretch of the imagination, fair to people of a certain colour. And, a notice at the office of the England Cricket Board (ECB) at Lord's has a pompous statement entitled "Clean Bowl Racism", which talks of "Going Forward Together" and "Achieving Racial Equality in Cricket", that are purportedly objectives of the ECB as outlined in its Mission Statement on Equal Opportunity/Equity Policy.

It is obvious the authorities at the MCC, and ECB are sweeping the mediapersons incident under the carpet.

Of greater importance is the matter of safety and security of the Indian players.

The Board of Control for Cricket In India (BCCI) should again take up the issue of the players' security with its English counterpart in all seriousness and, in the event of not getting adequate assurances, call off the tour.

And, since the media is a partner in the BCCI's progress, it should also realise that it just cannot wash its hands off looking after its interest.

The time has come for the BCCI to take up the Bhogle/Bhimani matter with the police.

Players' 'jhagda' with the BCCI a blessing in disguise

MID-DAY • August 26, 2002 • LEEDS

Whatever its long-term fallout, the dispute between the touring Indian Test cricketers and the Board of Control for Cricket in India (BCCI) has done wonders for team solidarity and morale.

Sachin Tendulkar

On balance, the 'jhagda' has been a blessing in disguise for the team, uniting the players like seldom before, making them fiercely determined to prove a point or two to all concerned.

The result is there for all to see: Sourav Ganguly and his boys have been away from home for almost two and a half months now - enough time for homesickness to set in and for them to feel jaded and fatigued, as evidenced by innumerable instances in the history of Indian cricket.

Not so this time around. After capitulating rather meekly to the opposition in the first Test at Lord's and after ignoble defeat staring them in the face at the end of the fourth day in the second at Trent Bridge, the team has suddenly, if not inexplicably, came to terms with itself.

The magnificent fight-back at Trent Bridge could only have done a power of good for the players' self-belief, but ever since the dispute with the BCCI erupted, the players have demonstrated a rare—and burning—desire to excel, a resolve amply discernible in their body language and cohesiveness for a common cause, if not against a common enemy.

This is not to suggest in any way, as is often implied, that it only takes the lure of lucre to "make the mare go," although money is, undeniably, a vital consideration for our present-day cricketers.

It is nobody's case that some players make, what some critics consider, obscene and undeserving amounts of money.

Good luck to them if they do, as long as they justify it to their promoters—and the nation's cricket fans.

Be that as it may, it behooves the BCCI to solve the imbroglio ASAP.

Ganguly, Tendulkar and their teammates justifiably feel let down by the seemingly uncaring attitude of the Board after placing them in an awkward position, which is not of their own making.

Also, it cannot be denied that the Board has acted in a suspiciously secretive, high-handed, if not devious, manner in this entire unsavoury episode.

It redounds to the credit of the players that they have not let it distract them from giving of their best in the Headingley Test—and what a performance has it been thus far!

The fast-approaching Champions Trophy in Sri Lanka and, indeed team considerations before the Test at the Oval early next month, make an early resolution of the impasse imperative.

When, as the saying goes, "an irresistible object meets an immovable force, something's gotta give".

BCCI president Jagmohan Dalmiya should eschew ego considerations, drop all other matters in hand and, expeditiously, come across to Britain, sit across the table with the players and solve the problem.

Rather than mere lackeys, it's time the Board treated the players as partners in its (financial) progress.

Don't insult our intelligence, BCCI

***MID-DAY* • November 26, 2002**

Please don't insult our intelligence, Board of Control for Cricket in India (BCCI) Honorary Secretary Karunakaran Nair.

S. K. Nair

"Anil Kumble is being dropped for "personal reasons" and Javagal Srinath "rested" (whatever that means) is what you told the media yesterday, while releasing the names of players for the tour of New Zealand on the crucial run-up to the World Cup.

"Personal reasons"? "Being rested"?

What do they mean, Mr Nair? Surely you, as spokesman and worthy official of the august body that presides over the destiny of our cricketers, whom millions of our fellow countrymen venerate, owe an explanation.

Why this ambiguity, that has characterised the notorious cloak-and-dagger working of the BCCI over the years?

In Kumble's case, does "personal problems" denote domestic, health or perhaps financial reasons?

In the eyes of our increasingly cynical cricketer-worshiping public's lexicon, nothing is "personal" as far as the players are concerned.

They are national property. You cannot pull the wool over their eyes, therefore the need for absolute transparency.

If the cricketing world at large were made privy to the "personal problems" that prompted England batsman Graham Thorpe to opt out of the current Ashes tour, and Australian vice captain Adam Gilchrist and leading New Zealand all-rounder Chris Harris to miss important matches last year because of well publicised "domestic problems," what is so sacrosanct about Anil Kumble's "personal reasons" and Javagal Srinath's "being rested"?

Srinath was recalled to the Test and one-day squads, despite all conventional wisdom and his well-known reluctance, and official "retirement" from Test cricket, as knight in shining armour, the answer to all our problems, despite his shoulder injury, lack of athleticism and ineptitude while facing genuine pace bowling.

Is this a face-saving device to a player who has performed yeoman service to the country?

If so, cricket lovers would love your saying so in so many words, and fully commiserate with your reasoning, instead of having you indulge in doublespeak.

It's time you, and your ilk in the BCCI, came clean with millions of our fellow Indians who, given the state of our nation - and the shenanigans of our so-called *netas* - are left only with cricketers as heroes.

Money root cause of India's woes

MID-DAY* • *December 30, 2002

What is it about the Indian cricket team on the ill-starred tour of New Zealand that prevents it from getting its act together?

The more one thinks about it, the more inescapable the conclusion that it is the impasse between the Indian players and the International Cricket Council (ICC) over money, money, money that could jeopardise their participation in the World Cup and even their careers, that is coming in the way.

How else can one explain the shocking lack of focus, the amazingly lacklustre, out-of-sorts performance by the Indian players in yesterday's one-day international (ODI) in Napier?

His own worrisome continuing lack of form with the bat apart, captain Sourav Ganguly's seeming obliviousness, if not insouciant lack of urgency, to ensure that the team bowled its full quota of 50 overs in the stipulated time was inexplicable.

As it turned out, only 47 overs were bowled and the team was lucky to be penalised by only two, and not three, overs.

No matter what coach John Wright may have to say by way of defence ("they haven't suddenly become poor players"), the fact of the matter is that the Indians have been playing not poorly, but ignominiously.

In the two-Test series the trumpeted "world's best batsmen" played like cats on hot tin roofs.

In the first one-dayer at Auckland, they resembled Bharat Natyam dancers with two left feet rather than world beaters on a bouncy track similar to the kind they must expect in the World Cup next year and which will distinguish the men from the boys.

True class lies in the ability to bat on all kinds of surfaces without demur.

Yesterday, on a wicket that even the nit-picky, whinging captain could not fault, and on which the mediocre New Zealand batting line-up managed 254, the star batsmen, barring the majestic Virender Sehwag, failed yet again as India were handed down their fourth successive defeat on tour.

If India were without master batsman Sachin Tendulkar, the home side did without as many as four leading lights—Chris Cairns, Chris Harris and Andre Adams because of injury—and tear-away fast bowler Shane Bond, who was left out of the squad to give others a chance to establish their credentials for inclusion in the World Cup squad.

As mentioned in this column yesterday, today was a "when the going gets tough, the tough get going" occasion, for heroic deeds by the Indian players to show determination and fortitude in adversity, to redeem prestige, and to regain confidence with the world's premier event round the corner and just six matches remaining in the interim.

Instead, Sourav Ganguly and Co. turned in another frustratingly spunkless performance after winning the toss and putting in the opposition on a sporting track that smiled benevolently upon India's pace bowlers in the morning and evened out progressively when India batted.

The most embarrassing aspect was the fielding, which the skipper described after the match as an area "in which we have worked very hard and improved."

Considering the shoddy, slipshod, lacklustre display by the fielders bar none, in which no less than 25 runs were gifted to the opposition, innumerable catches dropped and stumping chances frittered away, the captain's claim is downright laughable.

Despite the sterling bowling performance by Javagal Srinath (three for 36), the home side came up with their best batting performance to-date thanks to the professionally-crafted 146-run partnership between Nathan Astle and Matthew Sinclair.

Ganguly's dismissal, bowled off the inside edge through the 'gate' was an action replay of the manner in which he lost his wicket in Auckland and should be a matter of great concern for the team in that it is a technical flaw which perceptive opposition teams will exploit to the hilt.

After a torrid time when facing the new ball, which he repeatedly played and missed, Sehwag batted with imperious authority, that is the hallmark of his style, to raise visions of an Indian victory, first in association with Rahul Dravid, then with Mohammad Kaif, with whom he put on 78 runs.

But disciplined bowling by the home team, notably Kyle Mills (three for 45) and Daryl Tuffey (three for 35) and superlative wicket-keeping by Brendon McCullum, who dismissed five batsmen, aided and abetted by some asinine running between the wickets that resulted in the departure of Rahul Dravid and, finally, Sehwag himself, put paid to the brave bid for victory by the last-named.

To have to comment on the same dismal aspects of the Indian team's performance match after match is getting to be tedious.

Singles and twos are the flesh and blood of cricket. This is what cricketers are taught at school level. Sadly, the pampered maharajas of Indian cricket still have to come to terms with this cardinal rule.

BRIEF SCORES

New Zealand 254 for 9 in 50 overs (N Astle 76, M Sinclair 78) beat India 219 all out in 43.4 overs (V Sehwag 108)

India's media relations a disaster

MID-DAY* • *December14, 2003* • *Adelaide

Sourav Ganguly

The BCCI's illogical—and asinine—refusal to appoint a media manager on this tour is certainly not in its own interest and is giving Indian cricket, in general, and the team's captain and manager in particular, an extremely bad name.

Matters have come to such a pass that the media, especially the Australian press, has stopped taking the utterances of Messrs Sourav Ganguly and Shivlal Yadav at face value.

Three recent instances have prompted journalists here to wonder if Ganguly suffers from a bad case of amnesia, the extent to which he is aware of what's going in his own camp and whether, plain and simple, he has acquired a new gift for dissimulation.

First there was the confident assertion by Ganguly on the eve of the match press conference that Zaheer Khan's injured hamstring had improved sufficiently to enable him to play in the match. Zaheer was declared unfit on the morning of the match.

Then, there were the shenanigans concerning Murali Kartik's arrival, the captain giving the impression that he was not really au fait about details of the spinner's arrival.

Finally, there's been l'affaire Harbhajan Singh, which has got curiouser and curiouser, with Ganguly blowing hot and cold about the injury to his spinning finger which, it now transpires, has virtually ruled him out of the series and could well be career threatening.

True, the BCCI has taken many commendable decisions in the recent past in the interest of the game.

Knowledge, it is said, comes but wisdom lingers. One wonders when the BCCI powers-that-be will realise that the price for neglecting professional media relations in these days of instant global communication can be astronomical.

Can we prove 'intent'?

MID-DAY* • *January 24, 2004

Describing the Rahul Dravid ball-tampering issue as a "storm in a tea cup", former Australian Test pace bowler Geoff Lawson has called upon cricket officials to address themselves to more important issues.

Rahul Dravid

"Dravid's actions cannot be proved and the International Cricket Council's ruling needs to be changed to reflect this," he told *The Daily Telegraph* newspaper yesterday.

"If intent could not be proven, then punishment should not be handed out," Lawson said. "Nothing can be proved that it changed the cricket ball. Sure it can be argued. But I didn't see the ball start to move after that."

A theory being propounded here is that Dravid was trying to keep one side of the ball shiny to help it swing, as in English county cricket. But, according to Lawson, who was at the SCG to witness India's thrilling encounter against Ricky Ponting's men on Thursday, "What you want is to scuff up the white ball, not make it shiny. It's bizarre," Lawson said.

He also called for greater scrutiny on the action of bowlers. "There seems to be a lack of attention paid to the fundamentals of the game—those who throw the ball," he said.

It was an accident: Dravid

MID-DAY • January 25, 2004

Indian coach John Wright and captain Sourav Ganguly must be commended for the eminently sensible manner in which they handled Rahul Dravid's ball-tampering incident.

Rahul Dravid

With television cameras around the ground repeatedly and conclusively showing that Dravid did apply a foreign substance (energy lozenge) to one side of the ball, match referee Clive Lloyd was left with no option other than to fine the Indian vice-captain under rule 2.2 of the ICC Playing Conditions. Lloyd told KHALIDOSCOPE he had no doubt, whatsoever, that Dravid, for whom he has the highest respect as a person of integrity, had no intention to gain unfair advantage by his action.

"Intent apart, I had to go strictly on the basis of the evidence provided by television. Quite simply, I just had no choice in the matter. The rules are quite explicit in this regard."

A distraught Rahul Dravid told me he had no intention of cheating. "It was an accident. I didn't realise what I was doing and what the consequences would be."

When I met them before start of the thrilling one-dayer against Australia at the SCG, Wright and Ganguly both stoutly backed Dravid's self-righteous denial of guilt.

Their captain and manager both handled the matter admirably in dealing with the probing press and were largely instrumental in calming the atmosphere among teammates, in persuading them to treat the incident as an aberration and stressing the importance of moving on.

One's heart goes out to Dravid, a man of scrupulous rectitude. Time will heal the personal pain and the unfortunate stigma the incident has brought about.

But then, it is in the nature of things for mere mortals to be judged by their actions - and intent cannot always be proved. Sadly, both Sachin Tendulkar and Rahul Dravid have had to learn this the hard way.

POSTSCRIPT: A letter in *The Australian* newspaper: "Perhaps fining the Indian cricket team half Dravid's runs rather than half his match fee might be a more effective deterrent in these "honest mistakes."

What about Brad Williams, Sirs?

MID-DAY* • *January 25, 2004

International Cricket Council (ICC) match referee Clive Lloyd's decision to fine skipper Sourav Ganguly and his team members on one charge of slow over-rate and a level two breach of the ICC's code of conduct during the tri-series match against Australia last Thursday is not a matter of debate.

Lloyd was under obligation to impose the fine in his capacity as match referee.

Failure to do so would have been tantamount to gross breach of duty.

India's slow over rate and time wasting tactics to prevent 25 overs being bowled and thereby having the match treated as abandoned were a matter of fact, not opinion.

The offences were palpable and in full public view not only of those present at the SCG but millions of television viewers worldwide.

However, Brad Williams' hostile behaviour directed at Ganguly after he had dismissed him caught and bowled in the Brisbane match against Australia on January 18 was a matter of opinion.

Spectators at the Gabba, as also television viewers, were almost unanimous in their opinion that Williams' menacing gesture towards the Indian captain was not just a spur-of-the-moment reaction but constituted behaviour that cannot be construed as being in the lofty traditions of the game.

The ICC has recently tightened rules to ensure dignified and sporting behaviour on the field of play, including players celebrating a batsman's dismissal without waiting for the umpire's decision.

It would be unfair to attribute racial considerations—as is being done in certain quarters—in the failure of umpires Steve Bucknor and Peter Parker to report Williams' behaviour to the match referee.

But one cannot help feeling that the umpires, as also match referee Clive Lloyd, were remiss in not hauling the fast bowler over the coals.

Lahore game fixed? Rubbish!

MID-DAY* • *March 29, 2004

This writer has consistently rubbished in this column, on radio and television, maverick former Pakistan cricket captain Rashid Latif's incredible statement that India's fourth one-day international (ODI) against Pakistan in Lahore was "fixed".

Rashid Latif

Asked to react, former Pakistan skipper Imran Khan dismissed Rashid Latif's theory as "absurd".

Rahul Dravid said almost as much in diplomatic terms and Pakistan skipper Inzimamul Haq lost his cool when a reporter persisted in his silly line of enquiry on the subject.

The Pakistan Cricket Board (PCB) has threatened Latif with legal action, its chairman Shahryar Khan saying, "It's shameful for Rashid or anyone else to make such allegations without evidence in the midst of such an important series.

"We're looking into the matter and considering defamation and libel suits against him (Latif)," he is reported to have said.

"So far we've found nothing wrong in the way the matches have been played," Khan added categorically.

Last Friday's statement from International Cricket Council (ICC) Chief Executive Malcolm Speed on the subject has not come a day too soon.

Speed stated from ICC headquarters in London, "We have all seen the opinion of various people that have been aired in the media and they all share a common theme—they are long on speculation but short on evidence.

"If these allegations are to be treated seriously, the people making these claims need to substantiate their claims or withdraw them.

"To attack the integrity of the game and the players taking part in this series without proof is entirely inappropriate and does nothing to actually address the threat of corruption."

Speed stressed that the ICC's Anti Corruption and Security Unit (ACSU) has systems in place to deal with any malpractice in any international match.

As far as KHALIDOSCOPE is concerned, Rashid Latif's accusation is grossly unfair and casts baseless aspersions, particularly on the present Indian players.

When one of their predecessors—Mohammed Azharuddin—was proven to have been involved with match-fixing like the late Hansie Cronje of South Africa and Pakistan's Shoaib Malik, he was served his just desserts.

Having seen Sourav Ganguly's Team India at very close quarters at home and abroad for a few years now, I can go out on a limb to vouch for them.

I know just how dearly they value their own personal and professional integrity, their families' *izzat* and duty to their country.

I am convinced Ganguly and Co. would never consider selling these cherished values for pecuniary benefit, although some of them are, indeed, guilty of inordinate materialism.

The cascading speculation regarding match-fixing at Lahore is nothing if not the product of demented minds that are obsessed with conspiracy theories, the figment of imaginations of wink-wink, nudge-nudge know-alls.

Many, if not most, of these sporadic theories are floated by bookmakers themselves, and by people whose expertise in the game is limited to gambling and who have never played the game nor understood the elementary fact that it is well nigh impossible for eleven players to "fix" a match.

The proponents of conspiracy theories may have a point as far as "fancy fixing" with the abetment of a few players is concerned.

But for 22 players to conspire to fix a result in a series of historic importance with so much national pride at stake is an impossibility, especially with vigilant ICC watchdogs cynically scrutinisng every ball bowled and every little move of the players everywhere.

It is a well-known fact that Rashid Latif has a chip on his shoulder concerning the Pakistan Cricket Board, which handed out a ban on him.

The issue is best left to be sorted out by him and his board. As far as we are concerned, Latif's motivated kite-flying is an insult to our intelligence, which deserves to be dismissed with contempt.

That hurt, Mark, but Wankhede is no ground zero

MID-DAY* • *November 10, 2004

Ouch, that hurt, Mark Waugh.

Mark Waugh

The truth is known to hurt, and there is a lot of veracity in what you had to say in your *Sun-Herald* column last Sunday about Indian cricket.

Sadly, however, a lot of it is verisimilitude.

Moreover, the strident tone of your finger-pointing, coming from a well-loved personality, known the world over as much for your affable off-field demeanour as elegance at the crease, comes as a huge disappointment.

You write that Indians are "preoccupied" with pitches. You also opine that the team needs a change of leadership "if they are to improve their game".

It is shocking that as knowledgeable a person as you should say this because the entire cricketing world knows by now that it is the Australian side that has created such a hullabaloo over the Wankhede pitch, NOT the Indian team.

The question being asked even by Indian school children is: Would the Aussies have yelled blue murder, as they are doing day in and day out, had they won the Mumbai Test? Your captain, Ricky Ponting, while saying that he will express his "displeasure" with the "sub standard" wicket in his customary official captain's post-match report, has shown extremely poor taste and woefully bad sportsmanship, while trying to elicit the support of stand-in Indian captain Rahul Dravid in a formal protest to the ICC.

All sober, right-thinking individuals here in our cricket-crazy nation accept the fact that the pitch prepared for the final Mumbai Test assisted spin.

Is there anything wrong with that? After all, don't Australian Test venues prepare pitches—notably at Perth and Brisbane—with pronounced pace and bounce that assist your battery of champion pace bowlers to the detriment of opposing batsmen who are, often, all at sea against the furious barrage unleashed by your fast men.

In any event, what is the sine qua non of a "genuine" (a word your captain seems to fancy) Test wicket? And who is to decide whether it is dinkum or not in the absence of precise ICC guidelines?

Going by Ricky Ponting's trenchant criticism of the pitch, it would seem only green tops with exaggerated pace and bounce that favour your bowlers would meet his criterion.

No, Mark, Indians are not "preoccupied" with wickets, Ponting's touring team is.

It would appear the captain is disconsolate that he could not drive the final nail in the Indian coffin to win the series 3-0 in what your elder twin Steve, so flatteringly (for India) dubbed the Final Frontier.

It also seems he is disappointed he could not be an active participant, because of injury, in Australia's thoroughly well-deserved series win for the first time in 35 years, his team coming off second best in the only Test in which he led the side.

Indian skipper Sourav Ganguly suggests that Ponting was, perhaps, 'chicken' and, given his track record on Indian pitches, opted not to play in Nagpur, even though he was fit, because he did not wish to confront India's feared spin bowling. But that is his opinion and not the thesis of this piece.

The manner in which Ricky Ponting's world-conquering team prepared for the series just concluded in terms of meticulous planning, and the admirable execution of strategy devised for almost every leading player of the opposition, were object lessons.

However, in its impressive painstaking planning and strategizing for the Indian tour, the Australian brains trust missed out on a critical element—an understanding of the use of different types of rollers on subcontinental pitches.

Australia's batting debacle in the last innings was caused by their panic-stricken mind-set induced by nightmarish visions of what India's monstrous spin trio could do on a wicket on which their own 'pup', Michael Clarke, had taken six for nine on the third morning.

However, the only devil around was in the minds of the Aussie batsmen, who proved unequal to the task of negotiating India's spin bowling.

Earlier in the day, Sachin Tendulkar and VVS Laxman had demonstrated that there was nothing really wrong with the pitch when scoring 91 runs off 119 balls.

If the wicket favoured spin in the final passages of the match it was largely because of the decision of your captain to use the heavy roller before batting, first after winning the toss and—again—before the fourth innings.

As pointed out by former Indian Test captain Polly Umrigar, who supervised the preparation of the pitch, this led to the hard wicket breaking up later in the game and, thereby, assisting India's tweakers, who spun the match away from Australia.

You go on to write that India's record in away series is 'diabolical'. For the purpose of this discussion, it would suffice to quote the combative Harbhajan Singh who would like to remind you (MID DAY, November 8) that India "have not won matches only in India".

"We beat West Indies in West Indies, England in England, Pakistan in Pakistan, Sri Lanka in Sri Lanka and even Australia in Australia. I don't think we won there because we had friendly curators," the 'Turbanator' points out.

You say of Sourav Ganguly's captaincy, "Maybe a new captain might help their cause. Both personally and as a team leader, Ganguly's attitude and mindset does not seem able to cope with anything other than a pitch tailor-made for his team."

Whereas KHALIDOSCOPE does not go along with Harbhajan's comment that "Mark should keep his comment to himself", we would like to remind you that Ganguly is India's most successful captain with 15 wins, four of them overseas.

As batsman, he averages over 40 (41.47 to be precise) in Tests.

Not forgetting recent setbacks, Ganguly has been singularly responsible for rallying a dispirited rag-tag outfit into one that is respected, if not feared, in the cricket-playing universe.

In the process, he has instilled immeasurable national pride and self-belief not only among his team-members but also among most cricket-lovers in a nation of over a billion people.

Needless to say, Ganguly has his fair share of shortcomings, like any other captain including Ricky Ponting, but his contribution to Indian cricket is immense. To replace him at this stage would be an act of indescribable folly.

That said, some of your perspicacious observations about Indian cricket are on the mark (excuse the pun). Apart from setting its administrative house in order post haste, BCCI would do well to take note of some of your other criticism while addressing the many problems that afflict Indian cricket.

Paramount among them is the need to look ahead, take promising youngsters in hand right away and develop bench strength that would match Australia's daunting reserves. There are enough talented young players in the country for that.

You will agree, Mark, that the problem of replacing ageing stalwarts in Ricky Ponting's team is not very different from the one facing Sourav Ganguly.

Enough is enough

MID-DAY* • *March 15, 2005* • *New Delhi

Surely, enough is enough.

It's time to put an immediate end to the unending detestable jockeying for position, power and pelf in the Board of Control for Cricket in India(BCCI), and to get on with the all-important task of furthering the cause of the game, the players and the paying public.

Jagmohan Dalmiya and I. S. Bindra

For too long now, selfish interests in the supreme controlling body of the nation's favourite game have been allowed to distract attention from what should be single-minded concern for its well-being.

Sitting in at a press conference in Mohali last week during the excellently organised India-Pakistan cricket Test, and listening to former Board president Inderjit Singh Bindra and Rajasthan Cricket Association president Lalit Modi outline their eminently laudable plan for the BCCI to launch its own television channel, which would benefit players at different levels, state associations and the paying public, I could not escape one thought:

Isn't it unfortunate that the financial acumen, nay genius, of these two financially savvy administrators and other luminaries such as Jagmohan Dalmiya, NKP Salve, A C Mutthiah and Raj Singh Dungarpur is not being utilised unitedly in the interest of Indian cricket?

Reeling off mind-boggling figures to show the potential of a BCCI-owned television channel, which could be utilised to build infrastructure at the state level all over the country, Bindra delineated a scenario that would make Indian cricket a real powerhouse in the world.

Whatever the historical background and personal differences of the principal players, wouldn't it be wonderful if Messrs Jagmohan Dalmiya, Bindra, Lalit Modi and all other past and present presidents and office bearers of the BCCI and its constituents were to sink their differences, crush their egos and sublimate their considerable administrative qualities for the good for the game?

For too long now, personal and political considerations have been allowed to play ducks and drakes with a game which has not only become a national pastime but assumed attributes of a religion.

The money that the game generates from commercial avenues is not inconsiderable at present. But Bindra estimates the real value of Indian cricket to be an astronomical US$2 billion.

For the huge amounts of money being earned presently, despite shortfalls because of infighting, not to be utilised properly at the apex and state levels for the good of the game is, indeed, a shame.

Only recently, shocking details were revealed about the gargantuan amount of money from allotment of television rights that was allowed to go down the drain because of the squabbling and jockeying for power that is giving the cricket board such a bad name.

Moreover details that have recently come to light regarding the scandalous manner of functioning of the Rajasthan Cricket Association over the years which, if true, are a disgrace to all involved.

Lovers of the game of cricket have had just about enough of the political games that the powers-that-be have been indulging in to the great detriment of cricket, the players and, indeed, the paying public.

The time has come to put a stop to the crores of rupees that are being sunk into litigation by the warring factions and the nauseating washing of dirty linen in public.

The time has also come for all concerned to come together in a spirit of compromise, settle all outstanding issues such as Board elections, television franchises etc. post haste and work unitedly for the greater good of Indian cricket.

This entreaty may appear to be too simplistic (if not naive), idealistic and utopian to the cynical powers-that-be who are involved with a body that has been, and continues to be, a hotbed of dark intrigue and Machiavellian wheeling and dealing.

The millions of lovers of the game in the country are not interested in the personal equations of the prima donnas on the Board. Nor with their machinations, at which some appear to be past masters. Their only concern is honest and efficient running of the game. The fans are the ones who sustain it through gate receipts and, more importantly in today's context, television viewership that makes possible the income of crores of rupees (billions of dollars if the new proposal is adopted).

Surely, expecting efficient, politics-free administration of the game is not asking for too much.

Or is it?

Time for Board to back Bhajji

MID-DAY* • *April 5, 2005* • *Sydney

Now that the International Cricket Council (ICC) has dug itself in an unholy quagmire of confusion and controversy in l'affaire Harbhajan Singh, it becomes incumbent upon the Board of Control for Cricket in India (BCCI) to stand steadfastly by its worthy son.

Harbhajan Singh

The ICC's action (after the off-spinner had been reported by controversial umpires Steve Bucknor and Darrel Hair) upon the report of match referee Chris Broad, self-anointed upholder of ethics and morality of the game, is extremely unjust and high-handed.

The decision is bizarre in light of the fact that Harbhajan's 'doosra' had been cleared by the ICC's own physiotherapy gurus in Perth, Australia, barely a few weeks earlier.

In other words, not only is the 'Turbanator' being sentenced by the ICC repeatedly for the same 'crime' (his action was considered suspect twice before and cleared subsequently), the game's supreme body is also astonishingly implying that the naked eye is to be trusted more than its own latest scientific technology.

What also baffles comprehension is that although Pakistani all-rounder Shahid Afridi continues to bowl his patently illegal faster delivery (as the naked eye indicates) with impunity, Harbhajan is being singled out for treatment befitting a pariah.

It's extraordinary that Asian bowlers in particular (barring Afridi), are being singled out by the ICC for allegedly bending their arms to break its rules.

Pakistani all-rounder Shoaib Malik is currently under suspension as bowler.

The flip-flops of the ICC regarding the actions of Sri Lankan off-spinner Muttiah Muralitharan and Pakistani speedster Shoaib Akhtar are too notorious to warrant repetition. Both were cleared following outraged protests by their respective Boards after their actions had been questioned in Australia.

The Pakistan Cricket Board (PCB) is currently arguing the case of its captain Inzamam-ul-Haq over his fine and suspension, imposed by Broad after last week's Bangalore Test against India.

Born-again moralist Chris Broad's own record of shattering the stumps with his bat during his playing days was hardly worthy of the lofty traditions of the game he is now so zealously pretending to uphold.

It is hoped the BCCI—and especially its former president Jagmohan Dalmiya, who was largely instrumental in Shoaib Akhtar's clearance—will forcefully take up Harbhajan's case, as he so successfully did when Sourav Ganguly's Team India got the wrong end of the stick from ICC match referee Mike Denness in South Africa in 2001.

Too often in the past has the BCCI been guilty of spineless capitulation to the authoritarian and eccentric, if not inequitable, powers-that-be in the hallowed portals of the august ICC.

It's time it stood up for justice.

Pressing problems

MID-DAY • April 18, 2005 • Sydney

Mid-Day would like to place on record its appreciation of the Cricket Association of Bengal's (CAB) assurance that something will be done soon to improve the wretched working conditions at the Eden Gardens.

Jagmohan Dalmiya

Coming on the heels of the expeditious action by Jagmohan Dalmiya at the instance of present BCCI president Ranbir Singh Mahendra and secretary S K Nair, to prevent the ICC from taking punitive action against Harbhajan Singh until such time as it fine-tunes its own norms to define what precisely constitutes an illegal bowling action, the CAB's promise gives us reason for pride and joy.

The BCCI is finally showing sensitivity to complaints in the media, a development which, we sincerely hope, will now become par for the course. Before commencement of the Kolkata India-Pakistan Test, KHALIDOSCOPE had drawn attention to the abominable state of facilities for the media at our Test and ODI centres, with the possible exception of the Wankhede Stadium.

This column then noted with regard to the Eden Gardens press box, "You can safely bet a rupee to a rosogolla that the press box working conditions at the world-famous venue will be cramped and substandard in most respects, as always."

It went on to say, "Although allotted the best possible location and boasting the luxury of air-conditioning which many, if not most Test venues in the country do not possess, conditions in the Kolkata press box, set up with great fanfare in 1996, are below par and, therefore, the butt of trenchant criticism, especially from foreign correspondents."

Access to and exit from the school-bench type seating is decidedly inconvenient and, in the absence of microphones, the cacophonous yelling of details by the voluble scorer guarantees a headache by lunch time.

"One is at a loss to understand why elementary devices such as mikes and loudspeakers cannot be arranged."

And the less said about transmission facilities the better, as evidenced by numerous runs-in between communications staff, the notorious slapping of a Posts and Telegraphs employee by a despicable angrez saheb some years ago being the most outrageous.

"That said, the legendary stadium, over which administrator par excellence Jagmohan Dalmiya presides, does have many plus points for players, club house spectators—and VVIPs, mais oui!"

In a reference to the overall tenuous relationship between Indian officialdom and the press, KHALIDOSCOPE noted, "The press corps may not be the apple of the eyes of cricket administrators. There are, undeniably, some rotten apples in the media, as, indeed, in any other human endeavor.

"But surely, that ought not to be the reason for scurvy treatment of journalists, which only exacerbates the avoidable adversarial working relationship between press and organisers."

By way of conclusion, this column said, "It's time the Board of Control for Cricket in India set up a committee to inspect and approve press boxes in the country."

To his credit, Dalmiya phoned last weekend to say he had noted the points raised by KHALIDSOCOPE and, while expressing intent to redress cricket correspondents, grievances, requested written recommendations, as reiterated by Cricket Operations Manager of BCCI, Kunal Ghosh.

But of course, we will be only too happy to send our suggestions. Do bears sleep in the woods?

Meanwhile, we hope our other international cricket venues wake up to the urgent and imperative need to address the long-standing problems of the media—especially Delhi at its high-fangled, renovated Ferozeshah Kotla ground—which, over the years, has been the pits where press facilities are concerned.

What olive branch?

***MID-DAY* • December 9, 2005**

A report in a Mumbai morninger yesterday would have us believe that former BCCI president Jagmohan Dalmiya has offered his nemesis Sharad Pawar "an olive branch".

For his part, Dalmiya has described the report as "totally untrue, mischievous and motivated."

"There is a limit to lies and misrepresentation," he said to me last night. "I am surprised they have quoted from my letter. I do not know where the reporter got it from."

According to the Kolkata-datelined story, "Dalmiya is so impressed with Pawar's commitment to corporatise the Board that he has offered his team's full support to help achieve the goal by supporting the new dispensation's amendment to bring about professional managers."

The broadsheet—which, incidentally, considers the nomenclature 'tabloid' anathema—states that in a letter to Pawar, Dalmiya has also said that he was "convinced that professional management, as envisaged by Pawar in his blueprint for the BCCI, was the right way forward."

Dalmiya was attending a high-power meeting when KHALIDOSCOPE contacted him on his mobile phone last night for verification of the report. He was gracious enough to return my call promptly before MID-DAY'S deadline.

Dalmiya clarified that the new dispensation placed a mission paper before the Working Committee meeting in Mumbai on December 4, seeking to professionalise the working of the BCCI.

"I then told Mr. Sharad Pawar that he could either continue with the present system or go in for professionalism. I said the paper was a commendable move, something that I had been able to introduce in the International Cricket Council (ICC) and the Asian Cricket Council, in my capacity as president.

"I also said I had not been successful in professionalising the BCCI by removing honorary posts, because I could not garner the requisite majority. I said I hoped he (Mr. Pawar) would correct the situation even though he does not have the required majority and offered him all my votes to enable him to achieve the objective."

Terming the Kolkata-datelined report "nonsensical", Dalmiya added that it was also he who pointed out at the meeting that most of the national cricket boards in the world viz. Australia, England, West Indies, Sri Lanka, South Africa et al have a CEO.

He also cited the ICC, the International Olympic Committee (IOC), FIFA (the world's supreme soccer body), and the international tennis and swimming federations, which have professional CEOs.

"Even in our corporate world, bodies such as CII, FICCI and ASSOCHAM have CEOs," Dalmiya added. "But for it to work in the BCCI, the CEO must report to the president directly and not to the secretary. Otherwise, the CEO will be nothing more than an assistant secretary."

Dalmiya said he did not take any further part in the deliberations in the Working Committee meeting "because of all the shouting and accusations going on."

He confirms that he wrote to Pawar subsequently, reiterating the need to professionalise, and offering his support, if required, "in order to put an end to amateurism in the working of the BCCI".

The former president added: "I also suggested the appointment of an agency such as McKenzies or Tata Consultancy Services. Mr. Pawar later informed me that Tata Consultancy had been appointed."

Although this column applauds the former president for the spirit of cooperation shown in the interest of Indian cricket in this instance, it is distressed that Dalmiya vehemently denies his move is tantamount to "offering an olive branch" to Pawar and Co.

In MID-DAY dated December 1, KHALIDOSCOPE had made an ardent plea to all the warring factions in the sordid political chess game that has been a blight on our sport for a disgustingly long time now, to sink their differences, rise above egoistic and political considerations, and work together for the good of the game.

After the election victory, Sharad Pawar, while extending his hand of friendship, had appealed to Jagmohan Dalmiya for support.

Dalmiya, it would appear, has responded positively—but perfunctorily, restricting his support only as regards professionalising the BCCI, even as the wounds of the election defeat continue to fester.

It should be incumbent upon the former president and other heavyweights in the Board—past, present and future—to extend to Sharad Pawar and his team their fullest support in all their positive and constructive decisions.

A new spirit of selfless cooperation should be the lodestar for all concerned in the echelons of the BCCI. The national interest demands it.

Shame on you, BCCI

MID-DAY • January 15, 2006 • Sydney

The news that the touring team's management in Pakistan was coerced in the matter of selection against the expressed wishes of the captain and coach is a horrible blast from the past.

The report has come just when cricket fans were becoming smug following Team India's recent heartwarming performances and beginning to believe that the cataclysmic changes in the top echelons of the Board of Control for Cricket in India (BCCI) were making for efficient and responsible administration of the game.

According to an agency report datelined Lahore and widely published in Australia, "Sourav Ganguly was included in the Indian team for the first Test against Pakistan due to pressure from cricket board chiefs".

Attributing the report to a "team source", the story reveals that "coach Greg Chappell and captain Rahul Dravid did not want Ganguly to open and could not fit him in the middle order without disturbing a trusted combination.

"But team manager Raj Singh Dungarpur, under instructions from the BCCI, is understood to have urged Chappell to play the experienced Ganguly in the match.

"The manager was asked to convince Chappell to play Ganguly because of his vast experience," says the report.

The former captain was preferred over two regular openers, Gautam Gambhir and Wasim Jaffer after Chappell had told the media last Tuesday that two batsmen out of Sehwag, Gambhir and Jaffer would open the innings.

"Any two of the three will play because all three are in good form," the coach is reported as saying.

It goes on to add that during training on Friday, Dravid, Chappell and Ganguly "were seen having an argument in the middle, apparently over the batting order."

This makes one wonder whether the baffling decision for Dravid to open yesterday with Sehwag was their not-so-subtle way of telling the Board to go to blazes, even though it was a case of cutting the nose to spite the face!

By way of background, the agency story details BCCI president Sharad Pawar's meeting with Ganguly and senior players before declaring that India's most successful Test captain was not a "disruptive influence" in the team, contrary to Chappell's explicit belief in the leaked email to the previous dispensation.

All that I can say from this distance is that, if true, the report is shocking in the extreme.

It only reinforces my thesis over the years that the more things change in Indian cricket, the more they remain the same.

This piece is not about the controversy over Ganguly's merits and demerits regarding selection for the tour. In my view, Ganguly's services to the team and country as batsman and most successful captain ever need to be enshrined in letters of gold.

But that is not the issue. In my view, Ganguly's selection was flawed in the first place, since it was patently driven with political intent at the instance of interested BCCI bigwigs, who have no business to poke their dirty noses (to borrow an expression from Field Marshal SHFJ Maneckshaw) in matters of selection, and in shameful contravention of majority opinion in the Selection committee.

Personal, regional and (cricket) political aspects apart, the national selectors, had they been worth their salt, ought not to have countenanced any outside interference from any quarter, including from the very top, for any reason, whatsoever.

By virtue of being nominated on the national selection committee by their state associations, they are presumed to be men of unimpeachable integrity and expected to act only and exclusively in the national interest.

The selectors should have stood by their conviction and had the courage to resign. But does that ever happen in India?

No matter how you look at it: the BCCI 'diktat' to manager Dungarpur is despicable, smacks of political interference of the most disgusting kind and deserves to be condemned in the strongest terms, irrespective of the personalities involved.

It is obvious the current BCCI dispensation is hell-bent in establishing its credibility by projecting itself as being whiter than white.

Towards that end, an image of fairness towards Ganguly, who was perceived as being the raison d'etre of his so-called masters in West Bengal, their sworn enemies, is vital.

Needless to say, it is also craftily intended to erode Jagmohan Dalmiya's power base in a state where he is perceived in many quarters as being an 'outsider'. The way things have turned out, the change in the BCCI power structure has been a blessing in disguise for Ganguly who, in his wildest dreams, could not have expected their support.

That apart, the BCCI must, absolutely must, refrain from interfering in affairs that impact directly on the team's performance.

After all, the Board officials just do not have the requisite wherewithal in terms of knowledge and experience on the field of play, as compared with the captain, coach and selection committee members.

For another, in their obsession with matters of 'kursi', they often forget that the national interest should be paramount.

It's time they realised that they are merely the custodians of the hopes and aspirations of millions of cricket 'deewaane' in the country.

No party was wrong in saga

MID-DAY • September 20, 2005

Reports from Zimbabwe suggesting that all is again hunky-dory with Team India, now that skipper Sourav Ganguly and coach Greg Chappell have ostensibly kissed and made up, should be taken with a huge dollop of salt.

The fact of the matter is that, apart from bringing Indian cricket into disrepute all over the cricket-playing world, the spat between captain and coach has created a grievous divide among the players that will, willy-nilly, leave ugly, long-lasting scars.

In light of reports of a schism in the team, the public squabble has disinterred the ghosts of Indian Test captains past who, when deposed, deliberately worked towards their own team's defeat in shocking instances of cutting one's nose to spite the face.

In the present instance, versions out of Africa as to the 'guilty' party in the unsavoury incident have shockingly depended upon the predilections of reporters on the spot.

However, the truth of the matter is that in any such disagreement, no party is altogether right or wrong. The tragedy of the saga, which should have remained in the sanctum sanctorum, namely the players' dressing room, was leaked by a Deep Throat, apparently with malafide intent.

If Ganguly was within his rights to try and convince the coach that he deserved to continue as captain, Chappell was equally entitled to his daring (by Indian standards) opinion that the skipper step down for the time being in the team's interest—which ought to be paramount at all times.

I, for one, am dumbfounded and disgusted in equal measure, at the spin that has been given to the episode, depending upon the regional and national bias of individual purveyors of news.

I am sorry to say that, instead of applying the healing touch, some of the reporters on the spot have been grossly irresponsible in distorting and sensationalising an-honest-to-goodness difference of opinion between two strong individuals.

While sifting through the reams of muck, the sordid blow-by-blow accounts of the unpleasant incident in a section of the press, it appears indisputable that coach Chappell expressed his concern about captain Ganguly's below-par performances in characteristic blunt, no-nonsense, call-a-spade-a-shovel Aussie terminology.

In all likelihood, Chappell did suggest—and full marks to him for his professional honesty to team and country in doing so—that the skipper step down temporarily from the captaincy in view of his indifferent form, as evidenced by statistics and the fact that his previous Test century had come as far back as 21 months ago.

It should come as no surprise that Ganguly, being the proud captain that he is, took umbrage at Chappell's suggestion.

After all, he has been under tremendous mental pressure, and at the receiving end of a torrent of criticism, bordering on ridicule, for his patent temerity, increasingly apparent of late, against pace bowling aimed at his chin and rib cage.

If Ganguly was lionised by Indian cricket fans for setting an example to his team by standing up to the bullying tactics of some opposing captains (the shirt-removing incident being only one instance), it is unfair that he now be faulted for his spunk while arguing his own case to continue as captain.

However, Ganguly must accept blame, if reports about his making public his feud with Chappell, are true.

Equally culpable are the functionaries of the Board of Control for Cricket in India (BCCI) who sought to influence the selection process by remote control, as is their wont. When, oh when, will they learn that any self-respecting coach or selector cannot countenance their unwarranted interference for long?

Had the errant media and the ham-handed, never-ever-learn Board of Control for Cricket in India (BCCI) handled the matter with finesse and diplomacy, it would not have got out of hand, and Indian cricket would have been spared the indignity it has suffered worldwide.

But all this is in the realm of what might have been: It has now become incumbent upon the BCCI, the media and, most of all, the feuding parties to learn their lessons and bury this incident once and for all. To allow it to fester would be calamitous.

Events

Adhikari's reported comments—Cricket Board must explain this

SPORTSWEEK • June 2, 1974

According to an item from a London-based correspondent of a Kolkata newspaper, Col. Adhikari told a Press conference at Lords on the second day of the team's arrival in London that "ironically it was India who proposed the new experimental on-side rule, overlooking the tact that India's bowling strength lies in her spinners. ...."

Hemu Adhikari

It goes on to say that even English cricketers are not enthusiastic about this rule which did not receive the backing of England's representatives at last year's International Cricket Conference.

The reporter quotes Adhikari as saying that India were not happy about the rule, but "as good sportsmen" had agreed to give the rule a trial in the current series. "Win or lose, India will make the best of the bad situation," he is reported to have said.

The contents of the report are shocking. Knowing the Colonel as we do, we consider it highly improbable that the characteristically cautious manager would be so irresponsible in his utterances to the Press.

Cricket-Control Board secretary Professor. M. V. Chandgadkar when contacted by us stoutly denied that India had proposed the experimental rule. While expressing surprise at the report, he commented that it could only be the result of misreporting or misunderstanding of facts.

There is an increasing feeling amongst followers of sport in our country that officials who represent India at meetings abroad either do not participate actively in the proceedings, or if they do so, quite often do not advocate our interests forcefully enough.

The issue under discussion is of vital importance. Will the Board please come out with the true facts?

Now is the Time to Consolidate

SPORTSWEEK SPECIAL (Extracts from a speech)

YES, our series victory over England is one to be proud of by any count.

You know it better than I that it was not long ago that we were considered a second-rate cricketing nation, having earned the contemptible label of "duli dogs" from unkind English critics, a country which did not deserve even a full tour of England, of no more than 3 or 4 days Tests

But things have changed. It's taken us 30 long years but as we say in Urdu, *der aaye durust aaye.*

Even the most grudging English critic has had to admit that Indian cricket has come of age.

There is no such thing as a World Championship in cricket, yet—there are moves to organise one—and one cannot apply the rule of three in this context but who can deny that India is among the foremost cricketing countries in the world today.

Perhaps in no country in the world is cricket as popular a sport—both from the spectator and participation points of view—as in India. Well may one then ask: Why has it taken us so long to attain our present position in the international cricket hierarchy.

But then that is another subject which can be discussed—till the cows come home. Suffice it to say for the present that our cricket administration has had a lot to do with denying our cricket the glory which should have been hers a long time ago.

So much has been said and written already about the recently concluded Test series that it would be futile—and repetitive to dwell on the obvious although the members know that can be avoided.

OUR VICTORY IN A NUTSHELL

But if I were asked to put our victory in a nutshell I would have no hesitation whatsoever in saying that it is primarily attributable to TEAM SPIRIT. YES, TEAM SPIRIT, fighting qualities, able leadership, our spin attack and the failure of the much vaunted English batting to cope with our spin.

We at SPORTSWEEK have been most critical of all the loose talk of our so-called "team spirit" in the West Indies. One cannot deny that there was team spirit then. But to our way of thinking the talk of team spirit then was often inspired by political considerations, the politics which has always been the curse of Indian sport, be it cricket, hockey, football, tennis or any other game.

I maintain it was team spirit in England MORE THAN IN THE WEST INDIES which brought us victory. Look at the records and you will find that it was only a few who performed with any degree of consistency in the West Indies.

In fact most of the burden of our batting in the Windies had to be borne by Sardesai, Gavaskar and Solkar while the brunt of the bowling fell on the able shoulders of Bedi, Prasanna and Venkatraghavan. That was indeed a case of so many owing so much to so few.

In the series against England, on the other hand, there were NO tall scores, in fact not a single century from our batsmen, OR a really stand-out performance with the ball, with the exception of Chandrasekhar's deadly spell at the Oval.

This I maintain was team spirit.

One wonders why the people who parrot-like repeated the expression 'team spirit' in the context of our victory over the West Indies are today fighting shy of using it.

Ajit Wadekar's 100% series win record is indeed enviable by any standard. To have welded his unit into a cohesive fighting, one that could humble the redoubtable West Indies and England for the first time in their own countries in the short space of seven months is a staggering achievement, one which will take a lot of beating.

Most importantly, under Wadekar's leadership our players have demonstrated an admirable capacity to fight back when the chips were down as at that historic Oval Test.

No more, thank heavens, the sorry spectacle of throwing in the towel when the pressure was on.

FIGHTING CRICKET

Our victory in the last Test is a glorious example of fighting cricket. The manner in which our team struck back after being in arrears in the first innings and in the closing stages of the match blunted the stratagem of Illingworth, that master tactician, was proof of an abundance of guts and spine in our players.

Ajit Wadekar

Right through the series our boys have demonstrated a positive attitude, the will to win.

It is perhaps a tribute to the influence of Col. Adhikari that with the exception of the second Test when the chips were really down and we had no option but to try and play out time, our team always played for a win.

It was refreshing to see our batsmen, in most cases, stand up to the bouncers of the fiery English pace attack courageously, and without flinching, hook them to the boundary.

Yes that is how cricket should be played. And it was this positive approach which helped decide the fate of the series to a very large extent.

For it instilled in our batsmen the confidence that they could knock the much-feared English pace attack at will if they set their minds to it and at the same time also made it crystal clear to the opposition that our team really means business.

This coupled with the manner in which our spinners had awed the English batsmen in the first innings as in the earlier part of the tour against the counties, went a long way towards rattling the confidence of the England team.

PSYCHOLOGICAL ADVANTAGE

For as we all know, a psychological advantage of this kind can play a big part in swinging a series either way when the teams are more or less evenly matched.

I really must make a mention of the tremendous goodwill that our team has created wherever it has played. Other problems apart, the players have at all times conducted themselves with decorum.

Not once have they been guilty, as far as I know, of any unsportsmanlike behaviour.

The umpires' decisions, no matter how unpalatable, have always been accepted with good grace. There have been no tantrums or display of emotion on the field of play.

And the manner in which our team and Col. Adhikari, in particular, conducted themselves in that unfortunate "shoulder charge" episode has won for them, I am happy to say, tremendous respect and esteem all over England.

Col. Adhikari

Could we have won the first Test if rain hadn't intervened. "Yes, we could have, but I don't think we would have"

It was a matter of so near yet so far. And one must admit some of our senior batsmen let the side down by throwing caution to the winds in their quest for quick runs.

A MASTER STROKE

The promotion of Farokh Engineer in the batting order at that juncture was truly a master stroke. And the decision to go for quick runs deserves commendation, but one could not help feeling that some of our senior batsmen were somewhat irresponsible in the execution of the plan.

The ultimate result of the first Test was a just one. For on the run of play both teams had deserved to win.

It is said that in the second Test we were lucky in that bad captaincy of England was to some extent responsible for our finishing second best.

In my humble opinion, one has to reorient ones definition of "luck" in the English context, what is generally termed luck by our standards is an integral part of cricket in England due to the weather and the consequent conditions that obtain there.

Ajit Wadekar's performance as captain in the two Tests that I witnessed was of an exceptionally high order on the whole.

He demonstrated all the qualities of a good captain: shrewdness, sound strategy, an understanding of the strengths and weaknesses of the opposition, an intelligent deployment of the resources at hand and the capacity to inspire his team to play positively, to fight back from a losing situation against tough professional opposition. Most of all he set a fine example with his batting. His innings at Lord's was a true captain's knock and one learns he played an innings of real beauty at the Oval.

We are grateful

SPORTSWEEK CRICKET QUARTERLY

Our worst fears were confirmed when the charity match planned by SPORTSWEEK, in conjunction with the ROTARY CLUB OF BOMBAY MID-TOWN, did not come off last March.

We should like to place on record our sincere appreciation of the spontaneous response to our request for participation, by Barry Richards, Mike Procter, Younis Ahmed, Anura Tennekoon and David Heyn, all of whom agreed to play in the proposed match for the Prime Minister's Relief Fund *gratis* (barring actuals).

We are particularly grateful to Richards and Procter who went to the extent of offering to forego participation in a single-wicket tournament in South Africa, from which they stood to gain considerably financially.

We are also indebted to the Sri Lanka Cricket Board for agreeing to release Tennekoon and Heyn in the midst of the Sri Lanka team's tour of Pakistan, as also to the Pakistan Board for altering the itinerary of this tour to enable the Sri Lankan players to participate.

Barry Richards

By agreeing to raise funds for a humane cause, these cricketers demonstrated unequivocally that sport knows no barriers, that it can indeed build bridges between people, surmount all manner of artificial man-made differences. We salute them.

Hard-liners on the apartheid issue who advocate South Africa's isolation from international sport until such time as she plays non-racial sport at club level have an antagonist in Leslie Sehume, Sports Editor of the South African newspaper "The World".

According to Sehume, a black South African, "the majority of the 16 million blacks of African descent (who are almost three times as many as all other races put together) in my country are disillusioned and disenchanted with those overseas countries which have maintained vigorous campaigns to keep South Africa out of international sport."

Asks Sehume in an article in "Sportsword", "Who are these sworn enemies of South Africa trying to help? Certainly not black South African sportsmen . . . now we know that it is not only white South Africa which has become the polecat of the world. We, too, come into the unpleasant category. . .

Africans in South Africa are not racists, according to Sehume, who maintains that the agencies recognised abroad as representative of African sport in the Republic do not represent the present feelings of African sportsmen in the land of the Veldt.

"African sportsmen want dialogue and understanding with white sportsmen," says Schume. They realise that white sportsmen would like to see an end of all racial barriers in sport. But they realise, too, that both black and white sportsmen are faced with a rigid Government policy. Also, the fact that traditions die hard obviates overnight changes in the South African sports situation as far as the white electorate (which makes the laws) is concerned.

"African sportsmen," according to Sehume, "state that affiliation to white sporting organisations fosters good relations and creates an atmosphere of co-operation, which can only lead to progress for black sportsmen coupled with the vital financial assistance necessary for existence."

Food for thought, this, for the "hawks" in our sport.

Windies deservedly win an absorbing series

SPORTSWEEK • February 02, 1975

The deserving side has won. A most absorbing series has ended. As the popular band of talented cricketers from the Caribbean leave our shores, we bid them a fond farewell. And we're sure we echo the sentiments of millions of cricket lovers in this country when we say "It's been great having you here. We shall miss you".

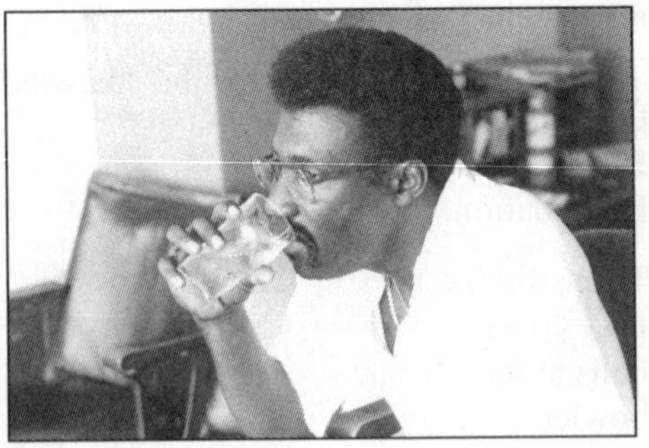
Clive Lloyd

In the ultimate analysis, the visitors had an edge over us in all departments of the game except spin. In the matter of fitness the West Indians were head and shoulders above our team. Most importantly, they brought to bear on their performances at Bangalore, Delhi and Bombay a thoroughly professional approach.

On balance, the nature of the Wankhede Stadium wicket, (about which so much rubbish was spouted), the spin of the coin, Bedi's indisposition on the first day and the atrocious Indian fielding determined the outcome of the final Test. One is tempted to conjecture as to what the result might have been, had India won the toss for the fifth consecutive time and accepted the catches that came her way.

That there is no substitute for class, was amply demonstrated by Lance Gibbs in the first innings and Vanburn Holder in the second innings, both of whom turned in superb bowling performances on an unhelpful wicket which remained chock full of runs until the very end and which made a laughingstock of the so-called 'experts'.

While it is no doubt true that our pathetic catching aided the West Indian batsmen, there can be no denying the fact that Lloyd, Fredericks, Kallicharran and Murray cashed in on their chances in thoroughly professional style.

From India's point of view, the series has thrown up two talented cricketers namely Gaekwad and Ghavri, but the former will have to learn that it is not much use scoring runs and gifting them away in the field and, more importantly, flooring catches which prove expensive.

The return to form of 'Mr. Reliable' Solkar was long overdue. Gavaskar was greatly missed in the series.

Intimidation or legitimate?

SPORTSWEEK • May 2, 1976

Mike Holding

The question on the lips of even those remotely concerned with the game of cricket is: did the bowling of Michael Holding, the toast of the Caribbean, in the final Test about which Bishan Bedi has said "it was not so much a match as a war," amount to intimidation?

To answer the question fairly and correctly it is necessary to examine Law 46 which states; "The persistent bowling of fast, short-pitched balls at the batsman is unfair if, in the opinion of an umpire at the bowler's end, it constitutes a systematic attempt at intimidation. In such an event if it continues, the bowler's end umpire must first caution the bowler, then inform the fielding captain and the other umpire and if it continues, call dead ball, instruct the captain to take the bowler off, the bowler being not able to bowl again in the innings," If we are to accept Lloyd's version, the Indian batsmen were themselves to be blamed for injuries insofar as they were frightened and technically not equipped to face the thunderbolts of local hero Holding who should now rank among the fastest in the world.

This point of view is supported by John Arlott who says, "Indeed, by the standard of modern Test cricket they (the West Indians) have been temperate in not employing that weapon (bouncers) to any great extent until now."

Says he, "The persistent use of the bouncer is virtually confined to Test cricket where careers are made and broken, publicity, standing and high income created. Indian batsmen of the modern period are invariably at a disadvantage against high pace because none exists in their domestic cricket and they encounter it only in other countries at Test level."

But Arlott also feels that the alternative is to prepare pitches of such pace, life or sympathy to spin that bowlers could beat batsmen by the traditional skill and, therefore, did not need to resort to intimidation.

On the other hand we have the opinions of Tony Cozier and the cricket correspondent of the *Jamaica Daily Gleaner*, both of whom maintain that Holding overused the bouncer, at times upto four times in an over. They maintain that umpire Gosein at Holding's end would have been justified in cautioning Holding on this score.

The subject of intimidatory bowling has been a vexed one for quite some time now. The problem stems from the vague definition of a bouncer vis-a-vis a fast short-pitched delivery, when a bouncer, a fast bowler's legitimate weapon may be termed intimidatory bowling and the vast discretionary powers which vest in the umpires in the matter of interpretation. But while the arbiters, and lawmakers at cricket's headquarters have been seemingly more concerned with the semantics of the problem, a young cricketer (Martin Bedkober) has lost his life in Australia and another, Ewan Chatfield, of New Zealand came close to losing his, as did our own Nari Contractor in the West Indies in 1962.

In our opinion the essence of intimidation is danger to life and limb. Chauvinism and fierce nationalistic pride put a premium on winning at all cost but intimidation should be viewed in relation to the ability of the batsman to handle bouncers safely. This is precisely why, traditionally, bouncers have been frowned upon when bowled at tailenders.

We submit, therefore, that ridge or no ridge (Bedi denies there was one) the 90 m.p.h, potentially lethal and persistent bouncers of Holding, delivered with a high arm action, around the wicket, were intimidatory to the technically ill-equipped Indian batsmen, who are slow to get in line or move away from the ball, although, they may not have been so against the Australians or even West Indian batsmen who have the requisite technical ability to face bouncers.

Holding can hardly be blamed for the shortcomings of the Indian batsmen but then surely human life is more precious than the winning of a cricket Test by any means.

It's hardly our intention to squeal, over our defeat but the facts, as reported by our correspondents must be viewed in proper perspective. It is during situations of the type that obtained at Sabina Park that the arguments of the advocates of neutral umpires even for a 'gentleman's game' which cricket is supposed to be, gain added weight.

Board President Ram Prakash Mehra has eloquently denounced the 'atom bombs' and 'nuclear-weapons' employed by the West Indies. It is significant that these were resorted to when the match seemed to be slipping out of the hands of Lloyd who was already under great pressure after West Indies' unexpected reversal at Port of Spain.

Having reportedly prepared an extra fast track on a side strip and having packed the side with four pace bowlers, the events which took place with India in the driver's seat at 191 for one were hardly surprising. Can we expect the Board president to take up the sorry episode as vehemently and eloquently with the International Cricket Conference when it meets at Lord's in a few months from now?

And more importantly, will the Cricket Board at last wake up and do something in the matter of producing effective pace bowlers of our own not only for their own sake but also to provide invaluable practice to our batsmen—a plea which finds more detailed expression in the latest issue of SPORTSWEEK's World of Cricket.

Bedi's much-debated decision to 'declare' or 'close' the second innings notwithstanding, our lads have emerged with much credit from the arduous twin tours. The future of Indian cricket appears bright once again. So rally round, ye cricket aficionados and roll out the red carpet for your heroes. Bedi and his gallant lads return home from the fray bruised and confused but strong in spirit. They have done India proud.

Of Vaseline, gamesmanship, clowns and insolent scribes

SPORTSWEEK* • *March 1977

England's well-deserved 3-1 win over India in what was often a remarkably painful, dull, agonising series between two mediocre, lack luster sides was largely the result of excellent teamwork.

John Lever

And, of course, the most admirable elements of dyed-in-the-wool professionalism characterised by a remarkable ability to adjust, adapt, improvise. Also to outwit, outmaneuver, 'psyche out', 'con' the opposition. A capacity to apply all the ruses, devices, gambits of gamesmanship and one-upmanship. Of 'psychological warfare', to win-Machiavelli-like at all cost, by means most often fair and within the framework of the rules but, alas, not always so.

Looking back—not in anger—after the dust of the 'battle' has settled, the conclusion is inescapable that the scales of the balance were tilted by the technical ability, dynamism, qualities of leadership and the do-or-die, win-at-all-cost determination of one individual—Tony Greig, the 'man of the series', who on arrival in India had rated his team's chances of victory "50:50".

It was Greig who through sheer personal example with bat and ball (is he really a bowler of Test calibre?) and the ability to command and inspire, rallied his side time and again (how often did the specialist batsmen lose their wickets early!), boosted its morale and in the end lead it to a most creditable victory on wickets which were presumably prepared to assist spin, a strategy which not only boomeranged thanks to the presence of 'Deadly' Underwood in the opposition but also demonstrated the sad fact that the so-called groundsmen are incapable of producing even wickets to assist spinners.

Verily can it be said that the 1976-77 India-England series marked a watershed in the modern history of English cricket. For it was here that an England captain about whose credentials there still prevail grave misgivings in his own country, transformed the mood of a nation which, after her dismal performances against Australia and the West Indies, had plummeted to abysmal depths of dejection and despair, to dizzying heights of euphoric ecstasy.

Many of the cognoscenti in this country still find it difficult to believe that the same side which they, only in moments of 'charitable' expansiveness, termed 'mediocre', could have come so close to defeating Australia (admittedly a depleted side) in Australia in the memorable Centenary Test. But then such has been the transformation in English cricket.

There have been post mortems galore. A great deal has been spouted and written about the reasons for India's defeat, the fact that the margin of England's victory was not a true index of the relative strengths and weaknesses of the two teams, that the Indian players were tired, stale, jaded, about the faulty itinerary which pitted the visitors against weak sides in the early part of the tour enabling them to strike form and boost their morale.

Enough verbiage has also been expressed about India's timid mental approach, the inability to take the fight to the enemy camp, about the lack of application, patience, determination, about gutless, spineless, technically inept batting especially against the moving ball, about faulty footwork and even more faulty selection. Also about atrocious fielding and the need for pace bowlers who can move the ball (the one effective pace bowler available—Ghavri—was treated scurvily).

By contrast, England were perhaps the best-ever fielding side to visit India. The only silver lining in the home team's performance in the fielding department were Yajurvindra Singh's seven catches on his debut in the Bangalore Test to equal two world records. On the whole, however, the spin trio strove manfully but was let down—yet again—by the batsmen and fielders.

The umpiring, too, for the greater part of the series, left a great deal to be desired. True, umpires today officiate under tremendous pressure, both from players and spectators, the more so from the huge crowds at Test matches in India. It would be most unfair to impute motives or to accuse the umpires of dishonesty.

But the fact remains that although quite a few doubtful decisions did go against the visitors, all in all, the home side suffered considerably more by comparison, with Gaekwad, Patel and Viswanath being the worst sufferers.

On balance, it would appear that some of the umpires are technically and physically incompetent. And the old 'hang-up', being sympathetic towards 'phoren' guests (the brown-man's burden?) persists. It is interesting to note that whereas one umpire ensured that the prefix 'Mister' was always used when addressing the England players, it was just "Bedi" or "Gavaskar" or plain "batsman" for the Indians.

No essay on the series can be complete without a reference to the obnoxious 'Vaseline' episode. Both Greig and Barrington have acknowledged that vaseline was used in the Madras Test, a fact confirmed by the chemical analysis. In an article in the London *Daily Mirror*, former England captain Ray Illingworth and fast bowler John Snow have admitted in so many words that 'greasy substances' such as vaseline and lip-ice have been used by past England sides. They have mentioned Geoff Arnold, Basil D'Oliveira and Tony Greig as those responsible for what they term 'cheating' on this score.

What is most surprising is the hurry with which the MCC treated the matter as closed, exonerating Greig and his team even before the report of the technical committee of the Board of Control for Cricket in India had been received by it. We now learn that the committee did not recommend action against the team and decided merely to refer the matter to the MCC because Bishan Singh Bedi did not wish to press the issue.

According to the India skipper, the use of vaseline by the England side started in the very first Test in Delhi. Bedi is said to have brought this to the attention of a high Board official who promised to get the ball chemically analysed. Instead, the 'rogue' ball was given as a souvenir to John Lever for his 'outstanding performance'.

It is futile to argue that the outcome of the series would have been any different. It is also arguable as to whether India could have reduced the margin of defeat had she adopted bold, aggressive methods, gone for runs at the end of the fourth day of the Bombay Test and declared after about an hour's batting on the fifth morning when the tourists' over-rate fell to a pathetic 11 in the first hour. It would not be incorrect to state that the tourists' bowling and scoring rates were largely responsible for making the series such a huge Y-A-W-N.

If the attempts of the British journalists touring with the team at defending and denying, playing down the Vaseline episode were laughable in the extreme, the partial, prejudiced reporting of some of them (at least one of them reported through 'instinct' and 'rumour') was highly unethical and, therefore, contemptible. So were the constant appeals, indecent, vulgar gestures and 'chatting up' tactics of Tony Greig which hardly brought honour to the cap he was wearing.

The British press was quick to rush to print and damn 'Sunny' Gavaskar for running down the Wankhede Stadium wicket, totally forgetting the fact that Lever and Greig had done likewise right through the series and for which Lever was warned.

Willis broke the stumps in protest against a leg-before decision. Greig stamped on the ball to supposedly bring it back to shape after an appeal to the umpires on the crucial last day of the Bombay Test was turned down.

Vice-captain Brearley waved his bat in anger at the crowd when given out caught in the second innings of the last Test and Randall whose boorish antics and juvenile attempt at humour wouldn't amuse even his own six year old son if he had one, made it a point of stressing to the press, as he returned to the pavilion in Bangalore, the fact that he had been given wrongly out.

In his attempts at raising cheap laughs, Randall thought nothing of bodily lifting up a Test umpire, of grabbing a constable's cap to don it on his own head. People in India respect their police and umpires. Would this clown ever dream of doing the same to a London bobby or to umpire Frank Chester? Or any other English umpire for that matter.

We salute England on her victory. But for many cricket-lovers here, the regard for the country which taught the world a gentleman's game called cricket, has diminished considerably. In this fiercely competitive age, many hallowed traditions have gone by the board, as has the precept that "winning is not the important thing". But, need it be the ONLY thing?

And, what of the gentlemen of the British press? Should reporting be based on 'instincts' and 'rumours'? What of the venerable member of the Fourth Estate who publicly rebuked and insulted a hapless Bombay photographer whose only 'sin' was to request payment from a foreign correspondent for a long-overdue four-year old bill for camera repairs? What of the insolent scorer who kept gate-crashing into press boxes, demanding the best seats, picking up arguments with Indian journalists, making an absolute nuisance of himself? This worthy had his comeuppance in the Garware Pavilion of the Wankhede Stadium when he was reprimanded for walking on seat cushions and, made to clean the cushions in full public view.

Traditional Indian hospitality is well-known. Visitors to this land are always considered 'honoured' guests. But, as Mr. S. K. Wankhede stated at a function organised by the Bangalore Sports Journalists Association, Indian hospitality should not be mistaken for weakness.

Bedi blasts the umpires

SPORTSWEEK* • *February 05, 1978

India's captain Bishan Singh Bedi blasted Australian umpires at the end of the third day of the final Test at the Adelaide Oval.

Bishan Singh Bedi

"India has had the rough edge of umpiring decisions," he said.

He also accused umpires Max O'Connell of Adelaide and Dick French of Sydney of being "not very competent."

"Toohey was out caught behind. Simpson was lbw, both to me, but that's not important," Bedi said.

Both appeals were turned down by O'Connell who also had declared Amarnath (Ghavri was given out by French) out to a controversial catch in India's first innings when he gave French the all-clear from square-leg although he was unsighted by Cosier who held the catch.

"The scene with Simpson in the last over of the day was not about that however. Wicket-keepter Kirmani wasn't ready. It was my fault."

Simpson explained that "there was a lot of noise coming from Vengsarkar fielding close at point." (Vengsarkar later said he was drawing the attention of Kirmani, who was not ready, to the fact that Bedi was coming in to bowl).

"Vengsarkar obviously was shouting at the wicket-keeper, so I pulled away."

Bedi said Simpson and some of the Indian players had exchanged words. "I just wanted to cool everyone down. No one wanted to get excited," Bedi said. "It should have been the one day there shouldn't have been any fuss over.

"A lot of unpleasantness can be avoided in such cases. But we didn't start it. We couldn't help it.

"It was a terrible pity it happened after having gone through such a tour. We don't swear on the field but how can you hide your emotions? We are human after all.

"Australia play hard and we accept that. We play hard ourselves but we play fair," he said.

Bedi said Australian cricketers always waited for the umpire's verdict when they were obviously out and had the habit of appealing for catches from half volleys.

"I haven't come across one touring team which was happy with the Australian umpires and the Australian players, approach to them," Bedi added.

"But I am not squealing. I am not saying this because we are in a mess at the moment.",

Bedi said he was not complaining as much about the Australian players as the Australian umpires.

"The umpires haven't been terribly competent in this game. And they're the best we have had so far in Australia. We came into this Test happy with anyone they gave us. We left the selection to the good judgment of the Australian Board.

"Other umpires on this tour have committed a lot more blunders., We've had the rough side of it—and not only in this Test."

The opinions of Bedi's teammates and Indian correspondents covering this tour are similar to those of Bedi. Australian umpires are known to invariably give the batsmen the benefit of the doubt for appeals for leg before when the batsman has played off the front foot. But it does appear as though right through the series starting from the Brisbane Test, Australian players, particularly Simpson, have benefited more by comparison from doubtful decisions

Bedi was right when he stated he was not squealing. The feelings of the Indian players' about what they consider "incompetent" if not "unfair" umpiring has been pent up for a long time and Bedi was merely giving vent to his and his teammates' emotions.

The timing of the complaint is unfortunate and may give the impression of being in bad taste or of poor sportsmanship.

But facts are incontrovertible and they have been corroborated by other visiting teams to this country. Rohan Kanhai, who is presently in Australia, and former Pakistan captain Mushtaq Mohammad too have been very bitter in their criticism of the standard of Australian umpiring.

India, Pak to sponsor World Cup?

MID-DAY • February 18, 1980

A World Cup, jointly sponsored by the cricket boards of India and Pakistan, is among the proposals informally proposed by Pakistan as part of a move to strengthen sporting relations between the two countries.

MID-DAY understands from reliable sources that Air Marshal (Retd.) Nur Khan who recently took over as president of the Board of Control for Cricket in Pakistan (BCCP) is keen on "reaching out" to India with the objective of breaking barriers and building bridges between the people of the two countries.

He is of the opinion that more frequent sporting encounters between India and Pakistan are "absolutely essential" to raise the overall standard of sport in the two countries.

It will be recalled Nur Khan offered India the use of Karachi's astro-turf stadium for preparation for the Moscow Olympics.

Eminent cricket commentator Omar Qureishi, who is director of operations, Pakistan International Airways, and former Test spinner Haseeb Ahsan were in Bombay over the weekend for exploratory talks with Indian sports officials and are understood to have sent out feelers to cricket officials for closer sporting ties between the two countries and the response is said to have been "encouraging".

They also met government officials, office-bearers of the Indian Olympic Association; organising committee members of the next hockey World Cup scheduled to be held in Bombay in 1982 and officials of the Indian universities and railways sports control boards.

The proposal for the hosting of the cricket World Cup is still in the embryonic stage. It envisages cosponsorship by India and Pakistan with Bombay and Karachi as venues.

Other avenues suggested by Pakistan are regular exchange of club, school and college teams.

Gavaskar unhappy

SPORTSWEEK* • *February 01, 1981

Indian captain Sunil Gavaskar is most dissatisfied with the umpiring in the second India-Australia Test which ended in a nerve-wracking draw at the Adelaide Oval on Tuesday.

Sunil Gavaskar

He told SPORTSWEEK after the match that he had expressed his feelings to Mel Griffin, the chairman of the umpiring sub-committee of the Australian Cricket Board, but clarified that no official protest had been lodged.

Gavaskar did not lambast South Australia's Tony Crafter and Victoria's Rex Whitehead, who umpired the Adelaide Test in so many words, but said the Indian captain at a press conference on Tuesday, "When cricketers from all over the world come to India and say things about our umpiring, all I can say is that they are moaners and grumblers".

The Australian journalists were amused at Gavaskar's choice of expletives but seemed to take it in their stride.

"I've said it before and I'll say it again", continued Gavaskar, "Australian umpiring is as good as Indian umpiring", but he would not give his opinion of the standard of Indian umpiring.

Australian captain Greg Chappell did not, however, agree with Gavaskar's assessment. "They're welcome to their opinion," said he "There were a few mistakes," said he. "I do not know of any Test in which there are not some debatable decisions. You have to expect the mistakes and the batsmen to be given the benefit of the doubt—as they were given."

Gavaskar told SPORTSWEEK, "It's a good feeling to go to Melbourne with a chance to square the series. India would put up an improved performance on the slow Melbourne wicket which assists spin bowling and fight back strongly."

Gavaskar told newsmen that India deserved to draw the Test.

Question: Does that mean that Australia did not deserve to win?

Gavaskar: Yes.

Question: Were there anxious moments in the Indian dressing room?

Gavaskar: Naturally.

Question: Doshi didn't look nervous after his brilliant cover drive in the first innings?

Gavaskar (Smilingly): He may not have been but we were.

Question: Any comments on the Indian batting?

Gavaskar: Our specialist batsmen—and that includes me—let the situation get out of hand. They succumbed to the pressure after Chetan and I had got out before lunch. Our senior batsmen—Vishy, Dilip and I have been struggling for runs and this has imposed a great burden on the lower order. In fact it was they who saved this match for us. What we are lacking in is application.

Question: Have your early dismissals been responsible for your batting collapses?

Gavaskar: Not really. There have been many occasions in the past when I have got out early but the other batsmen have carried the team.

Question: How do you feel now about your decision to put Australia in to bat after winning the toss?

Gavaskar: As I've said before it was a team decision. The feeling was that it would be better to have to chase 450-runs plus. We expected Australia to get at least that many on this wicket—than to be 80 for 5 as we were at Sydney and then have to fight back. Besides we didn't want to give Australia the advantage of bowling first on a fresh wicket.

Question: Faced with a similar situation would you take a similar decision.

Gavaskar: You bet.

Australian skipper Greg Chappell told pressmen he was not disappointed with the result when you take into account the nature of this wicket and the weather. Chappell stated that Hogg was tired after his first innings stint so he gave Lennie Pascoe a go because he had a disappointing first innings and he bowled magnificently to put Australia in sight of victory by sending back the first three Indian batsmen.

The Aussie skipper was all praise for Dennis Lillee whom he described as the only bowler in his team who can cut the ball. He added that Dennis was a tremendous team man with a lot of personal and team pride.

Yashpal and Vengsarkar told SPORTSWEEK that they were most dissatisfied with the decisions responsible for their dismissals. Yashpal thought the ball from Yardley which he missed while playing forward would have gone outside the leg stump.

Vengsarkar said it was the first time that he had been given out wrongly. "The ball that Chappell caught clearly went off my boot as everybody saw on the television replay. And the ball to which I was out leg before in the first innings—from Liliee—would have gone over the stumps. It struck me high on the thigh."

Be that as it may, the Indians lived to fight another day and the organisers are assured of sizeable gate-money at the Melbourne Test commencing on February 7. The Melbourne fans are the most enthusiastic supporters of traditional cricket in all Australia.

The Benson and Hedges award of Rs. 10,000 (approximately.)—this writer was one of the judges—went to Kim Hughes who on Tuesday failed in his bid to enter the hall of greats of those who have scored a double century and a century in a Test.

When cricket died at the MCG...

SPORTSWEEK* • *February 08, 1981

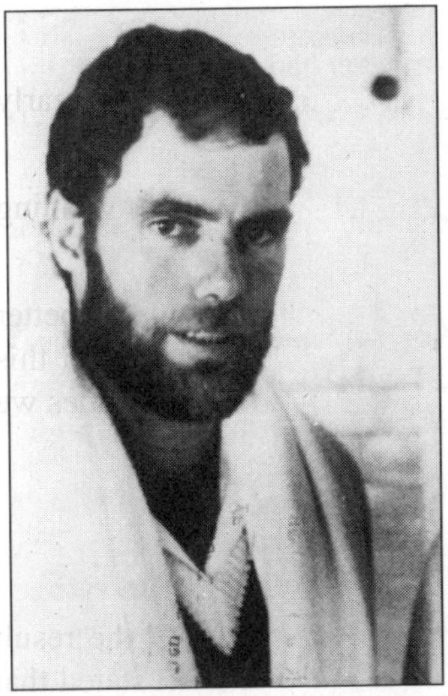

Greg Chappell

A storm of protest erupted on Sunday night after Greg Chappell ordered the last ball of the Benson and Hedges match between Australia and New Zealand at the Melbourne Cricket Ground to be bowled underarm.

Switchboards at newspaper offices and the Channel Nine network which televised the third game in the best-of-three series were jammed by calls from irate cricket fans condemning the Australian captain's match-winning tactics.

And Monday's newspapers were full of angry editorials and letters from outraged fans and vitriolic comments from columnists. With New Zealand 229 for 8 requiring six from the last ball of the game to tie the match, Australian captain Greg Chappell asked younger brother Trevor, bowling the 50th over of the New Zealand innings and the last ball of match, to bowl underarm. He informed umpires of the action so as not to render the delivery a 'no ball'.

NO OPTION

Kiwi Batsman Brian McKechnie had no option other than to block the ball as it rolled towards him. He threw away his bat and walked off the field before a crowd of 52,990 which could not believe its eyes and which made no secret of its disgust. Boos and hisses greeted the Australians as they left the field. Wicket keeper Rod Marsh showed his disapproval of his captain's decision by shaking his head as Trevor Chappell ran up to bowl.

New Zealand captain Geoff Howrath obviously unaware of the fact that the rules of the Benson Hedges World Series cup permit underarm bowling rushed out to the field with the umpires correcting him that the Australian bowler's action was perfectly in keeping with the rules.

The Australian Cricket Board is meeting shortly and is expected to legitamise underarm bowling with immediate effect. Greg Chappell said later he didn't run the risk of the match being cancelled which would have forced the two teams to play another game, in the best-of-five $55,000 (Rs. 5,50,000 approximately.) finals.

"It's within the rules and if it's within the rules of the game, it's fair play," he said. "We'd played our guts out and I wasn't going to see us forced into another game."

"I didn't want that to happen again. I knew when I made my decision I would upset many people but I was prepared to put up with it"

Gre Chappell admitted his decision was made "in the heat of the moment".

Former England captain Tony Greig has called for the sacking of Greg Chappell as Test captain. Greig said he was surprised and disappointed at Chappell's decision. "He did something very stupid" he said. In another incident in Australia's innings in which the home side scored 235 for 4, off the allotted 50 overs, Greg Chappell was given not out when Kiwi fielder Mark Snedden dived to hold a spectacular catch at mid-wicket off a pull from the Australian captain when he was on 58.

Chappell went on to score 90 before he was out to an equally brilliant catch by Bruce Edgar at the same position. Both umpires stated they had not seen the catch because they were "watching their respective crease at the time."

Television replays confirmed that the catch, which changed the outcome of the match and enabled Australia to go up 2-1 in the series was a clean one.

New Zealand captain Geoff Howarth and manager Ian Taylor said they would strongly suggest that the rule regarding underarm bowling be changed. Taylor said, "The way things are at the moment, you could get a team bowling all 50 overs underarm to prevent high - scoring and it would be ludicrous."

Trevor Chappell's underarm delivery, bowled under the explicit instructions of captain Greg Chappell, has been condemned throughout the length and breadth of the country and denounced as "shameful." "spineless,", "disgraceful", "churlish", "gutless" and the like.

The point of view is near unanimous that good sportsmanship "an honoured Aussie trait" as exemplified by heroes such as Donald Brahman and Victor Irumper "has been hit for a six".

Newspapers have published cables and letters from followers of the game many of who say they are "ashamed to be Aussie".

Telephone callers have asked for the telephone number of the hotel where the New Zealand team stayed so they could phone and apologise to the visitors. The Australian Broadcasting Corporation, which broadcast the running commentary on radio was flooded with angry calls from all over the country.

"Underarm or underhand?" Australians all over the country are asking. Former Australian Test spinner Bill O'Reilly says, "As a patriotic Australian, I felt humiliated."

BRIEF SCORES:

Australia 235 for 4 in 50 overs (G Wood 72, G Chappell 90) beat New Zealand 229 for 8 in 50 overs (J Wright 42, B Edgar 102) by 6 runs

Cricket Down Under Greg Stays

SPORTSWEEK • February 08, 1981 • Sydney

AMid Prime Ministerial intervention and an outcry unmatched since bodyline bowling, Australian cricket captain Greg Chappell on Monday apologized for last Sunday's underarm incident in the Benson and Hedges World Series match against New Zealand at the Melbourne Cricket Ground.

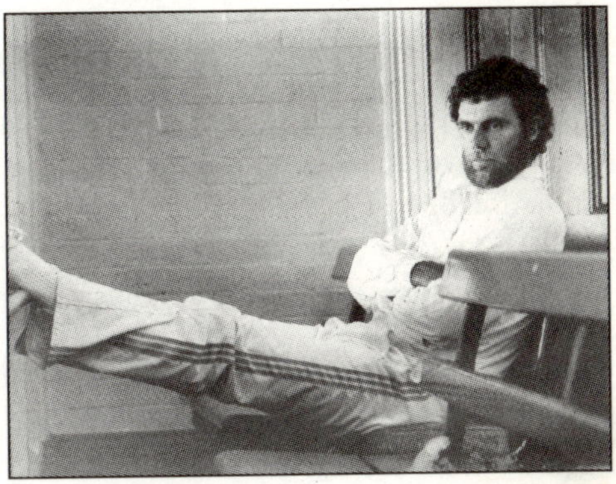
Greg Chappel

The Australia Cricket Board (ACB) reprimanded Chappell and said it had been greatly embarrassed by what he had done and formally reminded the skipper of his responsibility in upholding the spirit of the game.

Chappell issued a statement saying he regretted his decision to bowl a final mullygrubber to deprive the Kiwis the chance of scoring the six runs needed for a tie.

Chappell said it was a spur of the moment decision, taken under pressure, which would not be repeated.

Many of the delegates at Monday's ACB meeting pressed for Chappell's replacement as captain but his retention in the team as a player, but Chappell was retained as captain for the remaining matches against New Zealand and the Melbourne Test against India, starting on Saturday.

The ACB acted promptly to block the loophole in the rules and outlawed underarm deliveries in the remaining two games against New Zealand.

New Zealand captain Geoff Howarth, preparing for the fourth clash of the series was philosophical about the ACB decision to let the result of last Sunday's controversial match stand.

Said Howarth, "I'm probably contradicting myself, but we have no reason to demand a replay. The members of my team have not sought the match to be replayed. I have said all along that Greg Chappell was playing according to the conditions of the competition although his action was not within the spirit of game. I suppose his statement is an expression of wrongdoing. I do not think I expected an apology. You don't have to apologise if you stick to the rules of the game and as far as I am concerned his statement is a good form of apology."

Chappell said in his statement "The decision was made while I was under pressure, in the heat of the moment. I regret the decision. It is something I would not do again."

Sir Donald Bradman expressed strong disapproval.

The post office in Auckland, New Zealand, was flooded with people conveying their anger to the Chappell brothers.

Former England captain Tony Greig, now settled in Sydney and managing director of an insurance brokerage firm opined, "I think the time has come to make a few examples of people when they do things not in the interest of the game. I would sack Greg immediately and give the captaincy to Rod Marsh."

"It pains me to say this", continued Greig, "because Greg is a good friend of mine, but I don't think he has behaved in keeping with his position as captain of Australia."

And the man at the centre of the controversy, bowler Trevor Chappell, refused to comment on the incident. He did say, however, that he has heard of underhand bowling before.

"I have never had it bowled to me, and I haven't actually seen it happen but I believe it has happened in the past."

Former Australian Test captain Richie Benaud writing in the *Mirror* calls it, "a gutless performance from a captain who got his sums wrong. That's what I felt and I said it and nothing in the intervening 24 hours has changed my mind.

"The batting side needing six to tie off the last ball in a Test could be faced with an underarm delivery that would give them no chance at all of having a go for the runs. That is why it is ludicrous to blame one-day cricket for what happened. It just happens that it was a one-day match. It could happen again in next week's Test match against India."

"It was a disgraceful performance and should never be permitted to happen again. It was one of the worst things I have ever seen done on a cricket field and to compound the act, it came about because, I feel, the captain couldn't count. In my opinion, the Australian captain panicked. What other reason can there be for denying the opposition the chance to play a normal stroke at a cricket ball simply because there is a way of taking advantage of the rules?"

In a scathing article, former Test cricketer Keith Miller says, "I say abandon the one-dayer at the SCG, boot Greg Chappell out of the captaincy, free the Benson and Hedges prize money and hand it over to charity. The Kiwis who have had the rough end of the stick throughout the tour but behave impeccably should be winging their way across the Tasman Sea instead of becoming engaged in what must be the greatest grudge match played in this country since the volatile bodyline series in 1932.

"Greg should go to England," says Miller, "but not as captain. England, has a hotheaded leader Ian Botham and it won't be in cricket's best interest if a tired and irate Chappell plays for the Ashes."

In New Zealand, Australians were sworn at and refused service on Monday, "It's the land of the long white knives for Australians here on Tuesday," reported one Australian journalist from New Zealand.

The flag flew at half mast in Wellington over the office of a big Australian insurance firm. In Auckland T-shirts with the slogan "Aussies have an underarm problem," went on sale. A Wellington (New Zealand) disc jockey asked his listeners if they, had heard of a new underarm deodorant on the market. "It's called Chappell and it stinks," he said.

In Adelaide an advertisement in the public notices column of the Adelaide Advertiser proclaimed, "Death—Australian cricket died of shame last ball before stumps, February 1, 1981. C'mon, Aussies, C'mon".

Monday's *Daily Telegraph says*: "Regrets, are not enough from Greg Chappell. His mean act of captaincy demands nothing less than an unqualified and humble apology—to New Zealand for his poor sportsmanship and to his own country for the anti-Australian feeling he has aroused. His statement contained no such apology. One must be made if he is to continue as captain of Australia".

Brian McKechnie, the batsman, who had to face the unorthodox delivery from Trevor Chappell said he thought the umpires were joking when they advised him of the Australians' plan.

"I could not believe that would happen," he said. "It was totally against the spirit of the game. I could not believe they would stoop to that." Incidentally the rugby union All-Blacks does not consider himself a big hitter of the ball and it would have taken a mighty heave to clear the MCG fence. "The chance of my hitting a six must have been one in thousands", said McKechnie.

Three cheers India, despite near walkout

SPORTSWEEK • February 15, 1981

Dispirited, demoralised and beset by injuries, India stormed back to score a memorable 59-run victory over Australia at the Melbourne Cricket Ground to level the three-Test series one-all.

The hero of the last day's proceedings was Kapil Dev Nikhanj who returned to the fray in the morning after a leg injury and bowled unchanged for 16.4 overs to capture 5 for 55.

Kapil received excellent support from Dilip Doshi who bowled a nagging, accurate length right through to keep the Australian batsmen on a tight leash. He returned figures of 22-9-33-2.

When play commenced on the last day, India were given only an outside chance of victory by the pundits. But Gavaskar rallied his boys to great heights.

Kapil Dev is escorted to the pavilion after performance

The Indian bowlers and fielders exerted relentless pressure on the Australian batsmen despite injury to Shivlal Yadav. The undoing of the Australians was of their own making. Their approach was timid in the extreme and panic, so characteristic of Indian teams of the recent past, was incomprehensible.

Whereas the wicket had a low bounce, there was certainly no devil in it.

Sunil Gavaskar said after the historic win, the second successive one at the Melbourne Cricket Ground, which enabled India, for the first time ever to level a series against Australia in Australia, that the victory was the result of team work.

Asked if he was happy he didn't walk off after the fourth day's controversial umpiring decision, Gavaskar said, "I had no choice. I was given out and had to walk off. But I'm glad Chetan didn't."

The Indian captain said he was not very confident on the fourth evening about winning. "I gave ourselves just a 40 per cent chance." He said the turning point was Border's dismissal on the last morning:

Gavaskar said that most teams would have been hard pressed to score 140 on the last day because of the low bounce in the wicket.

Referring to Kapil Dev's recovery, Gavaskar said "Miracles do not happen in cricket but they seem to happen with physical injuries." The skipper stated that what was at first suspected to be a torn muscle turned out to be a bruise on the thigh.

"We set out for a meal to an Indian doctor's place at night on the fourth day when Kapil said he wanted to field this morning."

Gavaskar denied he had given Kapil any pep talk but said what made the adrenaline run for the all-rounder was the bad stroke he played in India's second innings.

"He was conscious of the fact that he had played a bad shot and wanted to make amends," said Gavaskar.

"I think our chances in New Zealand should be very good after this win. The morale of the team is high. I hope we get good wickets."

Gavaskar said he had not yet made up his mind about giving a report to the Australian Board on the umpires.

Gavaskar declared the victory as "one of the better performances ever from India."

As regards his instructions to Chetan Chauhan to leave the field, Gavaskar said he would have proceeded down and proceeded with the match.

"It was a spur of the moment thing. It perhaps brought out team's feelings about the umpiring. Something snapped inside. I later realised that I have a responsibility to the team. I have no regrets, mind you, but I realise that as a captain it was not the right thing to do. All along the team has been accepting the umpiring in the right spirit."

BRIEF SCORES

India 237 (G Vishwanath 114; D Lillee 4-65) and 324 (S Gavaskar 70, C Chauhan 85, D Vengsarkar 41; Lillee 4-104) beat Australia 419 (A Border 124, G Chappell 76, D Walters 78) and 83 (Kapil Dev 5-28) by 59 runs

Chappell blames his batsmen

SPORTSWEEK • _February 22, 1981_

Writing in his column in the Sydney Sun newspaper, Greg Chappell has blamed a woeful attitude and approach from Australia's batting line-up for the team's failure in the third Test against India.

Said Chappell, "We didn't lose that Test on the last day. We lost it in the first innings when the attitude and approach of our top line batsmen were woeful.

"We had the best of the batting conditions and we should have made at least 500 runs. Then we would not have been in the position we were. There were some mitigating circumstances, in the second innings—the wicket was again a disgrace—but that doesn't excuse us from not making 143."

*****

Most of the major Australian newspapers lauded Kapil Dev and criticised Australia's second innings flop, the lowest score ever by the hosts in a Test match against India,

The *Melbourne Sun* said both captains agreed that Kapil was the essential difference between the two sides.

"It was a tremendous effort from a bowler who had been hampered by a thigh injury," said the *Sun*.

The Melbourne Age printed a cartoon on its front page depicting a thunderstruck batsman walking away from shattered wickets.

"Australia's underarm batting" was the comment. "Australia bows to Kapil Dev" was the headline on the sports page.

*****

INDIA'S victory in the Melbourne Test was its third win in Australia (the other two were during the 1977-78 tour) and its seventh against Australia. Eleven Tests between the two countries have been drawn and Australia have won 20.

*****

The Melbourne Test was the eighth occasion when Greg "Chappell won the toss and put the opponents in to bat. He has won five of those Tests for Australia, drawn one, and lost two—the other defeat was against the West Indies in Adelaide last season. The series, just concluded was the first ever which India did not lose to Australia in Australia and only the second drawn series. Australia's second innings 83 was their lowest total against India and was well below their 105 in Kanpur in 1959-60. Australia's previous lowest at home against India was 107 in Sydney in 1947-48. But the lowest ever scored by Australia was 78 against England in 1968

INDIA'S refusal to continue playing would have given Australia the third Test and the series and India would have gone down in cricketing history as the first team to concede a Test.

Gavaskar's action rivalled that of England captain Ray Illingworth who led his team off the field in Sydney 1971 after an altercation near the hill between England fast bowler John Snow and a spectator. Persuaded by the umpires to return, England went on to win the Test and the series.

*****

INDIA Test captain Sunil Gavaskar has described as "distorted" and "highly irresponsible" a news item in a Melbourne daily that "the Indian team had been prepared to walk off the Melbourne Cricket Ground after an incident involving Australian batsman Allan Border"

The paper quoted Gavaskar; as saying, "If Border had not been given out by the umpires, I would have been the only Indian left on the field. The rest of the team would have walked off."

In the incident, Border tried to sweep offspinner Shivlal Yadav and had his leg stump knocked back. But the Australian did not walk, and it took a discussion between umpires Rex Whitehead and Mel Johnson to rule him out.

"The newspaper in question has twisted what I said at the press conference and published my comments out of context," Gavaskar said to SPORTSWEEK.

*****

This correspondent was present at the conference at which Gavaskar was questioned about his instructions to Chetan Chauhan to come off the field. Stating that he was 'not proud of what happened' Gavaskar clarified that the feelings against umpire Whitehead, who stood in all three Tests, ran high. Many members of the team felt that the umpire did not apply the laws of the game uniformly to both teams.

Gavaskar, said his action was the result of something "that snapped inside me." He added, "Now that I think about it coolly, I should have acted with more responsibility. As captain, I should have been leading by example. I'm not proud of it."

Continued Gavaskar, "in asking Chetan to walk off the field I was in a way expressing the feelings of the entire team."

Indian umpires are not 'butchers'

SPORTSWEEK • December 27, 1981

Reader Rohit Patel of London has very kindly sent us clippings of some of the gems of "brilliant" gems from the British press gems during the present India- England Test series.

Umpires Madhav Gothoskar and Swaroop Kishen

Says Patel, "Some of the things reported are (petty) lies and absolutely dishonest."

He continues, "I can assure you, however, that this is rediculous just a sample, some other reports especially by J.T. are ten times worse than what I am enclosing."

Rohit Patel has sent us photostats of some of the reports. For reasons of limitation of space, it is not possible to reproduce all the clippings, nor for that matter quote any of them in any detail. However, readers who are interested in knowing just how "impartial" the visiting English correspondents have been in their reporting and their response to India and her people are requested to write in for copies.

By way of providing a teaser trailer, here are a few gems:

"At Nagpur, M.V. Gothoskar was considered no better than his partner, K.B. Ramaswamy, the butcher of Bombay....Bangalore was the only Test England lost on Tony Greig's tour five years ago....umpire Mohamed Ghouse made himself notorious on that occasion."

"Swaroop Kishan, somewhat the larger of the two umpires who incurred the wrath of England's management for their role in India's first Test victory, has been branded such a monster that when his door opened at the Wankhede Stadium where he was lodged, one half-expected a white-coated Frankenstein.

"At best," continues the writer, "Swaroop in his cowboy (hat?) has been characterised as the mean old gangster who just rode into town for a shootout with the sheriff. Several England batsmen would readily swear that he and his first Test colleague K.B. Ramaswamy were quicker on the draw than Wyatt Earp, and deadlier by far with the right forefinger."

Talking about England's complaint about the umpiring in the first Test (which was an unsurprisingly thrown out with the contempt it deserved since there were no specific incidents mentioned), the genius writes, "it was also rather fruitless to complain as no constructive suggestions were made. The ritual noises about neutral umpires were made, but there is obviously not the slightest intention of asking a Pakistani and Sri Lankan to umpire a Test match at Lord's. What England honestly means by neutral umpires is having English umpires everywhere..."

Describing India as a country that "naturally prides itself on its hospitality towards foreigners," Scyld Berry of *The Observer writes*, "An official complaint about the arrangement which the host country has laid on is a serious step to take. This is also the country of bribe, baksheesh and string-pulling where a word in the right ear has more effect than all the outpourings of righteous indignation." (One supposes one should accept the criticism with legendary Indian resignation, offer the other cheek and not even stand up and say just how "beautiful and perfect" in every respect the "OLD COUNTRY" is!)

Continues Berry, "For the moment therefore, England have to take the rub of the green, just as Australia's Kim Hughes did last summer in spite of receiving six lbw decisions in his 12-Test innings. Offcialdom works in an inscrutable way in India. England will just have to accept. That's the way the chapati crumbles."

So does it, one would like to add, in England.

Ask any visiting Indian, Pakistani, Australian, New Zealand or Sri Lankan side and they will tell you horrendous stories about the standard of umpiring, the wickets and, of course, the disgustingly partial reporting. For heaven's sake, spare us this repulsive indignation and self-righteousness from people who live in glass houses.

Frank Keating of *The Guardian* while quoting an England cricketer's diatribe against Indian umpiring on the last day of the Bombay Test says, 'The 19 Indian wickets we have taken should have been at least 25, but we only get every other, bat-pad catch or leg-before."

In all fairness, however, the writer goes on to say, "I am not personally able to comment on decisions given 100 yards away...indeed it would be tragic if the series was so soon to become swathed in controversy. How professional sportsmen love a good bellyache against amateur officials."

Writes Alan Lee of *The Times* in glee, "The fall of an Indian wicket is like prayer time at the mosque. Silence reigns, but only until the wretched man out is within booing distance..."

Visiting the gents in Bombay for Lee presented the "hazard of total darkness underground." "Underground" Mr. Lee? What underground? The toilets in Bombay, especially those for the press which you probably used when you were here, are very much on terra firma.

Concludes Lee, "In India the battles are not over at stumps. You duel with a kamikaze taxi driver over the price he is charging to try and kill you, or you join the ragamuffin beggars, the crouching street traders and the occasional lost Englishman on the dusty walk to the hotel bath."

Thank the Lord, Mr. Lee, that you can walk the streets in India. That is certainly more than what is safe for some people in England. If you don't believe us, try asking Mihir Bose who is now in India covering the series for a London newspaper. Ask him how he was roughed up returning home to London by train from a football match.

The 'ragamuffin beggars' that you speak of are certainly more civilized than your Skin-heads and Paki-bashers.

Incidentally, gentlemen sports-lovers in this country are hoping there will be no repetition of the infamous Vaseline incident of the New Delhi Test.

The sahib bad loser—best he stay home!

SPORTSWEEK • 1981 - 1982

Almost as one man-and woman- this nation heaved a sigh of relief when Mrs. Indira Gandhi finally gave the long-awaited green signal which made the tour of the England cricket team of India a possibility.

The skulduggery involved was obvious enough to insult the intelligence of even the moronic cricket dewanaa.

A desire to get on with the game, and to hell with political exigencies was the mood of the nation. Personal predilections concerning South Africa were neither here nor there for lovers of sport in this country.

Geoff Boycott

A gentleman christened Geoff Boycott had been at the vortex of the storm of the almost aborted tour. He decided, reason best known to himself, to turn home midway through the tour whys and wherefors are matters of conjecture and therefore to be avoided. The fact, however known that on the tour he cover himself with glory in erasing the batting record of the legendary Sir also as well known that he had behind the near cancellation of dawn of a series to which we been witness.

Be it as it may, the series will unfortunately, go down in the annals of Indian cricket certainly of the game as one in which to all norms of decency and liness are aware of the "sins" of the present English cricket have come in the way of its where as popular as previous sides which have unquestioningly king long way towards breaking and building bridges between countries.

Deliberation on the doings of the journalists and radio commentators accompanying the touring cetenty unnecessary in so far as of the game in India are sick to and are anxious to treat the incidents, as aberrations which will not sour future relations between lovers of the game.

Cricket lovers in India are ever willing to forget.

But memory is notoriously short the world over.

Future England sides visiting Indian shores will do well to remember that things have changed—how do they say it—"baby"

The brown man—as he has been labelled—is no longer willing (able he may be) to shoulder the burden. For him the sun (howsoever unpalatable this might be for the 'honoured' guest) has set. He is no longer willing to be called a fool for his seemingly asinine desire to be a good host. He is sick and tired of being the wise man in the Arabic (or is it Chinese?) proverb who "knows he knows and knows he knows" but looks the other way. He is no longer willing to be taken the "mickey of."

In case a translation is asked for, there are a hundred variations for the expression to describe the smart ass, who is in essence a naive visitor to this nation. Any inability to empathise with the soul of the seemingly materially poor culture of this country is only a reflection on those who rush to point a finger, who look at it through jaundiced eyes.

From the sublime to the ridiculous, one last quote from a member of the touring England press party which is too contemptuous to deserve comment. Says Pat Gibson in a despatch to the *Daily Express*. London:

"England's cricketers could not have been more shocked at Cuttack if they had seen a ghost...or Geoff Boycott emerging from the pavilion for a net.

There, inspecting the pitch for the third and deciding one-day international against India was K.B. Ramaswamy, the umpire they thought they would never see again.

"Fearfully, captain Keith Fletcher approached him. "Are you standing in this match?" he asked.

"The reply was in the affirmative and suddenly England knew why the Indian officials had been evading all their requests for the umpires' names."

If they had known one of them was going to be Ramaswamy they would have tried to get him removed.

"Ramaswamy is the man they called the Assassin after his performance in the first Test at Bombay where England were all out for 102 in a little over two hours to lose by 138 runs, having complained informally about the standard of the umpires before that match.

"England protested officially afterwards and got the impression that Ramaswamy would not be appointed again on the tour.

"Now he has been sprung on them at such a late hour that there would be no time to fly a replacement to this cricketing outpost in the eastern state of Orissa.

"Even if the Indian Board agreed, all England could do is discuss what at best is a rude and discourteous act, at worst the dirtiest of dirty tricks and let the Indians have their comments in no uncertain terms...

"To make it even worse, Ramaswamy will be partnered by Polly Punjabi, the umpire who gave Fletcher out caught behind before he angrily knocked the bails off in the second Test at Bangalore."

As the slave said to the sahib, during the friendly golf match. "Forgive me sir, I'm sorry to say so sir, but you are not winning."

Well may the slave say. "The sahib bad loser—best he stay home."

Why Vengsarkar was denied entry

***SPORTSWEEK* • April 11, 1982**

The chief organiser of the Sharjah cricket festival week, Abdul Rehman Bukhatir, discussed certain aspects of what has come to be known as the 'Vengsarkar incident' at a press conference at which Sunil Gavaskar, Mansur Ali Khan of Pataudi and Asif Iqbal were present.

Dilip Vengsarkar

He made it clear that there had been a strong reaction in certain circles in India because it had been incorrectly reported that Vengsarkar had been deported. According to him Vengsarkar had been denied entry into Dubai because the immigration official with whom he had a "hot exchange" of words had interpreted the rules strictly according to the book and refused entry because Vengsarkar had been identified as a "student" in his passport.

It was on this point that the immigration official had sought clarification and had not cleared him immediately.

Bukhatir was sorry that the incident had been wrongly interpreted, and Vengsarkar was welcome any time. He still hoped he could make it in time for the last match of the international series on Friday. He was glad to receive a telex from Vengsarkar thanking him for the invitation.

The message read: "*It was unfortunate that I could not play. Wish Sunny a successful benefit match*".

Bukhatir hoped that this would not interfere with his plans to promote a tournament which has been acclaimed as a success by principal players of India, Pakistan and invitees from England and the West Indies, including a fair number from the British media present here.

He had plans to enlarge the scope of the tournament to entertain teams from England and Australia. He hoped to keep it going, notwithstanding the unfortunate episode, with the cooperation of the Indian cricket authorities and the players.

Why West Indians are rebelling

SPORTSWEEK • March 23, 1983

Although it is now over a month since the "rebel" West Indian cricketers returned from their controversial tour of South Africa, the topic of discussion wherever sports aficionados congregate in the West Indian islands, is the decision of the players to place pelf above principle.

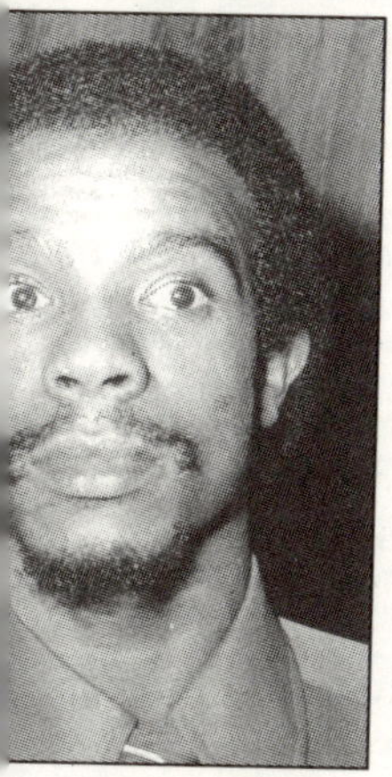

David Murray

With inflation rampant as elsewhere and with the battle to make both ends meet getting ever fiercer, the point of view that an individual should be at liberty to earn his livelihood wherever he pleases, is gaining ever-increasing currency—and to hell with principles and politics.

Typical of this school of thought is a letter to the editor from a Jaglal Susankar in the *Guardian* of Trinidad in which the correspondent writes, "Please convey my sympathy to fellow Trinidadian Bernard Julien for the amount of humiliation and stripping of his medal by the government, in my opinion he went to South Africa to play cricket as a sportsman. Secondly he was paid damn good. Who doesn't like money?...People of the same race who term him Judas are wrong and foolish".

Recently, Alan Rae, former Test cricketer who is now president of the West Indian Cricket Board made an eloquent appeal to try and retain cricketers by offering them lucrative jobs as coaches, welfare officers and in public relations.

The nub of the matter is that the average West Indian cricketer earns precious little outside of Test cricket—because of the way the game is structured in the various cricket-playing islands which constitute the West Indies and because of the poor state of financial health of the various associations in the territories.

It is for this reason that West Indian cricketers have been seeking greener pastures outside the islands, especially after their playing days are behind them.

A notable case in point is that of Alvin Kallicharran who now resides in England and regularly plays and coaches in South Africa (in fact he may be said to be a pioneer in this respect), because of his disillusionment with the West Indies Board for the alleged scurvy treatment he received after the so-called "big guns" of West Indian cricket returned to the fold following the winding-up of the Kerry Packer "circus".

Kallicharran was the only leading cricketer to have decided to "stand by his country". He led what was a second eleven to India in the absence of the super stars and was later summarily dropped from the side at a time when he was hopeful of being appointed captain.

One aspect of the recent controversial tour which is not fully appreciated in India is that barring two or three, all of those who decided to say "Ya, maan" (in the local idiom) to South African bait were players who were either past their prime or whose chances of being selected to play for the Test side were remote.

It is not generally known that Colin Croft's shoulder injury has virtually spelt "finis" to his Test career and that wicketkeeper David Murray would probably have lost his place to Jeffrey Dujon following a string of disappointing performances despite the patronage that he is said to enjoy in the West Indies Board. Perhaps only Sylvester Clarke, Everton Mattis, and Collis King may be said to have jeopardised their Test careers because of their decision to play for "blood money".

With the fabulous sums of money which the South African Cricket Board is willing to fork out—with undoubted help from hidden quarters—in order to frustrate the Gleneagles agreement and to get back into the international circuit, it is not surprising that cricketers in England, Sri Lanka and here in the West Indies who do not have very much to lose career-wise should decide to brave public opinion and risk possible censure and condemnation for the sake of pecuniary gain.

In any event, situations such as those which now obtain in regard to sportsmen's' remuneration in most countries of the world make the lure of money irresistible and "rebels" easy picking.

The absence of a responsible press and informed public opinion which unequivocally condemns sporting contact with South Africa because of that nation's hated apartheid policy is unfortunate. And in the absence of a vocal majority of people who, without wishing to inject politics into sport, favour the ostracisation of South Africa from the comity of international sporting nations not as an end in itself, but as a means to an end namely, the dissolution of all manner of barriers in that nation's sport, the likes of Lawrence Rowe and other mercenaries will continue to defy authority with impunity.

It is only when half-baked sanctions sought to be imposed by cricket boards are made more effective, that the hypocrisy of those who equivocate and talk glibly of "the right to earn ones living without hindrance" will be exposed. The West Indian rebels who toured South Africa have been banned by the Australian Cricket Board from playing as professionals in that country. But this decision is not likely to make the boat-rockers fall in line.They will have no other option only if they are barred from playing in the English County cricket championships which enables cricketers to earn a decent livelihood.

But will Lord's, which is increasingly under pressure from the persistent South Africans, have the courage of its convictions to stand firm? To expect anything of the sort would appear to be a tall order considering the latest move, said to be mooted by Denis Compton and "Bill" Edrich to propose a resolution which will enable English Club teams (ostensibly including past and present Test players) to tour South Africa without incurring sanctions.

* * * * *

Indian spectators are among the great supporters of the game in the West Indies. Trinidad with its high concentration of "Indians" is now the only Test centre in the West Indies (Guyana is no longer in that category following large-scale emigration of people of Indian origin from that country under the present regime) which makes a profit out of Test cricket. And verbal duels and clashes, friendly and otherwise, are the rule rather than the exception during Test matches here.

The local radio station has daily Hindi film music and devotional programmes. Hindi films "Kaalia", "Love Story", "Anurodh", "Naseeb", "Daulat", "Bobby" and others are having extended runs at Port of Spain cinema houses.

Amitabh Bachchan is said to have been mobbed when he visited Trinidad last year and Lata Mangeshkar drew a crowd of over 30,000 when she performed here. Her sister Asha Bhonsle is expected to give two concerts in May. Vinda Ramsingh, the chief promoter, has stated that he was proud to get the singer to perform "after years of protracted negotiations in the face of fierce competition".

During meeting with local Indians one discerns a strong sense of identification and a growing awareness of "roots". A local Indian tour promoter—in the true tradition of Indian ingenuity—has organised a tour called "Journey to the Roots".

One hundred and forty-seven Trinidadians of Indian origin are currently in India to commemorate the departure from Calcutta on February 22, 1845, of indentured labourers recruited largely from U.P. and Bihar to work on the sugar and coffee plantations in the West Indies. (They reached their destination after three months.)

The group landed in Bombay by air on February 22, moved on to Calcutta and is now touring the country. It is expected back next week.

Indians in paradise

SPORTSWEEK • March 30, 1983

Flushed after their resolute and successful fight-back in the second cricket Test against the West Indies at Port of Spain, the Indian team arrived in Grenada for the four-day match against the Windward Islands in exceedingly high spirits.

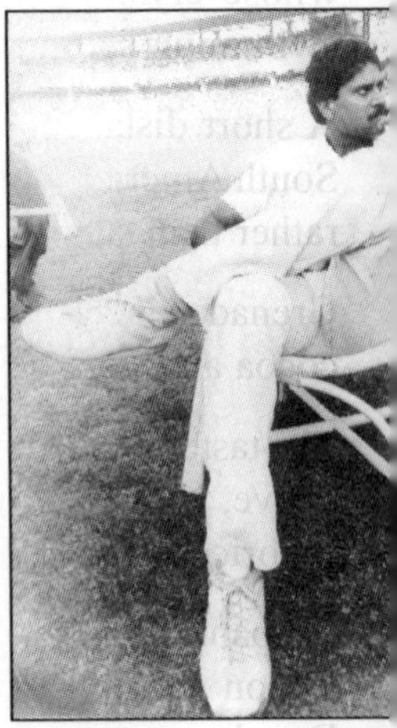

Kapil Dev

Enchanted with the beauty of the airport, which is a cricket ball's throw away from the azure blue waters of the seas with tropical forests forming a backdrop of various hues of green, members of the team reached for their cameras and clicked away.

The spontaneous reaction of skipper Kapil Dev on arrival at Secret Harbour Hotel which overlooks a cove was, "This is paradise, wish my wife were here". Members of the team were unanimous in their praise for the breathtaking location of the hotel and the beauty of the island considered the "Emerald in the charming Caribbean chain"

Volcanic in origin, with a backdrop of mountains running along its entire length, the island abounds in scenic wonders visible on the spectacular one-hour drive on the curving forest-covered mountain road from the airport.

The Queen's Park Oval where the match was played is situated against a naturally sawed-off rock rising up from the sea.

And lovely little houses dot the hill slope overlooking the ground.

Mr. Paul Scoon, governor general of Grenada (not to be confused with Granada in Spain which, incidentally is pronounced "Grenada") hosted a reception for the Indian team.

The informal function (it is good to see the team always smartly turned out for such receptions and while traveling) provided the team and the four members of the Indian press now here, the opportunity of meeting leading members of the Indian community, most of whom are businessmen or professionals, (the first batch arrived in the early sixties from Africa when forced to leave).

The inescapable impression was that the small and closely-knit community is extremely well-settled and happy here, unlike some of the other islands in the Caribbean where racial discord, very often beneath the surface, and an alarming crime rate, as in Forbes Burnham's Guyana, has compelled people of Indian origin to emigrate.

The quality of life in this the "piece de resistance" of the Windward Isles is halcyonic and the even tenor continues unabated despite the ravages of international recession, the revolutionary stance and leftist ideology of Prime Minister Maurice Bishop.

The renowned Grand Anse Beach of Grenada (discovered by Columbus in 1948) with its pure white sand, absence of waves and excellent facilities for water-skiing, fishing, snorkelling, scuba diving and yachting is among the most beautiful beaches in the world.

Just north of the capital is Annadale Falls which is surrounded by lush vegetation and whose crystalline freshwater 'Soda Pool' makes it one of the island's most delightful swimming spots.

A short distance away is Caribs Leap where the fierce Caribs, who like the Arawaks of South America were the original inhabitants of these West Indian Islands, leapt off the cliffs rather than submit to the French and English who colonised this 'spice island'.

Grenada, incidentally produces one-third of the world's nutmeg, in addition to bananas, cocoa and sugar.

The tastefully appointed suites at the Secret Harbour Hotel are therefore appropriately named Clove, Nutmeg, Ginger, Coriander, Cocoa, Allspice, Cinnamon, Coffee, Paprika, Saffron, Licorice, Vanilla, Tankabean, Mace, Anisette, Bay Leaf, Khus Khus, etc.

A spanking new airport is now under construction at an estimated cost of Rupees eight billion with financial assistance from Cuba, Algeria, Libya, Syria, Iraq and the European Development Fund.

The airport will not be ready by the time the Indian cricket team leaves after this and the one-day international against the full West Indies team.

But one thing is certain, Grenada will remain forever etched in the memories of members of Kapil Dev's team who were fortunate to visit it.

We are the Kings of one-day cricket

SPORTSWEEK • July 06, 1983

THE nation salutes you, Kapil Dev and your intrepid lads.

Kapil Dev with Mohinder Amarnath (centre) and Krishnamachari Srikkanth

Not in a long time in this nation's history—sporting or otherwise—has so much been owed by so many to so few.

It is not too often that our people have the opportunity to stick their chests out, hold their heads high over the exploits of their fellowmen on the field of sport.

By winning the Prudential Cup cricket tournament in England against all odds you have proved to the world that Indian cricket has come of age.

You have made the prophets of doom who predicted that India would once again as—in 1975 and 1979—eat humble pie.

You have dealt a resounding slap to the faces of the doubting Thomases in India and abroad who never tire of dubbing Indian cricketers 'dull dogs'.

You have proved to the cricketing universe that you can conquer the very best in the world

And this you have proved beyond a shadow of doubt right from the first day of the tournament when you upset all calculations by humbling the mighty West Indians, twice winners of the prestigious tournament

The fainthearted were justifiably annoyed at what at one stage looked like characteristic 'Indian chicken-heartedness' when you succumbed to Australia and to the West Indies in the return encounter.

But you proved your mettle by crushing England on their home soil in the semifinal.

And after what was described by all pundits as an inept batting display in the final at Lord's, you came storming back to break the back of the mighty batting lineup of the rampaging West Indians.

Who can deny the fact that you have been worthy winners? And that you have played in the best traditions of the game?

The world loves a winner. The more so when he happens to be the underdog. But your victory has been all the more heartwarming because of the stirring team-spirit which you demonstrated.

To single out achievements in your winning of the coveted Cup would be grossly invidious.

Some of the stars in your line up lit up the firmament on your way to the championship. But after all's said and done, your victory has been the result of extraordinary teamwork which is all the more remarkable engendered as it has been in the short time after the traumatic defeats at the hands of Pakistan and the West Indies.

We may be forgiven for a seemingly emotional outburst.

But we are only expressing the feelings of people all over the country.

So bring out the crackers. Strike up the band. And let the dancing in the streets continue unabated.

We are the KINGS of one-day cricket

Unsporting Pakistan

SPORTSWEEK* • *September 28, 1983

The walking off the field by the Pakistan players before 'time' had been called by the umpires on the fifth day of the first cricket Test in Bangalore on Monday was unfortunate, inexcusable and unsportsmanlike in the extreme.

Zaheer Abbas

If one were to go by what Pakistan captain Zaheer Abbas said in the course of the television interview after conclusion of the match, the decision was caused by misunderstanding and rnisinterpretation of the rules of the game.

But it is curious that a player of the experience of Zaheer Abbas who has played cricket in all the Test-playing countries of the world, and Intikhab Alam, the professional manager of the team, who too served his national Test team with distinction for many years should be ignorant of the rules of game.

Fortunately, the spectators conducted themselves with commendable restraint while the visiting team's management wrangled for half an hour over the rules which, in any event, are explicit in so far as the provision for the 20 mandatory overs on the final day are concerned.

Rule 17.6 of the game is unequivocal and there is no question of the requirement of the minimum of 14 overs per hour and 77 per day taking precedence over rule 17.6 regarding the 20 mandatory overs on the last day of a Test.

The unsavoury and avoidable episode could have triggered off a riot. And it was only the possibility of the umpires asserting their authority and awarding the match to India that prompted the Pakistanis to take the field reluctantly.

This is unfortunate in the extreme, because Zaheer ('Zed') Abbas is such a good sport and an exceedingly affable person. Knowing him as we do, we are inclined to put it down at an aberration, and, hope there is no repetition of the gripes which so characterised Asif Iqbal's behaviour as captain on the 1979-80 tour of India.

One would like to believe that the visiting team's behaviour was not motivated by a desire to deprive Sunil Gavaskar of his 28th Test century. But then, can one be certain especially when one takes into account the fact that seamer Tahir Naqqash generally bowled outside the off-stump with a packed offside field and offspinner Nazir (Jr.) attacked the middle and leg stumps with seven men on the onside perfectly? Within the rules of the game, mind you, but not cricket, what with the result of the match unalterable.

If one were to judge by the masterly touch of old which the 'Little Master' revealed in Bangalore, it is only a matter of time before he surpasses the legendary Don Bradman's coveted record of 29 Test hundreds and Geoff Boycotts Test aggregate of 8114 (of which Gavaskar is just 345 runs shy at the moment.).

One hopes the former Test skipper will achieve both distinctions during this twin series itself. What with two remaining Tests against Pakistan and six to follow against the West Indies, there is every reason to believe that he will.

BRIEF SCORES :

India 275 (S Gavaskar 42, R Binny 83*, Madan Lal 74; Tahir Naqqash 5-76) and 176 for no loss (S Gavaskar 103*, A Gaekwad 66*) drew with Pakistan 288 all out (J Miandad, 99, W Bari 64; Kapil Dev 5-68)

(MAR)shell shocked at Kanpur

***SPORTSWEEK* • November 2, 1983**

The victorious West Indian cricket team had hardly returned to the pavilion after its resounding victory over India at the Green Park, Kanpur last Tuesday when the disgusting chant of 'Kapil *hai hai*' rent the air.

The scenario was a familiar one for the Indian cricketers: Worshipped and idolised by millions of cricket 'deewane' all over the country one day, ground in the dust by the same fanatics the next.

But, then, we are a very emotional people. And we react as sharply in defeat as we do in victory on the field of sport as, indeed, in life generally.

Amid all the breast-beating, it is hardly surprising that not many self-proclaimed lovers of the game are giving sufficient credit to the visitors who outplayed the home side in all departments of the game in a little over three-and-a-half days the uneven contest lasted.

The West Indians, Greenidge, Dujon and Marshall in particular, gave the lie to the oft-expressed point of view that they are incapable of responsible, restrained batting. In the process, they exposed to the hilt the notorious limitations of the Indian attack.

And the West Indian fast men, in sharp contrast to the amiable, medium Indian pace bowlers demonstrated in no uncertain fashion that they are capable of extracting pace from even docile wickets.

Kapil Dev, while paying handsome tribute to the victors after the match, confessed that there was nothing wrong with the wicket.

Although the bounce tended to be uneven—the deliveries which accounted for Gavaskar and Gaekwad in the second innings rose awkwardly—no devil lurked in the region of the wicket prepared with characteristic tender care by groundsman Sitaram.

One conclusion is inescapable: India's specialist batsmen are technically inept and psychologically ill-equipped in the face of truly fast bowling of the variety dished out by Malcolm Marshall (and Imran Khan when we last toured Pakistan). Marshall, in the opinion of this writer, is undeniably the most lethal bowler in the world today in terms of sustained pace and hostility.

Marshall struck terror in the minds and hearts of India's top-order batsmen who should learn a few lessons from the likes of Madan Lal, Binny, Kirmani and Shastri. Only Vengsarkar (in the second innings), from among those having pretensions to being specialist batsmen, inspired some confidence.

The rest were (Mar) shell shocked, plain and simple, by the fury of the Man of the Match who bowled (as he had batted earlier) like a man possessed.

The outcome of the first Test is reminiscent of the 1974-75 series between the two countries which the visitors had opened with an equally emphatic victory at Bangalore.

Clive Lloyd stated after the Kanpur match that the Indians did not apply themselves and Kapil Dev remarked that his teammates will have to take control of themselves.

Kapil Dev admitted that his team batted badly, fielded miserably and that the bowling lacked penetration. He confessed that his side will have to work out a strategy to bowl the West Indians out.

In all fairness, the selectors deserve to be commended for refusing to panic. They have retained the same 14 for the second Test starting in. new Delhi on Saturday. Their sensible decision should go a way towards helping the team. Not much would have been achieved by reverting to the notorious chop and change policy of the Board.

But viewed in correct perspective real damage was done during the series against the experimental Pakistan team, when the selectors in their anxiety to continue basking in the World Cup victory euphoria adopted a negative shortsighted approach. The trauma they experienced at Kanpur was just reward for their own 'sins'.

A bold, innovative policy against Pakistan would have paid dividends now.

BRIEF SCORES:

West India 454 all out (G Greenidge 194, J Dujon 81, M Marshall 92; Kapil Dev 4-99) beat India 207 all out (Madan Lal 63; Malcolm Marshall 4-19) and 164 (D Vengsarkar 65, R Shastri 46*; Malcolm Marshall 4-47) by an innings and 83 runs.

Umpiring biased: Kapil

MID-DAY* • *December 31, 1985

Indian cricket captain Kapil Dev is of the opinion the umpires who officiated in the Melbourne cricket Test—Messrs. French and Henwood—should retire.

Kapil Dev

He was answering questions put to him by the press at the conclusion of the second Test at the Melbourne Cricket Ground. "Some of the decisions were pathetic," said he. "We are most disappointed with the standard of umpiring. The Board should not appoint such umpires."

Kapil, when asked if he thought India had been "robbed" of a win, retorted, "Whatever's happened has happened. You can't change that."

When asked if his team needed improvement in the next Test, Kapil replied, "Only umpiring", going on to add that India would win. He said he was very happy with the demeanour of his team which had not shown any anger against the umpiring at any stage.

"That is the sign of a good team," he said. Kapil also opined that if the umpiring had been fair even on the last day, India would have been required to score just 50 to win. "The match would have been over by lunch," said he.

He was referring specifically to the decision concerning Gilbert off the first ball he faced when he came in the second innings and when an appeal for a glove-bat catch by Srikkanth at shortleg was turned down, and to an appeal by Gavaskar at first slip off a top edge by Border when he was on 127. "If umpires cannot see clear deflections, all I can say is that I feel sorry for them," opined the Indian skipper.

When asked if he had sent any instructions to the batsmen to accelerate the run rate, knowing the rain was coming, Kapil said, "We expected the rain at 5 p.m.. not 4 when it came. Besides how do you ask a batsman like Srikkanth to score faster?"

He also maintained that he had done the right thing by sending Mohinder Amarnath at No. 3 because of his ability to play spin bowling.

Was there any move to lodge an official complaint?

"That's the manager's job."

Queried about his decision not to take the new ball sooner on the last day, the Indian captain replied that had he done so at that stage, there was the danger of the Australians appealing against the light.

Earlier, speaking to Tony Greig on Channel 9 Television, Kapil said he was not personally unhappy about not being able to achieve his first Test victory. “If I win I win, if I don’t I can’t help it,” said he.

Asked if he was disappointed the rain gods had not come to his team’s rescue, Kapil said, “Too many gods complicate matters.” He opined the wicket was not a good Test wicket to begin with but that it had improved as the match progressed.

BRIEF SCORES :

Australia 262 all out (D Hookes 42, G Matthews 100; R Shastri 4-87) and 308 all out (Allan Border 163; R Shastri 4-92) drew with India 445 all out (K Srikkanth 86, M Amarnath 45, D Vengsarkar 75, R Shastri 49, Kapil Dev 55; B Reid 4-100) drew with Australia 308 all out (Allan Border 163; R Shastri 4-92) and 59 for two.

Sackcloth and ashes for India

SPORTSWEEK • April 29, 1990 • Sharjah

Judging by the reaction — or over-reaction, to be more precise — to India's disappointing performance in this year's Australasia Cup, Mohammed Azharuddin and his team are in for a sackcloth and ashes reception on their return home.

Mohammed Azharuddin

But then, such is the lot of venerable Indian sportsmen who fail to measure up to the uncompromising expectations of their starry-eyed supporters. In their view, it was bad enough for the team to have snatched defeat from the jaws of victory in the match against the greenhorn Sri Lankans. It was unforgivable for them to have been 'humiliated' by arch enemies Pakistan, this being the eighth successive defeat at the hands of that team in 10 matches.

In the encounter against the Sri Lankans, the Indian batsmen betrayed astonishing complacency when failing to add another 25 runs in the closing stages of their innings; a feat which was well within their reach.

Then, their innocuous attack wilted under the controlled aggression of the majestic Arjuna Ranatunga who steered his team to an unexpected but extremely well-deserved victory.

In the crucial game against the Pakistanis, a side plagued by injuries to Imran Khan, Javed Miandad and Wasim Akram, the much vaunted Indian batting line-up revealed gross ineptitude and technical incompetence, woeful lack of application and the kind of positive professional attitude implied in the aphorism "When the going gets tough, the tough get going".

Having evaluated the performance of the Indian team in unsparing, critical terms, one must spare a thought for the players, give credit where it is due.

First of all, captain Azharuddin's gallant knocks, especially against the Pakistanis when he stood courageously amid a burning deck, will rank among the memorable deeds of the tournament. He seems to thrive under the burden of captaincy.

Ravi Shastri demonstrated a most welcome return to bowling form. Under the tutelage of Bishan Bedi, that old magician, Shastri has come to grips with the subtleties and mysteries of flight, line and length.

Navjot Siddhu, Kris Srikkanth and Manoj Prabhakar revealed only glimpses of what they are capable. But Anil Kumble has shown in his first foray outside the shores of his homeland that he has the makings of an accomplished spinner in the quickish (although not freakish) leg-spin mould of Bhagwat Chandrasekhar.

Here, alas, end the redeeming features of the Indian team's performance. The rest is a tale of woe, a saga of missed opportunities, a litany of unfulfilled hopes.

Since serious maladies call for drastic remedies, an accurate diagnosis of the state of the game in the country is in order.

To begin with, Indian cricket is still reeling under the turmoil and vicissitudes it has experienced in recent times. The eyeball-to-eyeball confrontation between the Board of Control for Cricket in India and the Players Association has left deep scars.

It has also deprived the country of an outstanding, experienced player like Dilip Vengsarkar who, despite his recent loss of form, cannot yet be said to be past his prime. It takes tremendous ability, not to mention consistency and application, to belong to the exclusive 6000 Test runs club.

It is hoped that the selectors will not let his adversary role in their run-in with the Players Association cloud their judgement when selecting the team for England where experience is an irreplaceable asset. The void left by Sunil Gavaskar's retirement makes the inclusion of experienced players in the squad that much more necessary. There is a lot to be said in favour of blooding deserving youngsters early enough. The moot point is one of definition: what is "Early enough"? In order to be an efficient fighting unit, a team must have a judicious blend of youth and experience.

The votaries of radical change are quick to point to the encouraging performances of Sachin Tendulkar, Sanjay Manjrekar and to some extent, Atul Wasson and Vivek Razdan. They just cannot wait to see the likes of Ajaysinhji Jadeja and Subroto Banerjee get their breaks.

These advocates for raw youth point to the "heartening" performance of the new-look England side in the West Indies, following the ban on senior Test players who preferred South African blood money to the honour of playing for their country. (That they did not relish the prospects of broken bones and flattened noses at the hands of the West Indian demon fast bowlers is another matter).

What the proponents of total overhaul forget is that the so-called England "new look" side consists of players who have cut their teeth on the exacting crucible of English county cricket. Most of them have been playing for their county for a few seasons now.

On the other hand, one cannot help concluding that Sanjay Manjrekar and Sachin Tendulkar, despite their undisputed talent, were baptised into one-day cricket in a bit of a rush because of the extraordinary circumstances in the cricketing set-up. If they have not entirely come up to scratch, the fault is not really theirs.

The confrontation between the Indian board and some of the senior players has sadly led to a situation in which the present Indian team has to consist of insufficiently tested, even mediocre youngsters.

The Australasia Cup has demonstrated that Kapil Dev and Krishnamachari Srikkanth, worthy cricketers both, are reaching the end of their illustrious careers. Nor is Ravi Shastri's inclusion as team member, leave alone as captain, a matter of certainty.

All of this makes for a situation in which the Indian cricket administrators must address themselves in real earnest to the task of organising the domestic cricket structure which will ensure a steady flow of talented youngsters.

Until that happens and until the crop now donning the country's colours matures and fulfills its promise, Indian cricket must be prepared for some more disillusionment and disenchantment.

One hopes that Camelot is not too distant a prospect.

Woodcock's 100 greatest cricketers

MID-DAY • July 7, 1996

John Woodcock, doyen of English cricket writers has published his list of 100 greatest cricketers of all time.

At the top of the list is W G Grace (1848-1915), who else? Former Sportsweek correspondent Woodcock says of him, "it is 81 years ago now that W G died and he remains the most magnificent figure in the game's history." Woodcock quotes Lord Hawke as saying of Grace, "no monument, no portrait, no book can adequately represent either his vitality or his superb skill in the game he loved."

And Lord Harris who captained W G in his first Test match (the first to be played in England at the Oval in 1880), "it is difficult to believe that a combination so remarkable of health, activity, power, eye, hand, devotion and opportunity will present itself again."

Included in the top 20 are (in order): Don Bradman, Garfield St. Auburn Sobers, A Mynn (England), Syd Barnes (England), Walter Hammond (England), Viv Richards ("he was strong, confident, handsome, athletic, sensitive and fiery, and he had a swagger of which no one could be oblivious"), Ian Botham ("because there were times when he was wayward and others when he was gauche, not everyone sings the praises of Ian Botham....but he was a towering figure with an incomparable record."), Denis Compton, Len Hutton, Frank Woolley (England), Shane Warne ("were he never to bowl another ball, his light would not go out; so salutary has been his effect on the game that it never will"), Victor Trumper (Australia), Barry Richards (South Africa), Imran Khan ("for as long as he wanted to be, Imran Khan was the prince of Pakistan cricket, and he played the part to perfection. When he gave the game his full attention he was a great all-rounder"), Keith Miller, Richie Benaud, Dennis Lillee, Alec Bedser.

No Sunil Gavaskar or Kapil Dev, Johnnie Woodcock? Your prejudice is showing, Wooders.

Sachin's forget-me-not

MID-DAY • March 11, 1998 • Chennai

Sachin Tendulkar scores a glorious 155

In the ultimate analysis, exemplary teamwork, some brilliant attacking batting, bold and astute captaincy and sustained, intelligent spin bowling largely enabled India to score her first victory over Australia in this southern metropolis since the inaugural India-Australia cricket Test in 1956-57.

Until commencement of this match, the Test record had read a dismal: played six, lost four, drawn one and tied one in favour of the tourists from Down Under.

Although one does not set much store by the "captain's luck" factor, it is, nevertheless, significant that the win has coincided with a change in captaincy and is the first victory after 12 Tests played abroad over a 15-month period.

More than anything else, it has buttressed the theory that India is a very difficult side, indeed, to defeat at home.

Although fully meritorious, India's convincing 179-run victory somewhat devalued by umpiring decisions which did not find favour with some of the batsmen of the world Test champion side.

It will be interesting to see what action match referee Peter van der Merwe of South Africa, who passed a draconian sentence against Indian wicketkeeper Nayan Mongia for allegedly showing dissent against an umpiring decision, takes against the Australians for the same "offence".

For too long now, we Indians have been the favourite whipping boys of the racist czars in the International Cricket Council (ICC) and their Uncle Toms.

Despite the transfer of power in the corridors of the once high-and-mighty ICC to the non-white nations, the current state of affairs indicates that it is still the brown man's burden as far as international cricket administration is concerned.

This Chennai Test will be long remembered for Sachin Tendulkar's luminescent batting technique, Nayjot Singh Sidhu's savage second innings blitzkrieg against Shane Warne when the spin wonderkid was threatening to induce spondylitis in the Indian batting line-up, Mohammed Azharuddin's self-effacing second knock and courageous declaration, Rahul Dravid's consistency, Anil Kumble's return to form, the impressive batting and, keeping of Nayan Mongia, especially to the spin trio, and the refreshing improvement in the overall fielding and physical fitness standard of the Indian team.

The Australians, on the other hand, known for their no-nonsense approach, will understandably want to consign this Test to the dustheap of history as an aberration. They were outplayed in every department. Thirty-one-year-old Gavin Robertson made an impressive debut with both bat and ball but of the others only Ian Healy and Mark Waugh, the latter only to some extent, lived up to their formidable reputations.

The Australians are accustomed to playing in oppressive heat in their country but they were clearly drained with the humidity in Chennai. They will be looking forward to the cooler northern climes for the rest of the series.

Had Azharuddin's bold declaration boomeranged it would have been characterised as foolish, even suicidal. By the same yardstick since nothing succeeds like success (or excess, as Mark Twain would have us know), the Indian national selectors predictably will want to claim "we-told-you-so" glory for their wisdom which made victory possible.

Without in any way detracting from their judgement, we would like to remind them that in our cricket-crazy country, the life-span of glory is only as long as the next defeat. It would, therefore, be churlish to deny them their transitory moment in the sun.

That rise and fall of reputations in matters of sport as a microcosm of human endeavour is axiomatic. Unfortunately the stock of Indian sport internationally tends to languish at a consistently low level. At this point in time it is soaring in inverse proportion to the Titanic-like sinking of the world cricket Test champions' stature.

Of one thing one can be reasonably sure: It won't be long before our pugnacious but friendly visitors from Kangarooland bounce back.

BRIEF SCORES :

India 257 all out (N Mongia 58, N Sidhu 62, R Dravid 52; S Warne 4-85, G Robertson 4-72) and 418 for 4 (N Sidhu 64, R Dravid 56, S Tendulkar 155*, M Azharuddin 64) beat Australia 328 all out (M Waugh 66, I Healy 90, G Robertson 57; A Kumble 4-103)

Lessons from Kolkata

MID-DAY • March 16, 2001

Starting with Pullela Gopichand's All England Badminton win last Sunday, down to India's thoroughly well-deserved Test cricket victory over Australia yesterday, it has been an ecstasy-inducing five days for Indian sport in the midst of the *tehelka* in New Delhi and the turbulence in the nation's Stock Exchanges.

VVS Laxman

For helping put the brakes on Steve Waugh's Dominators' run of 16 successive Test wins and recording only the third victory in 1535 Tests in history by a team following-on, the names of VVS Laxman, Harbhajan Singh and Rahul Dravid, in particular, will be written in letters of gold.

Nothing succeeds like excess (oops, success) as the truism goes. But, even as the nation celebrates, one cannot but help express the point of view—and one is being churlish—that India's magnificent win at Kolkata's Garden of Eden came perilously close to not being achieved, given the fact that only 6.3 overs remained to be bowled when Australia's last wicket fell.

Without in any way detracting from the team's heroic performance or Sourav Ganguly's successful captaincy, a constructive, dispassionate assessment of at least one aspect—the skipper's declaration yesterday—is called for.

Sourav Ganguly is not known to be steeped in the richness of English literature

However, he would do well to commit to memory the following well-known quotation from Shakespeare following his negative leadership that, more than any other factor, almost came in the way of his Bravehearts pulling off their spectacular victory:

"*There is a tide in the affairs of men,*" wrote the Bard in *Julius Caesar*,

"*which, taken at the flood, leads on to fortune,*

Omitted, all the voyage of their life

Is bound in shallows and in miseries."

Faced with the option of either grabbing opportunity by the forelock and staking a heroic claim to victory or of playing safe to avoid an unlikely defeat—no team has scored more than 300 runs in the fourth innings in India—the prince of Kolkata betrayed a lily-livered mental make-up when he played safe in a manner that defied comprehension.

Having maneuvered itself to a (now) unusual position of dominance, thanks to the magnificent batsmanship of VVS Laxman and Rahul Dravid, the captain inexplicably decided that not losing—in the hope of levelling the series in the last Test at Chennai—was preferable to forcing a gallant win in Kolkata itself on a turning fifth day track and, from there, boldly going for a series win in the deciding Test.

It was mystifying in the extreme to see Sourav Ganguly languidly watching the meaningless proceedings on the fifth morning as Laxman, Dravid, Mongia, Zaheer Khan and Harbhajan increased the lead to 383 in the hour before wisdom dawned on him and he applied the closure, (thus forfeiting the opportunity of inducing the Aussie's to go for a win) and leaving his side only 75 overs to bowl out the opposition.

History will record that Ganguly's judgement was spot-on, his mathematical expertise akin to that of Shakuntala Devi.

However, viewed in correct perspective, the morning's logic-defying decision denoted not just flawed tactics. It also demonstrated, on the part of the Indian captain, a demoralising lack of faith in his bowlers and an exaggerated awe of the Australians' batting ability.

More importantly, it needlessly exposed specialist bowlers Harbhajan Singh and Zaheer Khan to the risk of injury in an attack which was already depleted because of the absence of match-winner Anil Kumble and Javagal Srinath.

Worse, it was pathetic to see the Indian bowlers' and fieldsmen's languor and lack of urgency at a time even when they had the Australians on a perilous 116 for three. It was a time to go for the kill, not procrastinate and aimlessly slow down the over rate.

It is hoped that this criticism will be taken in the right spirit. As we all know, those who refuse to learn from the mistakes of history are condemned to repeat them.

BRIEF SCORES:

Australia 445 all out (M Slater 42, M Hayden 97, J Langer 58, S Waugh 110; Harbhajan Singh 7-123) and 212 all out (M Hayden 67; Harbhajan Singh 6-73) lost to India 171 all out (VVS Laxman 59; G McGrath 4-18 and 657 for decl. (VVS Laxman 281, R Dravid 180) by 171 runs.

Return home, Ganguly and Co.

MID-DAY* • *November 20, 2001

If reports about the disgraceful, draconian action taken yesterday by match referee Mike Denness against Sachin Tendulkar and as many as five other Indian cricketers in the second Test against South Africa at Port Elizabeth are factual, our team should return home IMMEDIATELY—and to hell with the consequences!

Sourav Ganguly

At MidDay press time, various news agency reports from South Africa concerning hanging judge Mike Denness' Banana Republic-type sentence have been described as "unofficial". However, there is no reason to doubt their authenticity.

If reports are true—but prudence dictates that we await fuller details of Denness' damning 'fatwa'—we should call off the tour in protest in the strongest possible terms against an unprecedented autocratic action, which palpably vitiates all canons of natural justice, and which will rank in the annals of the game as a heinous scandal which is as, if not more, despicable than the Richter Scale-shattering, match-fixing drama that rocked the cricketing world not so long ago.

Prudence dictates that we await receipt of details of the official report that decreed the damning 'fatwa' and the incredible action - on the basis of unsolicited South African television coverage - against India's pride and joy Sachin Tendulkar who is acknowledged the world over as being the epitome of fair play and sportsmanship, apart from being one of the greatest batsmen of all time. His well-wishers would be justified in suspecting a diabolical plot to unsettle him in his pursuit of greater glory.

The harsh sentences pronounced by Denness, England captain by default, but whose performances hardly matched his own arrogance, upon skipper Sourav Ganguly for allegedly "not being able to control the players" (whatever that means!) and Harbhajan Singh, S S Das and Deep Dasgupta for alleged "excessive appealing" are patently prejudiced, especially in the light of the repeated, intimidating appeals during the Indian innings at Port Elizabeth by South African skipper Shaun Pollock against whom no action has been taken.

Much as one hates to believe it, cricket continues to be a white man's game—witness the allegations of suspect bowling action concerning Harbhajan Singh, Muttiah Muralitharan and Shoaib Akhtar.

And, the fact that cricketers of a certain pigmentation, to name only a few, notably (former England captain Michael Atherton, (in the infamous sawdust in-the-pocket incident), Michael Slater and Glenn McGrath were let off, the former in India and the latter in Australia recently for behaviour that certainly does not do much good for a game that is already in the pits of disrepute!

The governing cricket body of Sri Lanka stoutly stood up for Muralitharan until his action was cleared, and the Pakistan Cricket Board (PCB) president is on record as saying that he is contemplating taking action against the International Cricket Council (ICC) for finding fault with Shoaib's action after he was cleared by the august body last year.

Will our high-and-mighty Board of Control for Cricket in India (BCCI) have the courage to stand up to the bullying tactics of an ICC-appointed bigot at a time when national honour and dignity demand it.

Your guess, dear reader, is as good as ours.

Well done Dalmiya, but...

***MID-DAY* • November 21, 2001**

To put things in proper perspective: First of all, this column salutes Deep Das Gupta and Rahul Dravid for their heroic batting display yesterday at Port Elizabeth which helped India draw the second cricket Test against South Africa with honour.

Jagmohan Dalmiya

For all one knows, bete noire match referee Mike Denness may have done the Indian team a huge favour by instilling in them a sense of pride which was woefully lacking hitherto.

Unfortunately, the heroic performance has been overshadowed by the disgraceful happenings instigated by Denness which, more than Tendulkar's behaviour as alleged by the referee, have brought the game into disrepute.

KHALIDOSCOPE also commends Board of Control for Cricket in India president Jagmohan Dalmiya for taking a no-nonsense stand against Denness for handing down preposterous punishment against national icon Sachin Tendulkar and five of his teammates.

It has now come to light that the Indian players were not prepared to take the field on the last day in protest against the miscarriage of justice.

They were prevailed upon by Dalmiya to do so out of consideration for the South African public and the United Cricket Board of South Africa.

Fair enough. But it remains to be seen what International Cricket Council (ICC) chief executive Malcolm Speed comes up with today, as promised, after meeting with his namesake, president Malcolm Gray in London.

If Speed's seeming lack of concern and sympathy for the concerned players and the sensibilities of millions of Indian cricket *deewane* as evident at a crème de la crème reception hosted for him in Mumbai last night by former BCCI chief Raj Singh Dungarpur is anything to go by, one should not expect much joy from the august cricket body, whose racist proclivities are becoming increasingly obvious.

Be that as it may, the Indian Board should stand firm in its demand to have Mike Denness replaced for the third Test starting on Friday by another ICC panel referee who should be acceptable to it. As we go to press this morning, a news despatch from South Africa indicates that the South African Board, too, is in favour of having Denness replaced.

This writer takes issue with Dalmiya as regards his announcement that "if no panel referee is available, any former cricketer of repute is acceptable to us."

This betrays a weak-kneed reaction. For one thing, "availability" ought not to be a problem in this age of jet travel. In any event, most of the match referees—many of them retired cricketers—are "holidaymakers", in the words of the irrepressible Geoff Boycott.

More importantly, for all Dalmiya knows, the replacement in the form of a "former cricketer of repute" may be more of a Rasputin than Mike Denness himself. The circumstances surrounding Denness' inquiry into Tendulkar's alleged breach of rules are extremely curious and need to be thoroughly investigated, especially since it appears as though the referee had acted suo moto.

Batting genius Tendulkar is acknowledged by his peers and the media the world over as being the epitome of sportsmanship and good conduct. His fair name, and, indeed those of his hapless team mates, have been besmirched by Denness.

Their honour can only be restored by the BCCI ensuring that the draconian and discriminatory punishment is revoked and, if possible, damages secured for loss of reputation of all sentenced players and loss of earnings in the case of Virender Sehwag compensated.

The entire sordid episode also raises important issues such as sentenced players' right of appeal, which is the cornerstone of jurisprudence in all civilised societies, the sustainability in a court of law of a ban on them as regards speaking up in defence and the consequences which miscarriage of justice can have on their careers and future professional earnings.

The nation's honour—and that of the sentenced cricketers, DEMANDS that the Indian Board act expeditiously to ensure that justice is not only done but seen to be done.

Hussain's tactics put India on backfoot

MID-DAY • August 23, 2002 • Leeds

Nasser Hussain

Whatever else you might say about skipper Sourav Ganguly, he is never one to fight shy of trusting his own better judgment even if it means swimming against the tide of conventional wisdom.

Many an Indian eyebrow was raised yesterday morning when Ganguly announced that his team would bat, under a huge cloud cover making for conditions which were palpably hazardous for batting, after he had won the toss.

Worse still, the cognoscenti were stupefied by his choice of Sanjay Bangar as opening batsman, in preference to S S Das, prompting the question all around as to what else the diminutive Orissa batsman needed to do to merit inclusion in the Test side after his brilliant 250 in the previous match against Essex.

As it turned out, Ganguly was vindicated on both counts. Though England's pace attack of Matthew Hoggard, Andy Caddick and Alex Tudor admirably exploited the overcast conditions to make the ball swing and seam perilously on a wicket of uneven bounce, Bangar and Rahul Dravid applied themselves to the job of building the innings with commendable concentration, discipline and technical prowess.

One-up in the series, England had obviously done their homework after their so-near-yet-so-far disappointment at Trent Bridge, where the four-pronged pace attack had wantonly pitched short outside the batsmen's off-stump.

England, under Nasser Hussain, have mastered the art of containment, a ploy devised primarily for Sachin Tendulkar, in a manner reminiscent of Douglas Jardine's leg theory to curb Don Bradman.

Howsoever effective in combating aggressive batsmanship, England's negative tactics make for extremely boring cricket, are grossly unfair to the paying spectators and deserve to be denounced.

Yesterday, Hoggard and Tudor seemingly willed the ball to climb steeply and menacingly from just short of a good length, tucking in the batsmen and compelling them to take evasive action. However, in two brilliant overs from Tudor on either side of the lunch break, Dravid, playing his 64th Test, was subjected to torrid treatment, which the vice-captain was extremely fortuitous to survive.

Twenty-nine year-old Dravid's achievement of 5,000 Test runs—the seventh by an Indian, was yesterday due in large measure to his commendable resilience and courage as evidenced by the numerous blows to his anatomy.

It must be said that the Karnataka stalwart was true to his word in that he did not let the contentious events concerning the senior Indian players, the International Cricket Council (ICC) and the Board of control for Cricket in India (BCCI) over sponsorship contracts distract him from the job at hand.

No praise can be too high for makeshift opener Bangar's fiercely determined application and his stubborn refusal to nibble at the forbidden apple offerings outside the off-stump.

Given the never-never-learn propensity of Indian batsmen of recent times to succumb to away-going balls pitched on or outside the off-stump, the sight of Mumbai-based Railways all-rounder Bangar, in particular, and of Dravid, frustrating the all-too-obvious gambit was a refreshing sight, indeed.

Midway in the afternoon, as the Indian batsmen seemed to be getting the better of the battle of attrition, Nasser Hussain, who always likes to be in control, seemed uncharacteristically, bereft of ideas.

However, all in all, the proceedings were painfully slow going for the substantial Indian audience in the West stand, weaned, as it is on slam-bang, instant cricket gratification.

Nevertheless, for connoisseurs, the manner in which Dravid and Bangar fended off lifting deliveries on their rib cages out of reach of the close-in leg side fielders and forced the ball to the on-side, made for absorbing viewing.

Speaking at a function the previous evening at the inauguration of a new stand at the Headingley stadium, at which Yorkshire legends Freddie Trueman, Ray Illingworth, Geoff Boycott and Brian Close were present, Sachin Tendulkar had spoken movingly about his experience of playing county cricket for Yorkshire 10 years ago, when he was 19, about its educational value and the love and affection he had received all around.

However, Flintoff was in no similar expansive mood when Tendulkar came out to bat in failing light after Bangar finally left for 68 runs, assiduously garnered in just a shade under five hours.

Bowling at full throttle and seemingly untroubled by his niggling groin injury, Flintoff greeted the imperturbable Little Master with a flurry of rising deliveries which Tendulkar left well alone, even as Dravid proceeded majestically to his 12th Test century, his second successive in the series.

Despite his deceptive lethargy on the day, Hussain had used his trump card—the rising delivery— to restrict India, 0-1 down, to just 236 at close of play, thereby putting them on the back foot in their quest for a series win.

BRIEF SCORES :

India 628 for 8 decl. (S Bangar 68, R Dravid 148, S Tendulkar 193, S Ganguly 128) beat England 273 all out (M Vaughan 61, A Stewart 78) and 309 all out (N Hussain 110; A Kumble 4-66)

Massacre!

MID-DAY* • *August 24, 2002* • *Leeds

Sachin Ramesh Tendulkar's Julius Caeser hairdo and designer goatee stubble may not win the approval of fashion pundits. But there can be no two opinions about the fact that the master batsman is wise way beyond his 29 years.

Sachin Tendulkar

Introverted to a fault, Tendulkar believes in the adage that handsome is as handsome does and that the best way to answer one's critics is through deeds, not empty words.

Yesterday, at Headingley, while surpassing the legendary Sir Don Bradman's feat of 29 Test centuries and overhauling David Gower's aggregate of 8231 Test runs (behind Allan Border, Sunil Gavaskar, Steve Waugh, Graham Gooch, Javed Miandad and Viv Richards), Tendulkar delivered a resounding riposte to the section of the British media which had proclaimed that his illustrious career was at an end.

Tendulkar's heavenward acknowledgment by way of thanks upon reaching a landmark has, by now, almost assumed trademark proportions. But his accentuated wave of the bat towards the press box yesterday after he had completed his sixth hundred against England was as uncharacteristic as it was eloquent.

Tendulkar's century, which has boosted his average against England to over 80, although nowhere near his best, was his first at Headingley, home of the Yorkshire Cricket Club, which he represented 10 years ago. This is also the venue where Don Bradman scored 304 in one day after the bodyline series in 1932-33.

Although Tendulkar modestly acknowledged the pat on his back from Nasser Hussain as he walked back at the tea interval, he could not have been amused at the sight of the streaker, after his experience with the intruder in the first Test at Lord's.

If India find themselves in a position of strength at the end of the second day, on which the sun never shone, it is largely because of the contribution of three Marathi-speaking gentlemen, apart from Ganguly: Rahul Dravid, Sachin Tendulkar and Sanjay Bangar, which should please a certain gentleman, who resides in Matoshri, no end.

No praise can be too high for Dravid's sterling knock of 148, his highest against England, in extremely difficult atmospheric conditions on a treacherous wicket of uneven bounce. This will, arguably, rank among his best-ever innings.

England coach Duncan Fletcher seemed as much at his wit's end as Nasser Hussain, while India rendered the England attack toothless with a precision that would warm the cockles of the heart of even the most fastidious dental surgeon.

Skipper Saurav Ganguly also joined in the party, to the unadulterated delight of the Indian spectators in the packed 14,000- capacity stadium, while compiling a polished century—his ninth in Tests—after his two consecutive fifties in the series, and helped amass what could turn out to be a match- winning total.

John Bunton, the spectator in the raucous West Stand, who ended with a bleeding head while attempting to catch Ganguly's six off Giles, must have been as repentant as the wayward England bowlers, who looked dispirited for the greater part of the day. Their insistence on consistently bowling short of a length and outside the stumps was incomprehensible.

The situation calls for urgency on the part of the Indian batsmen, when play resumes today, to enable an early declaration.

And, of course, for Messrs Kumble and Singh to weave their magic. The pronounced spin which Giles has extracted from the wicket should suit their wiles and guiles.

Headingley High

MID-DAY • August 27, 2002 • Headingley

Following disclosure in KHALIDOSCOPE of the inadequate security for the Indian cricket team at Nottingham, The England and Wales Cricket Board (ECB) has considerably stepped up arrangements at the team hotel and the Headingley ground.

This was confirmed to *Mid Day* yesterday by Trevor Crouch, ECB liaison officer, who is traveling with the team.

Crouch said that hotels in the UK are not quite seized of the kind of security needed for the team as cricket "is not a religion here as in India".

"I have had to emphasise to the hotels that nothing short of Manchester United Football Club-type of security will do," he said.

When Sourav Ganguly came for yesterday's press conference after the match, he was escorted by as many as three security guards.

This column had exposed the pathetic security arrangements at Nottingham during the Trent Bridge Test in an open letter to BCCI president Jagmohan Dalmiya, after which team manager Ranga Reddy took up the issue with the ECB.

Time for players to agree gracefully

MID-DAY • September 02, 2002 • London

Jagmohan Dalmiya

Now that the International Cricket Council (ICC) has agreed, in writing, to "have in good faith discussions (with the Board of Control for Cricket in India) concerning the issues of players' endorsements and pre-existing sponsorship contracts for future ICC events", it would be in the best interests of Indian cricket—and that of the players themselves—to agree to sign and comply with the Players' Terms for the forthcoming ICC Champions Trophy in Sri Lanka.

On the face of it, the touring Indian cricketers' refusal to sign the Terms was justifiable, given the unique situation of the Indian players, unlike none others, whose sponsorship contracts and players' endorsements run into millions of dollars.

Unfortunately, the manner in which the entire issue was handled queered the pitch and the situation soon got mired in ego considerations.

This brought about a totally avoidable long drawn-out dispute between the Board of Control for Cricket in India (BCCI) and the ICC, culminating in a situation at last Saturday's Board of Directors of ICC Development (International) Limited (IDI) in Dubai in which India was almost completely isolated.

It is understood that, but for the spirited stand taken by BCCI president Jagmohan Dalmiya in presenting the unique problems faced by the Indian players, a resolution, sponsored by New Zealand, would almost certainly have been passed.

This could have resulted in bestowing virtual pariah status upon India in international cricket, for however limited a period.

Yesterday afternoon, BCCI president Jagmohan Dalmiya, in the course of a half-hour international telephone conversation, reportedly summoned all his acknowledged powers of persuasion to get captain Sourav Ganguly and his team mates to agree to the BCCI's point of view.

Dalmiya followed up his conversation with a letter to the members of the team (through the captain) and enclosed a copy of the ICC's letter to him in which managing director Malcolm Speed confirmed the above-mentioned proposal.

The captain reportedly declined to commit himself without consulting his teammates, many of whom were unavailable for immediate consultations.

The issue was expected to be discussed by the players last night.

Details were not available at press time, but KHALIDOSCOPE sincerely hopes that better counsel prevailed.

By making a small concession and agreeing to abide by the commercial terms and conditions of the tournament, not just for the 18-day duration of the tournament (as agreed to by themselves), but also 30 days after the event, as suggested by the ICC, the players' ends would be met in the sense they would have a month's time after the end of the tournament on September 30 and the end of October 2002 to sort out the problem for the future once and for all.

Former Test captain Kapil Dev, presently in London in his capacity of brand ambassador for Sony, the entertainment giant who have an interest in the telecast stakes for the Sri Lanka Champions' Trophy, also met with senior Indian players at the team hotel yesterday to try and help. He, too, was in favour of a compromise in the short term to buy time.

What with vital elements of conflict of interest and restraint of trade involved, the dispute is of an extremely complex nature. But good grace and understanding at this stage can only help the players' long-term interests.

It's party time!

MID-DAY* • *October 01, 2002

Virender Sehwag

Ring those noisy bells, hoot those raucous horns, burst those deafening firecrackers. Our cricket champions return home today!

Even though they have been declared 'joint' winners in the ICC Mini World Cup, all things considered, in a notoriously unpredictable game, one may justifiably conclude sans bias that India were singularly unfortunate in not bringing home the coveted Champions Trophy.

The battle-hardened young warriors, mentally toughened by their inspirational captain, and technically and physically licked into shape by devoted coach John Wright, physiotherapist Andrew Leipus and physical conditioner Adrian Le Roux did enough right through the Mini World Cup to satisfy their uncompromising legion of followers that they deserved to be crowned world champions–albeit for the time being and in its 'mini' avatar.

If the victory over England was awesome, Sourav Ganguly's warriors' wins over Zimbabwe and South Africa proved the team's tenacity, their steely resolve, their do-or-die capacity to draw into deep reserves in times of crisis.

And the bowling attack, much maligned for its so-called inadequacy, rose gallantly to the occasion, not once but in both finals against Sri Lanka, who were generally considered impregnable at home.

It may appear presumptuous to conclude that India would have definitely won the second, if not first, final, but for the intervention by the elements.

However, given the state of the wicket and the impressive, consistent display by her batsmen, I have no doubt in my mind that India would have won on BOTH rain-affected days, Muttiah Muralitharan notwithstanding.

However, one does concede that this is applying empirical, not theoretical, data in an extremely fickle sport.

One would be eminently churlish to indulge in finger pointing in this hour of glory. However, the fact that the World Cup is just a little over four months away calls for some constructive introspection.

To begin with, the time for experimentation is over. It's time the practice of chopping and changing the team's line-up was put an end to.

Apart from disturbing the smooth running of the team's engine, experiments with individuals, as also their expected roles in the scheme of things, can be extremely unsettling and, therefore, deleterious to the players' morale.

The decision to fly Javagal Srinath almost straight from Leicestershire and Colombo airport into the first final—and to drop him for the second—smacked of panic (following injury to Ashish Nehra).

It was equally scatterbrained to drop stalwart Anil Kumble, who has captured no less than 299 one-day and 333 Test wickets in his star-spangled career, from the team in the first final. In characteristic gutsy manner, Kumble dealt a sharp reply to those who have rushed to write him off, in the second final with a fine display of restrictive bowling.

Equally incomprehensible, if not downright illogical, was the decision to pitchfork Dinesh Mongia into the opening slot to partner Virender Sehwag.

Ganguly and Sehwag have established their credentials as being, arguably, the best opening ODI pair in the world.

So why monkey around?

This is not to make a case for rigidity and to altogether discourage innovation in accordance with situations, but at this juncture the less the experimentation, the better - and this includes the important matter of Sachin Tendulkar's batting position.

Although the Little Master (he remains that, despite the unrealistic expectations of his fickle hero worshippers), has himself expressed a preference to bat at the top of the order, skipper Ganguly is on record as saying that he is batting at number four for "the team's sake".

The team's interest being paramount, that should signal the end of all controversy on the subject. I'm certain that Tendulkar himself, team man that he is down to his toenails, will be the first to want 'finis' to all discussion on this topic, for the time being, at least.

Having said that, two glaring weaknesses remain in our one-day team's composition: a wicket-keeper batsman and consistent, if not fiery, support for the fast-improving Zaheer Khan.

Taking all factors into account, it may be a trifle late in the day to find a replacement for Rahul Dravid as (reluctant, but uncomplaining!) wicketkeeper-batsman, risk of injury to the leading batsman notwithstanding.

The chances of injury are, indeed, real but there seems no other option, thanks to the seeds sown by the previous selection committee.

It must be admitted that Ajit Agarkar and Ashish Nehra have not, quite come up to scratch as operators of the new ball. However, no adequate replacements are visible on the horizon who can immediately fill the breach.

The youngsters, who could do so are as yet untried at the top level, and only a very optimistic bunch of selectors would hazard inducting any of them at this juncture.

Talking of selectors, all credit is due to the previous selection committee comprising Chandu Borde, Madan Lal, Ashok Malhotra, Shivlal Yadav and Sanjay Jagdale who have just relinquished office, for a sterling performance.

A few quirks notwithstanding, they have functioned in their thankless job with exemplary rectitude and with the national interest in mind.

To them should, rightfully, go a great deal of credit, for the state in which we find ourselves today - proud of our worthy one-day cricket champions.

Did we hear you ask: what about our Test team? Let's not spoil the party.

Admirable teamwork was the key

MID-DAY* • *November 04, 2002

Time was, not so long ago, when India's situation at the end of the fourth day in this Kolkata Test, would have heralded, almost certainly, a lacklustre Diwali.

But things have changed dramatically over the past year or so. That being the case, India's gallant fight back in the second innings here yesterday, reminiscent of the epic victory over Australia in January - 2001, has not come as much of a surprise.

The manner in which Sachin Tendulkar, that wondrous genius, and never-say-die VVS Laxman applied themselves to the rescue act, with India precariously placed on 87 for four, one knew that it would not require a miracle for India to remain undefeated in the series.

In a country which looks upon its cricketing heroes as super humans, expectations can at times be absurd. One bad patch is sufficient to set tongues wagging and fingers pointing that such and such is past his prime, over the hill.

The chorus of criticism directed at both Tendulkar and Laxman was becoming ridiculous. One can only hope that this magnificent display by both stalwarts will silence the detractors, at least for some time.

VVS Laxman

A colleague informs us that when she met Sourav Ganguly soon after commencement of play yesterday morning, the captain kept marvelling at Sachin's mastery.

Not known to speak to himself, Ganguly, reportedly, kept repeating "genius" to himself. Given the fact that Ganguly himself is today among the world's leading batsmen, the unabashed admiration for his former captain's God-given gifts speaks volumes of both.

From the moment he went out to bat, Tendulkar's body language bespoke grim determination. From the very first ball that he faced, it was obvious that he was determined to steer India to safety and in the process, dispel misconceptions about his abiding gifts.

The hard work at nets in honing his technique to perfection soon became evident. Tendulkar was more bent in his stance in order to "smell" the ball. He diligently eschewed the hook shot that has often been his Waterloo and minimising cuts and pulls, played straighter than is his wont.

This was vintage Tendulkar once again.

It would be invidious to single out contributions of individual players in the series win. Suffice is to say it was the result of admirable teamwork, with every member responding to the side's needs at different times. There is considerable merit in Raj Singh Dungarpur's thesis that the present team is the best Indian side ever, teamwork being an important contributory factor.

In all the adulation showered upon our cricket team, the role of selectors is often forgotten.

Also, that of coach John Wright, physiotherapist Andrew Leipus and physical trainer Adrian le Roux. Their involvement with the team, their single-minded devotion and hard work in making the players mentally and physically 100 per cent fit, in the process instilling in them feelings of confidence and self-belief are unfortunately not appreciated sufficiently.

Significantly, the success of the team in both versions of the game has coincided with the association of these foreign gentlemen and should silence critics who opposed their appointment merely because they are "phoren".

It is hoped that their contracts will be extended when they come up for renewal and that a performance-based incentive clause will be worked out to ensure the continuation of India's heart-warming performances.

India can win Cup: Kirsten

MID-DAY* • *February 28, 2003* • *Johannesburg

Former South African Test player Peter Kirsten fancies India's chances to win the World Cup.

Peter Kirsten (left)

He told *Mid-Day* yesterday that he has tipped India to win all along, even before the tournament started and despite their poor showing on the tour of New Zealand.

"They are peaking at the right time," he said, "although the absence of a fifth specialist bowler is a bit of a worry for them."

Meanwhile, the Pakistan team management is said to be incensed at umpire Srinivas Venkataraghavan's decision to adjudge Pakistani stalwart Inzamam-ul-Haq, who is passing through a wretched patch, leg before wicket.

Some Pakistani supporters are said to have been furious and even wanted to have a word with the umpire, some suggesting that an Indian umpire should not have been selected to stand in a match featuring Pakistan, especially since both teams are involved in a close race for the Super Sixes.

Pakistan team manager Shahrayar Khan indicated that Inzamam will not be dropped from tomorrow's crunch game against India.

"He is too great a player to be discarded for the match," he said.

The Pakistani team management is also said to have expressed its displeasure over a television commentator's remark that Inzamam, whom they consider among the world's best batsmen, walked to the wicket in manner akin to a man going to the gallows.

"A code of ethics should be framed by the ICC for commentators," remarked a player on condition of anonymity.

Team India had more *jazba*

MID-DAY • March 02, 2003 • Johannesburg

India crushed Pakistan by six wickets in a memorable Pool 'A' match in the ICC World Cup at Centurion Park on Saturday to secure a berth in the Super Six round of the tournament.

Sachin Tendulkar

India's epic victory, their fourth in as many World Cup matches against Pakistan, was largely the result of a classic knock of 98 by Sachin Tendulkar, ably assisted by some eminently sensible batting by Yuvraj Singh (50 not out), Rahul Dravid (44 not out) and Mohammad Kaif (35) after Pakistan had scored 273, thanks to an elegant innings of 101 by Saeed Anwar.

After all's said and done, it was largely India's superior jazba, allied to better team-work, discipline and self-belief that prevailed over a dispirited Pakistan team that has been rent asunder by internal strife.

Due credit must also go to India's bowling attack - to Zaheer Khan (two for 46), Javagal Srinath (one for 41) - and to the high level of fielding.

Even as he strode out to bat, Sachin Tendulkar's demeanour bespoke grim determination, a here-and-now urgency to not only set India authoritatively on course for victory but also to put to rest, on the world's biggest cricketing stage, all meaningless debate concerning the world's premier batsman.

He started off with a flurry of savage, bludgeoning strokes which seemed to suggest that, although they came in the aftermath of Mr. Jaswant Singh's Union Bill, he was not budgeting for runs in the initial stanzas of the run-chase.

Virender Sehwag followed suit almost dutifully, almost matching the genius stroke for stroke. It rained sixes and fours as the pair put Shoaib Akhtar, bowling at full throttle in the 150-kph speed zone, and Waqar Younis, now only a shadow of his devastating self, to the sword. The 50 of the innings came off only 32 deliveries amid frenetic waving of innumerable tricolours in the packed stands.

Ganguly departed without scoring to leave India in a somewhat perilous state at 53 for two. But Mohammad Kaif, who was on the verge of being excluded from this momentous encounter, helped Tendulkar put the innings back on the rails while helping him cross the 12,000 ODI run mark.

Kaif dropped anchor, remaining practically scoreless while Tendulkar, who was granted a reprieve by Abdul Razzaq at mid-on off Wasim when on 32, imperiously plundered runs from all points of the ground's meridian.

But once he had settled in, Kaif demonstrated a delectable array of strokes in an invaluable cameo of 35 runs. An inspired passage saw him cover drive Waqar for two consecutive fours, then flick the skipper to the square leg fence, followed by an immaculate straight drive that would have done credit to Sunil Gavaskar.

Tendulkar was beginning to feel the effects of cramps in his foot which he aggravated while going for a sharp single when on 98.

He collapsed at the bowlers' end and was attended to by physio Andrew Leipus.

The very first over after resumption saw him back away awkwardly from a snorter from Shoaib, who had smelt his prey.

The nasty delivery ricocheted off the bat to Younis Khan, who scooped up a brilliant running catch inches from the ground as he dived full stretch forward.

Tendulkar's 98 had come off just 74 balls and included two sixes and 13 fours.

Batting with circumspection, Rahul Dravid and Yuvraj Singh avoided further alarm to steer the team to a convincing win.

Waqar Younis's predictable decision to bat after winning the toss on a flat wicket in bright sunshine under an azure sky was vindicated when Pakistani openers Saeed Anwar and Taufiq Umar blunted the innocuous Indian pace attack to put on 58 before Umar was bowled by Zaheer through the 'gate'.

The stream of Indian fans, many decked out in the team colours, in the 18,000-capacity Centurion Park stadium, had further cause for rejoicing when the enormously talented Abdul Razzaq fell to a brilliant one-handed diving catch to his right by Rahul Dravid off Ashish Nehra to make it 90 for two in 20 overs.

The out-of-form Inzamam-ul-Haq, arguably among the finest batsmen in the world, having scored just 10 runs in his previous four innings, proclaimed his intent when he smote the first delivery faced—off Anil Kumble—over the bowler's head to the fence.

However, Inzamam, who looks a picture after having shed 14 kg fell to what has become the stuff of jokes— run out by Sehwag after scoring 6. Pakistan were now 98 for three at the end of 22 overs.

But a thoroughly professional fourth wicket stand of 73 between Saeed Anwar and Mohammad Yousuf (Yohana) put the Pakistan innings on a steady course until Javagal Srinath, bowling with nagging accuracy in the channel, had Youhana caught by Zaheer Khan at deep extra cover in essaying a lofted cover drive.

Indian skipper Ganguly failed to ring the requisite bowling changes that would have prevented the batsmen from settling down. In an unimaginative act of wishful thinking, he persisted inordinately with Nehra who went for 71 runs and bowled his two left-handed pace bowlers with almost metronomic tedium.

The incomprehensible tactic suited the batsmen just fine, thank you.

Anil Kumble, who was included in the side in preference to Harbhajan Singh bowled economically (none for 51 in 10 overs but one felt that Sehwag, Mongia and Ganguly himself could have bowled longer spells in preference to the profligate Nehra.

Saeed Anwar, who had been in the cricketing wilderness for six months for reasons ranging from loss of daughter to religious pursuit to injury to omission by selectors, rose to the occasion in an innings of pristine artistry that was replete with wristy cuts and exquisite flicks on both sides of the wicket.

Saeed fell for 101, scored off 126 balls, bowled by Nehra but not before he had helped stabilize Pakistan's innings in conjunction with Younis Khan (32) and Rashid Latif (29 not out) to set India a defensible score.

BRIEF SCORES

Pakistan 273 for 7 in 50 overs (Saaed Anwar 101) lost to India 276 for 4 in 45.4 overs (S Tendulkar 98, R Dravid 44, Yuvraj Singh 56) by six wickets

All's well that ends well

MID-DAY • March 03, 2003 • Durban

Sourav Ganguly

Last Saturday's clash between India and Pakistan at Supersport Park in Centurion had all the elements of its pre-match high drama.

The proceedings charmed the senses with fans chanting, waving fans, whistling and cheering raucously right through the day until the denouement.

A strong police presence at the stadium and extra security guards ensured that the good natured banter between the large number of Indian supporters and the considerably smaller Pakistani cheering squad did not get out of hand.

The organisers also laid on lunchtime entertainment with Hindi popular music, a parade of South African tribals, who danced as they went around the stadium, Gujarati Indian dancers and a flypast by a South African Airways jet, which has become standard practice for matches at the Supersport Park.

However, there was some trouble when frenetic flag waving turned into threats of violence before police moved in and gave the combatants a wee reminder of how much nicer it was inside the stadium than outside.

The night before the match, captains Sourav Ganguly and Waqar Younis had agreed to make a public gesture in keeping with the World Cup's theme of a unifying force once more on the brink of war.

Ganguly and Younis exchanged team ties and their teams shook hands before start of play in a public show of goodwill.

Old warhorses Javagal Srinath and Wasim Akram exchanged a friendly word and warm smiles.

Ganguly, of whom fans back home had demanded that India "beat Pakistan or not come home", had appealed to his team to subdue show of emotion because "it can cause problems off the field".

'Rawalpindi Express' Shoaib Akhtar had received phone calls from all over the world telling him that "you can lose the World Cup—but don't lose to India."

As it turned out, batting genius Sachin Tendulkar lived up to the assertion in a poster which read "1947: Gandhi was our God. Now it's Sachin."

Ganguly dedicated the victory to the team's fans as he gushed, "This is an absolutely fantastic day. It's great for all the people who came out to see us.

We're glad we could bring a smile to everyone. They closed offices and schools for this game (in India). It was a public holiday in some places and we did it for them. The way we batted, especially Sachin, was superb."

Touched by the occasion, Tendulkar said, "It's always a special match (against Pakistan). This is the fourth time that we have beaten them in a World Cup.

The ball was coming on to the bat well and I picked up the line and length quite early, so I decided to be aggressive. I had a cramp in my leg, which started getting worse."

Although some Indian spectators spoilt the mood by booing Waqar at the presentation ceremony, cricket provided a healthy distraction from the sordidness of politics, the incessant high-decibel spats between supporters of the two teams notwithstanding.

As so aptly described by a local newspaper, for a few glorious hours it actually seemed that there could be peace and understanding between the peoples of the two countries.

Shock reigns in SA after Black Monday

MID-DAY • March 05, 2003 • Johannesburg

Shaun Pollock

We clap our hands and wave our flag, shout "well done, chaps, it's in the bag!"

But if some day they miss the prize, Oh, aren't we quick to criticise!

Fortify—don't crucify!

Last Monday—03-03-03—was an auspicious day for the Chinese community in many parts of the world.

A large number of starry-eyed young lovers belonging to the community tied the marital knot on the palindromic day in expectation of health, wealth, longevity and the like.

However, for millions of South African cricket fans, it turned out to be a heartbreaking Black Monday with the team crashing out of the ICC World Cup in tragic circumstances after tying their last 'B' Pool match against Sri Lanka.

The rain-induced setback triggered shock, horror and despair bordering on trauma, across the length and breadth of this rainbow nation.

Suddenly, the World Cup was history for many hard-core supporters of Polly (Shaun Pollock) and his team.

As the doggerel goes: *Jonty has left His team quite bereft / And Shane's been sent home to his mummy / Ganguly has slumped Donald was dumped / And Polly's bought a dummy.*

In many respects, the high expectations engendered among followers of the game were sponsor and media driven in manner similar to that in India.

What was particularly poignant was the fact that South Africa's exit from the world's premier cricket event was the result of a tied result, hauntingly reminiscent of the 1999 World Cup semifinals which the Proteas lost to Australia as a result of a dramatic last-ball run-out involving Allan Donald and Lance Klusener.

It was also an action replay of the 1992 semifinals of the World Cup, at which the South Africans made their debut after their return to international cricket from the wilderness, when rain played spoilsport and brought the match to a premature end, with South Africa 229 for six chasing 269 to win.

Minutes after the shock exit, which continued the jinx afflicting World Cup host nations (no host country has won the tournament since its inception), a distraught Pollock said, "I don't think we got what we deserved at this tournament. I don't think we were that bad."

He continued, "I don't think we've failed. We're all disappointed, but we won't make excuses. It's third time unlucky. The World Cup is one event that seems to keep evading us.

"It's got to rank up there as possibly the most disappointing thing.

Two ties in the last two World Cups, and out of both of them. The players are gutted.

I felt we deserved better on the day."

The South Africans were under the impression that they had scored enough runs to win the game when the rain came down in sheets, unaware that one more run was needed under the Duckworth-Lewis method.

After lofting Muralitharan for a big six, Mark Boucher merely prodded the next ball defensively, without bothering to score - the last of the 45th over, which turned out to be the last ball of the match!

Asked if he was contemplating retirement, Pollock replied, "No, not at all."

But the knives are out already. Skande - Afrikaans for "shame" – appears to be the flavour of the day, the morning after the "tragedy".

Vox populi can be irrationally demanding in its expectation from sportsmen.

*****

Umpires Srinivas Venkatraghavan and Steve Bucknor, who officiated in the match, covered themselves with glory for the cool, evenhanded, efficient manner in which they handled the chaotic last moments of the Sri Lanka-South Africa humdinger.

As pressure from the home crowd and some players to resume the match intensified, the umpires did not lose their equanimity.

Their efforts to restart play having been frustrated by the pouring rain which cascaded in sheets, they consulted the Duckworth-Lewis calculations and after careful consideration, declared the match a tie.

*****

For those interested: Prior to the match, South Africa were being quoted by South African bookmakers at 33-10 to win the World Cup.

Australia were firm favourites at 33-10 and India 6-1. Other teams still in the tournament were quoted at 10-1.

ICC fields at silly point

MID-DAY • March 05, 2003 • Johannesburg

The International Cricket Council (ICC) has come in for severe criticism from various quarters for rules governing the World Cup.

Political factors, day-night matches, the non-provision for a rain day and most importantly, the format of the tournament are being blamed for the fact that strong teams like South Africa, West Indies, England and Pakistan have been knocked out, whereas Kenya and Zimbabwe have moved up to the next round, largely because of the four points gifted to them by New Zealand and England respectively.

But World Cup rules are being faulted most of all, for being iniquitous, thereby depriving the prestigious tournament of glamour and excitement.

England, in particular, feel aggrieved that the Zimbabwe and Kenya issues were handled in a ham-handed manner by the ICC, which resulted in their forfeiting four points for refusing to play in Zimbabwe (New Zealand in Kenya) and, ultimately, leading to their exit from the tournament.

As a result, Zimbabwe have become the second African country, along with Kenya, to move into the next round.

The rule, which stipulates that teams will carry forward points from the preliminary round to the Super Sixes and beyond to the semifinals round, has generally been considered illogical, after the conclusion of the Pool matches yesterday.

Australia, India and Zimbabwe proceed to the Super Sixes round from Pool 'A' and Sri Lanka, Kenya and New Zealand move up from Pool 'B'.

The points system under the carry-forward rule could win lowly Kenya, whose true class was revealed in yesterday's 142-run defeat by the West Indies, a semifinals berth even if they fail to win a single match in the Super Sixes round.

West Indies captain Carl Hooper has advocated a fresh look at the rules on match forfeits and washouts after his team was knocked out of the tournament on Monday.

He made no secret of the fact that the Kenyans had qualified because of refusal by New Zealand to play in Kenya. He also referred to his team's match against Bangladesh being abandoned because of rain, which cost his team two points.

West Indian great Michael Holding, too, questioned the qualification process for the Super Sixes, saying "blood and sweat counted for little."

He believes the points earned by Kenya and Zimbabwe have undermined the competition.

Holding writes in his syndicated column that the Super Six is meant to be those teams that have played the best cricket in the 42 preliminary matches and had finished in the top three positions.

"But, unfortunately," he writes, "off-field activities have ensured that is not the case.

"Should teams be allocated points as freely as this in such a prestigious and financially rewarding tournament?" he asks.

"Should teams who have played their guts out, giving of their best and, heaven forbid, suffered injuries in the process, be allowed to be sent home because another team pocketed unearned points and leap-leapfrogged ahead of them?" Holding asks.

Michael Holding

Former Sri Lanka captain Arjuna Ranatunga lashed out at the ICC saying that it is "stifling the World Cup with too many rules."

He said he had warned the game's governing body four years ago that it was making the game too complicated and detracting from its enjoyment for fans.

"I warned them there would be problems if they carried on adding to the rules. I said the system should be kept as simple as possible. But it made no difference.

"Every time you turn around there is another rule. Teams have no sooner worked out the current set of rules than another rule gets changed. It is not good for the tournament," Sri Lanka's captain in the 1999 World Cup said.

Move that was bound to fail

MID-DAY* • *March 08, 2003* • *Pretoria

The Board of Control for Cricket in India (BCCI) did not exactly cover itself with glory in asking the ICC Cricket World Cup 2003 Organising Committee to change the second semifinals in Durban on March 20 from a day-night match to a day game.

As explained in KHALIDOSCOPE yesterday ('India's Request Absurd'), the ill-advised, last-minute move was doomed to failure from the very start.

Although all teams in the Super Six could be affected by the timing of the Durban fixture, India were the only country, in their infinite wisdom, to ask for the change.

Apart from the fact that the move did not meet with the support of the other countries, it was also illogical to the extent that it presumed that India would reach the semi-final stage and did not take into account the fact that Ganguly could win the toss and bat first.

Importantly, it also betrayed a negative mindset and a lack of confidence unworthy of any claimants to the title of world champions.

The seeds of doubt and suspicion that have been planted in the minds of the players by our administrators could conceivably take a heavy toll.

The BCCI 'request' was given the short shrift it deserved. It may have brought president Jagmohan Dalmiya centre-stage for a brief period—but for all the wrong reasons!

India was hoist by its own petard

MID-DAY • March 24, 2003 • Johannesburg

y Ponting

Without taking anything away from Australia's extremely well-deserved victory over India in the final of the ICC World Cup yesterday, one cannot escape the conclusion that India had largely themselves to blame for their downfall.

And, without being unduly harsh, in the ultimate analysis, skipper Sourav Ganguly must accept a large share of responsibility for letting the team down—on two counts.

Firstly, he took the extremely curious decision of asking Australia to bat after winning the toss, thereby surrendering the initiative right away.

Then, with India chasing a victory target of 360, Ganguly batted in an irresponsible manner that defied all logic.

With Sachin Tendulkar back in the pavilion with the score just four, the need of the hour was for the Indian batsmen to mix caution with aggression, but the captain, who should have set an example, mystifyingly threw caution to the winds.

His buccaneering approach seemed to indicate that he had given up the ghost at the very start of the innings. Had he applied himself, the way Virender Sehwag, Rahul Dravid and Yuvraj Singh did, India could have run Australia much closer than they did.

All credit to Australia, who won the title for the third time. By far the best team, they went through the competition unbeaten.

India came storming back after a stuttering start in the tournament. They were worthy runners-up, even though the margin of defeat in the final does not do justice to their overall performance.

All Indian cricket lovers should be proud of Sourav Ganguly and his lads. Those who behaved in an abominable manner after India's defeat to Australia in the qualifying round should be ashamed of themselves.

Had Sourav Ganguly remembered the truism that those who refuse to learn their lessons from history are doomed to repentance, and taken a leaf out of Kapil Dev's 1983 World Cup book, he would not have committed the blunder of putting Australia in to bat after winning the toss.

Having elected to bat after winning the toss, Kapil's Devils could manage only 183 against the ferocious attack of Clive Lloyd's West Indians, but it sufficed to put pressure on the opposition and enabled India to eke out a stunning victory.

Australian captain Ricky Ponting said that he would have batted had he won the toss. To that extent, the toss was rendered "meaningless", in the words of former Australian Test opener Keith Stackpole, who told KHALIDOSCOPE that he was "amazed" at Ganguly's decision.

Even after allowance is made for the possibility of rain later in the day (as forecast), being a factor in Ganguly's decision, the fact remains that it betrayed a negative mindset and resulted in gifting to Australia on a platter, the considerable advantage of winning the toss.

Given the fact that most of the Indian players, including Ganguly himself, were playing their first-ever World Cup final (three Australians were playing their third), the skipper should have expected his team-mates to be afflicted with a case of nerves.

So it turned out and Zaheer Khan, obviously overawed by the occasion, gave away as many as 15 runs in the very first over of the match, which included two no-balls and two wides, to set the tenor of the final.

It may be said that, to a large extent, the 2003 World Cup was won and lost with the toss and in that very first over of the match, since India never regained composure after that.

Australia's openers Adam Gilchrist and Matthew Hayden, not ones to look a gift horse in the mouth, made the most of the benediction to rattle up 105 runs off only 92 balls.

The prodigal Zaheer Khan conceded 28 runs in his first spell of three overs and with Javagal Srinath, and Ashish Nehra, too, failing to find their rhythm, the Australians were off the block on a savage run scoring spree.

It rained fours and sixes as Ricky Ponting and Damien Martyn joined the party after Hayden's departure to set up a World Cup unbeaten partnership of 234 on a wicket that was the 'bowlers' graveyard.

Be that as it may, the Indian bowling attack looked pathetic in the face of the carnage that Ponting and Martin unleashed.

Zaheer Khan and Srinath took a severe mauling that they will not forget in a hurry.

As it turned out, the wicket, although true, assisted spin enabling Harbhajan Singh to extract considerable turn. From hindsight, Anil Kumble would have revelled on the bouncy track.

Ganguly tried every trick in his repertoire: switching bowlers' ends frequently, trying pace at one end and spin at the other, and used as many as eight bowlers—not himself for some curious reason—to stem the onslaught, but to no avail.

Sachin Tendulkar's early departure, to a rash stroke, got India on the back foot, a position from which they never recovered.

And, with Ganguly committing hara-kiri, all chances of winning evaporated, although the run rate was at par with Australia's for the greater part of the innings.

It is improbable that India could have overhauled Australia's formidable total of 359, but had Tendulkar and Ganguly not perished irresponsibly, the large Indian crowd would, at least, have had something to cheer about.

BRIEF SCORES

Australia 359-2 in 50 overs (A Gilchrist 57, R Ponting 140*, D Martyn 88*) beat India 234 all out in 39.2 overs (V Sehwag 82, R Dravid 47; G McGrath 3-52) by 125 runs.

'Naani yaad aayegi' in Australia? Don't bet your pants on it!

MID-DAY • December 02, 2003

Sourav Ganguly

So everybody says Sourav Ganguly and his team are in for the *"naani yaad aayegi"* hammering of their lifetimes.

On current form, the Aussies are runaway favourites to monopolise the forthcoming Test series against Sourav Ganguly's warriors commencing at the Gabba in Brisbane on Thursday.

Sure, if you were to go by conventional wisdom, India's preparation for the Test series against Australia appears akin to that of Laloo Prasad Yadav walking on the moon.

Yesterday's Sydney Morning Herald report would have us believe that even the prospects of India's putting up a game fight, is as remote as, "walking into the furnace," and its preparation akin "to dabbing on Coppertone for a trip to the sun."

At the grave risk of flying in the face of logic: I say "Rubbish! I do NOT agree".

Sure, the Aussies are world champions—by far.

To be certain, the cricket setup of that country—in its desire to be world champion—is seemingly imperialistic.

In its desire to remain at the very top, Cricket Australia's style of functioning is awesome for many reasons that other cricket playing nations would do well to emulate by even a minuscule margin in order to be considered worthy opponents at the world level today.

Coming to Sourav Ganguly's current lads Down Under, the fact of the matter is that the side has lost more than half its mental battle already, by pressurising, in an illogical knee-jerk reaction, former New Zealand captain and current Indian coach, John Wright, midstream to relinquish control and make way for Bruce Reid to take charge as bowling coach.

Former Indian skipper and SUNDAY MID DAY columnist Dilip Vengsarkar was on the button when he wrote last week about the devious gambit of former Australian cricketers, currently newspaper columnists, who "run down teams visiting their country".

The fact of the matter as all former Indian stalwarts, who have played Down Under will confirm is that any tour of that country is the last word in mental toughness.

Not only because of the playing conditions, but, more importantly, the psychological pressure that the media and genuinely partisan crowds (nothing wrong with that!) can exert on namby-pamby opponents.

If one goes solely by Ganguly's reported request for a bowling coach midstream during the tour (which has prompted former Test player Rusi Surti to exclaim "What's Coach John Wright Doing: Frying Eggs?"), panic has already set in the Indian ranks.

The Australian Board—Cricket Australia—craftily decided (while our Board pooh-bahs were obviously sleeping), that India's first match on tour would be on the historically bouncy track at Adelaide, given Indian batsmens' notorious unease on lively wickets.

Cricket Australia's gambit of fielding a palpably (Queensland) second XI in the match, obviously succeeded, what with the home team batsmen going hell-bent for leather. For the host side it was a win-win situation.

The gutsy Queensland Academy of Sport lads underscored the talent that Australia has in reserve.

It may have failed to force a win, but it was, after all, only a second XI! For quite some time now, the Australian Board has been playing mind games (nothing wrong with that!) with touring Indian sides as regards scheduling, wickets, opposition, which the powers-that-be back in India are oblivious about.

All logical indicators point to an Indian battering in both series.

Yet, having seen inspirational skipper Sourav Ganguly and his jaadugar lads from close quarters in both forms of the game, may I stick my neck out and say:

DO NOT WRITE OFF THIS INDIAN TEAM

When I say this I take into account factors both technical and mental.

The bookmakers would have you know that the Aussies will "yaad karaao" Ganguly's lads.

Silly, I. am not a betting man, there's no way I will wager on it.

'Poor travellers' prove a point with tour de force

MID-DAY • December 17, 2003 • Adelaide

Victory, sweet victory—all the more heady because it has been achieved against all expectations over a team that has proudly, fiercely, zealously defended its status as world champion in both forms of the game.

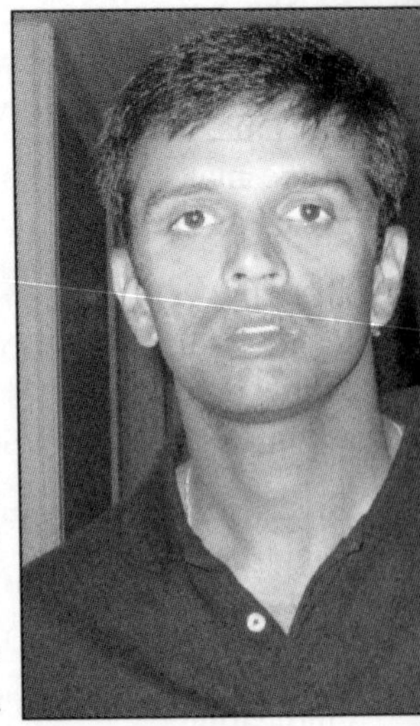

Rahul Dravid

As expressed by Ravi Shastri to Tony Greig in the commentators' box yesterday, "The pitch had nothing to do with the Aussie wickets that fell. They were the result of overconfidence, bordering on arrogance."

In fashioning the emphatic four-wicket win, Sourav Ganguly's warriors have exorcised the accursed mental demons that have earned touring Indian teams the dubious distinction of being the world's most homesickness-prone cricket side.

The victory, the result of one of the most dramatic fight-backs in the history of the game is at par with the epic 171-run win over Australia in 2000-01 in Kolkata.

In lighter vein, it has pooped Steve Waugh's turkey and plum pudding (Christmas) party and made a sad mess of his farewell series.

But, seriously, this was Waugh's only second Test defeat as captain at home.

Only three teams have scored more runs in the past to win at Adelaide.

Moreover, not for 110 years has a team scored so many first innings runs as Australia (556) in this Test and lost a Test.

And not since the 1993-94 series against South Africa does Australia find itself one-down in a home series.

The manner of Sourav Ganguly's doughty warriors' triumph made a mockery of the bookmakers' odds of 33-1 against India and raises hopes of an Indian series win, which will be the first outside Asia in 17 years and the first-ever in Australia.

It was obvious Indian manager Shivlal Yadav had not taken into account the Australians' pluck and fighting qualities when, at the end of the fourth day, he predicted an Indian win by lunch time yesterday.

On a wicket which had deteriorated marginally, Jason Gillespie (until he limped off the field with a groin injury), Andy Bichel and Stuart MacGill made the Indians fight all the way to earn their win in typically resolute Australian fashion. There is no room for free lunches in the Aussie Way.

Particularly commendable was the courage demonstrated by Brad Williams who, (refusing injections, took only a course of paracetamol) gave the Indian batsmen no quarters despite a shoulder injury.

The celebrated Indian batting lineup was pushed to the hilt in achieving the modest target of 230 on the Les Burdett-prepared wicket, which had remained true until the end.

It took the steely nerves of Rahul Dravid—yet again—to navigate the churning of the seas by the never-say-die Australian bowlers in enervating 39° C (103° F) degree heat in the shade.

The amazing Dravid, deservedly named Man of the Match, who scored as many as 305 runs in the match and was undefeated in the second innings, is inviting comparisons with the greats of the game.

After this match, his Test average (56.54; it was 55.89 before today's innings) is in the same league as the legendary Don Bradman (99.94), Herbert Sutcliffe (61), Ken Barrington (59), Walter Hammond (58.5), Adam Gilchrist (58), Jack Hobbs (57), Steve Waugh (51) and Allan Border (50.5).

Given India's notorious record of capitulating under pressure, one wonders what the outcome might have been had Adam Gilchrist not grassed a fairly simple offering by Dravid when the batsman was on nine.

In the end it was Steve Waugh's redoubtable Australians who cracked under pressure, vindicating the point of view that they are awesome only when they are allowed to dominate.

So, on to the third Test in Melbourne on Boxing Day. With fast bowlers Zaheer Khan and Brett Lee both expected to be fit for the fray, the resumption of hostilities between the evenly-matched combatants should be worth going miles to see.

BRIEF SCORES

Australia 556 all out (J Langer 58, R Ponting 242, S Katich 75; A Kumble 5-154, J Gillespie 48*) and 196 all out (S Waugh 42, A Gilchrist 43; A Agarkar 6-41) lost to India 553 all out (V Sehwag 47, R Dravid 233, VVS Laxman 148; A Bichel 4-118) and 233 for 6 (V Sehwag 47, R Dravid 72) by four wickets.

Beaten but not disgraced

***MID-DAY* • December 31, 2003 • Melbourne**

At the end of the fourth day in the third India-Australia Test here, the scenario was similar to the one at the same stage in 1981 when India pulled off a shock 60-run victory after setting Australia a 143-run target.

However, Steve Waugh's resolute world champion team turned the script around yesterday and shattered India's hopes of replicating the miraculous events of Melbourne '81.

The exultant high-fives and prolonged embrace between man-of-the-match Ponting and Matthew Hayden after the winning stroke yesterday reflected the closeness of the contest and the home team's relief at levelling the series for the Border-Gavaskar Trophy.

Matthew Hayden

The manner in which Sourav Ganguly's never-say-die team fought was heart-warming and has earned it lavish praise from fans and the media at large.

Written off before the series as a bunch of no-hopers who would be whitewashed, Ganguly's warriors have made their detractors eat humble pie.

And, despite Sachin Tendulkar's continuing disappointing form, the batting lineup of Virender Sehwag, Akash Chopra, Rahul Dravid, Sourav Ganguly and VVS Laxman has come to be acknowledged, almost universally, as among the most formidable in world cricket today.

Derided by the media as "toff" and "caricature," Ganguly has shown tremendous character while scoring a courageous century at Brisbane and fortitude and resolve in compiling a brave 73 here in the second innings, despite being hit on the helmet in each inning.

The self-effacing manner in which the skipper came out to bat in place of the off-form Tendulkar at the end of the third day has also earned him the respect and admiration of knowledgeable critics here.

In 1980-81, Kapil Dev's heroic five wickets for 28 had turned the tide for India. Needing 143 for victory, Australia were bundled out for a mere 83.

With Kapil Dev not around and with bowling mainstay Zaheer Khan absent because of injury, India's task was cut out due largely to the turnaround which saw the team lose six wickets for just 16 runs in the first innings after being an imposing 286 for two.

In retrospect, the Test was won and lost with India's catastrophic collapse in the first innings. The abysmal repeat performance by the lower order batsmen in the second innings in which the last six wickets fell for a mere 33 struck the proverbial nail in the coffin.

To really make a fight of it on the last day on a wearing wicket, which became the subject of an investigation by ICC match referee Mike Procter, India's lower order batsmen needed to buckle down to the task with grit and determination, which they twice failed to do in the Test.

The manner in which Ajit Agarkar and Ashish Nehra troubled Australia's batsmen yesterday morning upon resumption of play, raised slender hopes of a repeat of 1980-81 especially after Agarkar sent back Justin Langer with a magnificent in-swinging yorker with the score just nine.

The home team's position would have been precarious had umpire David Shepherd not shockingly disallowed a leg-before appeal when Hayden was struck on the pads palpably in line with the middle stump by Nehra, who soon thereafter failed to reach a catchable ballooned chance off Ponting's bat and pad on his follow through.

The overall fiercely determined attitude of the Indian team in this series was epitomised in Dravid's statement to the press at the end of the fourth day.

"There is always hope; that is one of the things we have done well in the series," he said.

"I think a lot of people expected us to come here and fold away and I think we have show everyday we have come back.

"We have had tough days which is expected, but we have come back and fought quite hard, like we did today, and we will do the same tomorrow and we might not win but there is always hope."

Then there was the spunky unbeaten 69-minute knock of 27 by Parthiv Patel in which he manfully stood up to the fury of the Australian pace bowlers who, having scented victory, were breathing fire and brimstone at that stage.

The all-conquering Australians, with their nerve-tingling brand of attacking cricket, have made it a habit of finishing off most of their Test matches inside four days.

But despite injury to key players Ganguly's team has dug deep into its inner reserves. Its admirable chutzpah has enabled it to take all three Tests in this series into the fifth day.

The last time this happened for the Australians was 11 years ago when they went into the last Test against the West Indies at Perth with the series level only to be swamped by the awesome West Indians.

Zaheer Khan is a doubtful starter for the fourth and final Test starting in Sydney on Friday, as is Harbhajan Singh, after surgery to his spinning finger.

The nature of the Sydney wicket would seem to make a strong case for the inclusion of Murali Kartik in the squad, but it remains to be seen if skipper Ganguly will give the gutsy left-arm spinner, who is also a useful bat and brilliant fielder, his deserved opportunity, especially in view of the Australians' lack of experience against bowlers of that genre. Left-arm spinners seem to have become dinosaurs Down Under.

With Jason Gillespie expected to be fully fit for the fray, India will have to play out of their skins at Sydney in all respects if they are to win the first series in this country since the advent of Test cricket between the two countries in 1948.

On the face of it, conventional wisdom dictates that Australia's grit and confidence after the Melbourne victory following the chastening setback in Adelaide, as also India's depleted bowling attack, its substandard, butterfingered fielding and spineless lower order batting will tilt the scales heavily in favour of the home side.

After yesterday's win, Steve Waugh stated that, having retired as captain from one-day cricket on a losing note, he has no intention of doing so from Test cricket.

That said, the fact of the matter is that Ganguly's grossly underrated Team India has been repeatedly turning logic on its head.

BRIEF SCORES:

India 366 all out (A Chopra 48, V Sehwag 195, R Dravid 49) and 286 all out (R Dravid 92, S Ganguly 73, Tendulkar 44; B Williams 4-53) lost to Australia 558 all out (M Hayden 136, R Ponting 257; A Kumble 6-176) and 97 for 1 (M Hayden 53) by nine wickets.

Cometh the hour...

MID-DAY • January 03, 2004 • Sydney

Sachin Tendulkar

Desperately battling loss of form and the disparaging comments of uncharitable critics who have no compunctions about demolishing idols quicker than they install them, Sachin Tendulkar played an innings that had true grit and grim determination as its underpinning.

It did not take the eye of a Don Bradman to know from the very first over that he faced, that the Australians, strengthened by the return of Jason Gillespie were in for a difficult time at the hands of the little master in their battle of attrition.

As a teenager, Tendulkar scored an unbeaten 148 on his maiden appearance at this venue 12 years ago that had critics in raptures. He lived up to his lofty reputation the next time around - in 1999-2000—when he composed a classy 45 even though India lost embarrassingly within three days, to take his tour aggregate to 278 runs which won him the man of the series award.

Tendulkar's innings yesterday, although nowhere near the best of his illustrious career, occupied three hours and 22 minutes at the crease during which he faced 164 balls.

It could only have had the benefit of doing his depressingly low confidence the boost that was long overdue. The opposition could be in for a torrid time in this Test and the one-day series to follow, unless they can devise a strategy to dislodge him early today.

However, on occasions Tendulkar's acknowledged flawless technique did desert him, as when he took a leaf out of the books of team-mates Sourav Ganguly, Virender Sehwag and Akash Chopra, who between them, ducked four times into perceived bouncers in the Melbourne Test.

He, nevertheless, summoned inner reserves of tenacity to resist the fury of a disciplined attack on an awkward drop-in pitch that had a grass cover.

That said, the platform for Dravid and Tedulkar was laid by Virender Sehwag and Akash Chopra, who have been the answer to India's long-time prayer for a reliable opening pair.

Sehwag once again kept his reckless natural aggressive instincts in check, as he had done in Melbourne, but savaged anything short of a good length, as evidenced by his swatted six off Lee to point and his 10 fours that sped to the fence like tracer bullets.

27-year old Delhi opener Chopra showed admirable temperament while negotiating the seam and swing of Brett Lee and Nathan Bracken in the early stages.

But he bore a charmed life when Simon Katich dropped a fairly simple catch at gully when he was on eight, the very next ball after being caught at the wicket off a Lee no-ball.

Chopra was also lucky when a direct throw from Stephen Waugh at mid-off missed the mark. The Australian captain, similarly, gave Sehwag a reprieve in the very next over, when the batsman was on 59.

Nevertheless, Chopra must learn to convert his 30s and 40s into centuries if he is to serve the team to his full potential.

Dravid was class, patience and elegance personified when he resumed from where he had left off in the last two Tests. He fell to Gillespie just when he threatened another big score.

One could not help feeling that Jason Gillespie, who bagged two of the three wickets to fall, sacrificed movement at the altar of speed.

Lee and Bracken exploited the helpful conditions much better comparatively, after Ganguly won the vital toss and boldly decided to bat on a wicket that is expected to help spin in the later stages of the Test.

All in all, it was a good day at the office for the Indian team, one that could lay the foundations on which Anil Kumble and Murali Kartik could make life difficult for the home team's competent batting on a crumbling wicket.

But the unfinished task at hand is the consolidation of the score into a match-winning one. The nerve tingling proceedings of the preceding two Tests have shown to both combatants that putting up a seemingly tall score on day one is not sufficient insurance against defeat.

BRIEF SCORES

India 705 for 7 decl. (A Chopra 45, V Sehwag 72, S Tendulkar 241, VVS Laxman 178, P Patel 62; B Lee 4-201) and 211 for 2 declared (V Sehwag 47, R Dravid 91, S Tendulkar 60) drew with Australia 474 (J Langer 117, M Hayden 67, S Waugh 40, S Katich 125, J Gillespie 47; A Kumble 8-141) and 357 for 6 (J Langer 46, R Ponting 47, D Martyn 40, S Waugh 80, S Katich 77*; A Kumble 4-138).

Run out got Bangar out?

MID-DAY • January 15, 2004 • Hobart

If one were to go by press reports, the Australian media seems to know much more than even the Indian captain about the dropping of Sanjay Bangar from yesterday's one-day match against Zimbabwe in Hobart.

Sanjay Bangar

"Bangar Pays Price For Run-out" shouts one headline.

"Now It's Bangar Run Out Of Team," yells another.

The gist of the stories is that the Railways all-rounder was excluded from the squad because of the mix-up, albeit caused by Bangar's fault, which resulted in the captain being run out.

At that time, Ganguly was in full flight after racing to 82 off 83 balls, and seemingly on course to steer India to victory over Australia.

Twenty-seven-year old Hemang Badani, left-handed Tamil Nadu batsman, left-arm spinner and outstanding fielder was included in the squad yesterday in place of Bangar.

In last Friday's match against Australia, when Bangar tentatively pushed the first ball he faced, Ganguly charged down the wicket only to be sent back by the batsman. The skipper failed to regain his crease as he turned back and was run out by Ian Harvey, the bowler.

One newspaper pontificated after the Indian team for yesterday's match was announced: "The fastest way out of the Indian team—run out the captain."

Another theorised, "Indian all-rounder Sanjay Bangar has learnt the consequences of being involved in a run-out with your captain."

And the captain's comment on Bangar's exclusion? "It did cost us the game but these things happen in cricket."

"It's hard on Sanjay because he's only played in one game, but we didn't bat well in pairs after that and it cost us the game."

Ganguly insisted Bangar's exclusion was also because of a desire to strengthen the team's fielding, which he said was a major factor in the narrow defeat to Australia.

Was the Prince of Kolkata indulging in prevarication? Or does the Aussie press know better?

Cricket, the winner

MID-DAY • January 23, 2004 • Sydney

It was not a finish for the faint-hearted and, on balance, judging from the course of the humdinger of a match at the packed Sydney Cricket Ground yesterday, a tie would have been a fair result.

Ganguly's expression at the finish spoke volumes. He needn't have despaired.

Australia deserved to win, but India didn't deserve to lose. Ultimately, the game of cricket was the victor.

The match had all the ingredients of a thriller: swashbuckling batting by Yuvraj Singh (139) and VVS Laxman (106 not out), followed by a typically torrid innings by Adam Gilchrist (95).

Then, a nail-biting run chase to meet a rain-curtailed target, and a missed stumping chance by Parthiv Patel offered by Michael Clarke before he had scored.

Next, a questionable turning down by umpire Steve Bucknor of a Symonds catch at the wicket off Irfan Pathan, television replays of which proved the umpire wrong.

At 150 for one Australia looked comfortably placed but three quick wickets by Irfan Pathan, followed by Gilchrist's dismissal by Murali Kartik turned the tide in India's favour.

In an inspired move, Sourav Ganguly brought himself on to bowl and swung the game India's way with three wickets for 41 in seven overs, but it was all in vain. The Australians, who had dedicated the match to David Hookes, emerged victorious. However India were far from disgraced.

India's fighting score of 296 for four was largely the result of Yuvraj Singh's audacious knock, which won him a standing ovation, and an unbeaten majestic innings of 106 by VVS Laxman, who continues to be a thorn in the side of the home side.

The target of 297 from 50 overs, reduced to 225 from 34 because of a torrential downpour, was not going to be easy, but Adam Gilchrist's 95 from 72 deliveries made Australia's hard -fought victory possible.

Bowling consistently in the 140/145 km/h region, Lee attained a top speed of 155.2, while returning the impressive analysis of two for 46 off nine overs.

His second was a ball of full length at 145.2 and the third (143.1) had the captain caught at the wicket, to give Gilchrist his 300th dismissal.

Ganguly's old failing of fishing at deliveries outside the off stump, one which has been endemic to Indian batsmen of yore, had been his undoing once again.

The spunky Parthiv Patel is vindicating the faith of his seniors and is developing into an aggressive opening batsman. His cameo of 28 off 33 deliveries contained four lusty hits to the fence.

However, his 'keeping leaves much to be desired. A clinic with former Test wicketkeeper Syed Kirmani, currently chairman of the national selection committee, should help iron out deficiencies in Patel's technique.

Rahul Dravid, who was booed for the ball tampering incident when he came out to bat, (however, a banner in the Swamy Army stand read "Rahul We Know You Are Innocent" and another in the Aussie section stated, "Suck On That, Oh What A Feeling") majestically drove Andy Bichel for three fours off the seven balls he faced, before he fell, caught at the wicket, to give Gilchrist his third catch of the innings.

The swashbuckling 213-run record partnership between VVS Laxman and Yuvraj Singh was refreshing as much for its controlled aggression as for the skilful running between wickets. Its most noteworthy aspect was the manner in which the batsmen kept the ball down while executing their extravagant strokes. On the occasions they decided to loft, they ensured the ball landed in untenanted areas.

The dynamic duo gave the capacity crowd plenty to cheer for the manner in which they dominated the disciplined bowling despite the Australians' brilliant, athletic fielding.

After Simon Katich, thrown in at the deep end at the top of the order after his recall to the one-day side, was consumed by Pathan for just one, Adam Gilchrist went on the rampage, as only he can, and despite rain interruption and revision of target to 225 from 34 overs, set Australia on course for a thrilling victory.

BRIEF SCORES

India 296 for 4 in 50 overs (VVS Laxman 106, Yuvraj Singh 139) lost to Australia 225 for 8 (A Gilchrist 95, R Ponting 42, I Pathan 3-51, S Ganguly 3-41) by two wickets (D/L method)

Why are we so secretive?

MID-DAY* • *January 23, 2004

A few days ago, KHALIDOSCOPE had faulted the Indian team management's secretive ways and its proclivity to provide the media incorrect information and half-truths.

Sourav Ganguly had categorically informed the media after last Tuesday's match against Zimbabwe that Sachin Tendulkar and Virender Sehwag would be fit to play: but both were left out of the playing eleven yesterday because of injury.

Anil Kumble

As clarified by coach John Wright to *Mid-Day*, Anil Kumble was rested, the team management being of the opinion that the veteran bowler deserved a break after fourconsecutive one-dayers.

Left arm spinner Murali Kartik finally got his long-awaited call to the one-day squad.

An unusually large number of tricolours fluttered in the stands as Sourav Ganguly won the toss again and opted to bat, as is his wont.

All eyes were on Brett Lee who, along with the off-form Damien Martyn, was given a last throw of the dice by the selectors.

Coming on to bowl in the enervating 30°C heat after Jason Gillespie had conceded one run in the first over of the match, Lee beat Ganguly outside the off stump with his first delivery timed at 137.5 km/h which was a portend of things to come.

Lee finished with impressive figures of two for 46 which, allied with his match-winning six off Laxmipathy Balaji, should cement his place in the team, at least in the short term.

Unfortunately, the same cannot be said of the stylish Damien Martin. His duck could result in his being sent to state cricket for redemption.

Forget the Perth experience horribilis

MID-DAY* • *February 04, 2004

Since belief and self-confidence are acknowledged essential ingredients in the mental make-up of a champion team, the Perth *experience horribilis* of the Indian team over the past three days should make Australia firm favourites to win the upcoming finals.

Fortunately for India, the Western Australia Cricket Association (WACA) ground at Perth is not a venue for the best of three finals beginning on Friday.

The Odyssey across the Australian continent to Perth was a nightmarish experience which is best forgotten if Sourav Ganguly's Team India are to put the finishing touches to an otherwise memorable tour.

To be fair, India's specialist batsmen, who have earned unanimous encomiums from the cognoscenti, were caught on the wrong foot on the fast wicket, which had a pronounced bounce, reminiscent of the ones in New Zealand that made life a misery for the Indian batsmen last year.

Having made hay on flat, slow wickets on this tour, the sudden exposure to a brutish pitch was more than the otherwise technically correct batsmen could handle.

Apart from the torment which Brett Lee, Jason Gillespie and Brad Williams inflicted in Australia's comprehensive win over India last Sunday, even Zimbabwe's mediocre bowling firm of Streak, Blignaut and Ervine made life difficult yesterday.

Brett Lee

It was sad to see world class players such as Sachin Tendulkar, VVS Laxman, Rahul Dravid and Sourav Ganguly completely at sea, unable to cope with the wicket-assisted hostility of the bowling.

Small wonder, then, that Sourav Ganguly expressed relief that the finals were not being played there, although he welcomed the prospect of testing their mettle on fast surfaces on future tours.

Adam Gilchrist, who captained Australia against India on Sunday, said: "What a delight it was to see the Indian top order finally ducking, weaving and jumping around on a true and fast wicket.

"I'd be quite a few bucks better if I had a dollar for every time someone has asked me why we didn't play India in a Test at the lively venue rather than just the one hit-out against Zimbabwe."

Gilchrist went on to say, "There are no prizes for correctly predicting what conditions we face whenever we head to the subcontinent, whether it be for one-dayers or Test matches.

"Just last November in the TVS Cup, the hosts regularly bowled 30 or more overs of spin in one-day matches on wickets that were dry, dusty and turning plenty. In fact, they even opened the bowling with Virender Sehwag in Mumbai."

Echoing a widely held-belief here, the Australian vice-captain asked, "So why, when the Indians arrive here for a major tour, do we greet them with flat, relatively lifeless wickets that are more in line with what they are used to?

"And why do we get only one crack at them on Australia's fastest pitch?

"Indian skipper Sourav Ganguly told me after the game on Sunday that he almost felt we were in a different country playing in Perth, such was the change in conditions they have become accustomed to so far on this tour."

Gilchrist quoted Ganguly as saying, "You would need a month of practice to get used to it. Thank God we didn't play a Test match here."

The world's leading wicketkeeper-batsman asked, "It does take some getting used to, but isn't that what touring in other countries is all about; testing yourself in conditions unique to that nation?" he asks with devastating logic.

Paying tribute to India's batsmen, whom he describes as "world class", Gilchrist says, "I'm sure the Indian fast bowlers would have loved a few more chances on wickets similar to the WACA Ground."

But he refutes the criticism that Australian curators have prepared wickets to suit their fast bowlers in the past.

"In the time I've played in the Australian side, never have I known administrators, captains or coaches to have even mentioned to individual curators what we would like by way of wickets.

"It just doesn't happen and rightly so. A groundsman should have control of his patch of turf and produce the best pitch possible from the resources available."

Gilchrist's comments do take away a lot of the gloss from India's brilliant batting performances on this trip.

However, for the present, they would do well to dismiss the Perth Experience as an aberration and focus on the stern test ahead in the knowledge that self-belief is half the battle won.

BRIEF SCORES

India 203 all out in 49 overs (Yuvraj Singh 47; B Lee 3-22) lost to Australia 204-5 (A Gilchrist 75, A Symonds 73) by 5 wickets

India lack steel on big occasion

MID-DAY* • *February 09, 2004* • *Sydney

India's abysmal performance in a hopelessly one- sided contest yesterday, in which they were crushed by 208 runs, could not possibly have done their morale much good before the forthcoming tour of Pakistan.

Ricky Ponting

The large number of Indian supporters from back home and abroad in the packed stands were understandably disappointed at the gutless capitulation. A placard displayed by an Australian supporter which proclaimed "We Should Have Played Zimbabwe," aptly summarised the lopsidedness of the two finals.

To be fair, overall India won innumerable friends and admirers for their gallant performances in the closely fought Test and one-day series which, truth to tell, were played in the best traditions of the game.

Unfortunately for them, Australia were mentally and physically stronger, and more ruthlessly - almost fanatically—driven and efficient when push came to shove.

As Australian skipper Ricky Ponting put it at the prize ceremony yesterday, "We showed character in the big games."

Yet again, Sourav Ganguly's India betrayed a lack of steel on the big occasion, as it had done twice against Australia last year - in the finals of the World Cup in Africa and the TVS Cup in Kolkata.

And, Indian captain Sourav Ganguly, while congratulating the opposition and thanking his own players, admitted that his team had played well "except for the last two games."

Although he did not quite spell it out, the captain must have had in mind the Perth Effect, the shell-shock that Australia's pace bowlers (notably Brett Lee) administered to the Indian batsmen on a fast and bouncy wicket at the WACA stadium.

The Perth Experience, which saw a number of Indian batsmen hit on the helmet in the two matches played there (against Australia and Zimbabwe,) patently affected their morale and marked the turning point in their mental make-up as regards confidence and self-belief at the end of a long and mentally draining tour.

Having said that, Australia were deserving winners of the one-day series and also deserve commendation for the manner in which they fought on the last day of the Sydney Test to deny India what would have been a stirring, hard-fought series win.

It was obvious from the outset yesterday that the objective of the Australian batsmen was to upset the rhythm of the depleted Indian attack and bat India's renowned line-up out of the match.

Adam Gilchrist and Matthew Hayden got their side off to the now-customary rousing start against an attack weakened because of the absence of Anil Kumble, who had a relapse of his rotator cuff indisposition, and Ajit Agarkar, who was advised by physiotherapist Andrew Leipus to sit out in order not to aggravate his shin injury.

Barring skipper Ricky Ponting, all the home team batsmen treated the bowling with disdain, with even the off-form Damien Martyn, a controversial inclusion in the side, joining in the fun.

With the placid wicket playing true to character, the Indian attack floundered in the face of the Australian onslaught on a fast outfield, which left it bereft of ideas about matters concerning length and direction in an effort at containment.

The Indian bowlers must have sensed a window of opportunity when Gilchrist and Ponting were back in the pavilion with 73 on the board off 11.2 overs, but world Test record holder Matthew Hayden was determined to see through his pre-match prediction about wrapping up the finals yesterday itself.

Hayden had stated categorically on the eve of the match that he and his team-mates would welcome the extra leisure time before the team's departure to Sri Lanka on Friday, the13th of this month.

Towards that end, Matthew batted majestically while plundering 126 off 122 balls which included 11 fours and three mighty sixes to help steer the score to 359 for five in 50 overs.

The total was identical to Australia's in the final of the last World Cup at the Wanderer's, the difference being that the world champions rattled up the match-winning score there for the loss of just two wickets.

However, at the Wanderers', where they lost by 125 runs, India managed a score of 234, as against the paltry 151 yesterday.

Farewell, Team India!

MID-DAY • March 10, 2004

The blessings and good wishes of millions of Indians go with Sourav Ganguly and his warriors as they embark today on the mother of all Odysseys for the epochal series against Pakistan.

It can be assumed that every member of the side is aware of the awesome history-making potential of the tour in political and diplomatic terms.

Although most players chosen—and their families—have expressed grave reservations in private about the tour they have, nevertheless, bowed to the dictates of the Government and the parent cricket body in the larger interests of country and sport.

They deserve the fullest support of our cricket *deewaney* who will, undoubtedly, follow every psychological gambit, the cut and thrust of the tumultuous battle in what promises to be a humdinger of a series.

Many political commentators, columnists and sports journalists - KHALIDOSCOPE included—have expressed their opposition to the tour for a variety of reasons.

Sourav Ganguly

Arguing that there can be no dispute with the imperatives of peace and friendly relations with Pakistan, indeed with all our neighbours, this column has been of the opinion (Mid Day, February 11) that despite the assurances of both governments, the tour poses a serious security risk for the players.

After all's said and done, it takes just one misguided individual to wreak senseless havoc.

The notoriously inept security set-up across the border hardly inspires much confidence, witness the three recent near-fatal attempts on the life of the Pakistani president. (Former fast bowler Javagal Srinath said as much to this writer in Australia during the last series Down Under).

KHALIDOSCOPE has argued that the tour is premature in terms of the continuing level of Pakistan-inspired terrorism and that the way to go would have been first for bureaucrats, foreign secretaries and ministers of the two countries to create the right climate.

This series betrays political expediency on the eve of the forthcoming Lok Sabha and Assembly elections and is tantamount to putting the cart before the horse.

But all opposition to this tour is now so much water under the bridge.

The series is a fait accompli. What we need to do is hope that both teams will play the game in the highest traditions so that we may enjoy the acknowledged gentleman's game in its true spirit. And may the better team win.

Most of all, let us hope that—win or lose—Sourav Ganguly's Team India brings credit to the country by its performances on the field and demeanour off it and, thereby, wins over the hearts of Pakistani fans, politicians and even those who harbour and promote terrorism.

Mother of all ODIs?

MID-DAY • March 14, 2004

Rahul Dravid

What a fitting rumbustious start Saturday's pulsating encounter between India and Pakistan in Karachi has provided in a historic series that promises heart-stopping excitement all the way!

Touted as a battle royal between India's illustrious batsmen and Pakistan's vaunted bowling attack, the opening stanza saw India's batting line-up live up to expectations in rattling off 349 even as Pakistan's bowlers turned in a shockingly profligate performance.

Pakistan's decision to put India in to bat on a good batting wicket was reminiscent of India's in the final of the World Cup in Johannesburg when Australia's rampaging batsmen put India's pace attack to the sword and virtually wrapped up the match in the first 10 overs.

On a day on which it poured fours and sixes, Sachin Tendulkar and Virender Sehwag got India off to a flyer to provide the platform for Rahul Dravid (wretchedly unlucky to fall at 99), Sourav Ganguly (45) and Mohammad Kaif (46) to mount a potentially match-winning score.

In the process, they were assisted by some rank undisciplined bowling by Shoaib Akhtar and Mohammed Sami who failed to temper raw passion and earnestness with levelheaded application. It reminded one of Brett Lee's misguided fire-breathing zeal in the Melbourne Test last Boxing Day.

The electrifying atmosphere at the start obviously got to the Pakistanis who made a bizarre start, sending down a plethora of wides and no-balls.

Rana dropped a simple catch offered by Sehwag (then on one) and Tendulkar was caught off a no-ball. (In the end, Pakistan's bowlers sent down as many as 10 wides and 20 no-balls).

On the other hand, the Indian openers slashed recklessly, played and missed repeatedly. The Alchemist was obviously hard at work on their behalf.

So, too, seemingly, was opposing skipper Inzamam-ul-Haq who failed to post third and fourth slips while the batsmen cut with impunity in the slip region. Nor did he deem it necessary to counsel his bowlers or offer them any encouragement even as the Indian batsmen cut loose.

Although Tendulkar's performance lacked conviction, Sehwag's was patently a case of fortune favouring the brave.

Ganguly showed a welcome return to form but Dravid and Kaif paced themselves with clinical *savoi-faire*.

Inzamam's classic effort was notable for its imperiousness and re-established his credentials of being among the world's best batsmen.

Pakistan were always in with a chance as long as Inzamam and Yousuf Youhana were at the wicket. Batting with commendable resourcefulness, they treated the India bowling with scant respect to help Pakistan break the world record for a team batting second.

Younis Khan and Abdul Razzaq possessed the requisite mental and technical attributes to swing the game Pakistan's way after Inzamam fell to a tired-looking stroke, but Murali Karthik and Zaheer Khan struck vital blows to take the game into a virtual sudden death stage.

Whereas Inzamam's dismissal marked the turning point in the nail-biter, Kaif's incredible running catch to dismiss Shoaib Malik provided the icing on the cake.

Although the curator's efforts resulted in almost 700 runs being scored on the day to the great delight of one-day aficionados, bowlers of both teams had themselves to blame for their discomfiture.

Coach Javed Miandad's theatrics and attempts at controlling proceedings from the pavilion to fashion a repeat last-ball sixer win for his team were of no avail.

Although on the run of play neither team should have lost, Sourav Ganguly's lads were fully deserving of the appreciative applause from the sellout crowd.

Howsoever narrow, India's win in the first match on tour should give them a massive psychological boost.

But there's a long, long way to go.

BRIEF SCORES:

India 349-7 in 50 overs (V Sehwag 79, R Dravid 99, S Ganguly 45, M Kaif 46; N Rana 3-73) beat Pakistan 348-8 in 50 overs (Inzamam 122, Y Youhana 73, Younis Khan 46; Zaheer Khan 3-66)

Open letter to PM Vajpayee

MID-DAY* • *March 15, 2004

Respected PM Atal Behari Vajpayee Saheb:Having read about your reported congratulatory telephone call to Sourav Ganguly after our team's stirring victory over Pakistan in the first match of the "Goodwill Series" against Pakistan in Karachi last Saturday, I feel constrained to address you:

Atal Behari Vajpayee

Coming, as it did, from an universally acknowledged statesman who, in a manner of speaking, has swum against the tide in his single-minded desire for peace with our neighbours, one cannot but help feel that your call was not only premature, but also ill-advised.

Don't we know all too well that we are an exceedingly emotional people and that overreaction of this kind can cause disastrous consequences? Who can deny that every Indian, worth his salt, would love to see our country win in any - and every - sporting encounter anywhere in the world, Pakistan included.

There can no denying your passion and unwavering goal of good neighbourly relations with Pakistan, which you have pursued with commendable single-minded dedication.

That said, dear PM, your telephone call after only the first match of a four one-day and three Test series, does seem premature.

It suggests that obvious considerations of the "Feel Good Factor" have clouded judgment.

Don't we all wish for Sourav Ganguly's Team India to return home winning every single match in this historic series that would help in your most commendable objective?

However, dear PM, that widely-reported telephone call does not quite fit in with your memorable advice to our brave warriors before they flew across the border—much against their own—and their families' —wishes, as we all know?

Your words : "*Khel hi nahin, dil bhi jeetiye*" to our young cricketers epitoimised all that is fair and noble in international sport, in keeping with the Olympic spirit. They deserve to go down in the vernacular of international sport.

Nevertheless, I, for one, no matter how hard I try, cannot escape the conclusion that your reaction which, although in keeping with our national mood after the match, can only add to the hysteria which previous India-Pak sporting encounters have engendered and which you, above all else, would wish to stamp out.

PM Saheb: May I, as a humble, unabashed lover of Indian glory in any and every sphere, especially in sport, ask you: " Will you congratulate our boys ever time they win on this tour—both in the one-day series and the Tests?

And, what if they lose—since winning and losing is what sport is all about?

Will you congratulate the rival team, should they win in the process of winning hearts, as you so eloquently expressed in Hindi?

May I, also, emphasise that our hockey team has barely managed to qualify for the Athens Olympic Games and that we lost to Pakistan on the very day that all of India's attention was focused on cricket, only cricket—and no thanks to the regionalism and arrogance in our hockey affairs, which starts at the very top with Indian Hockey Federation (IHF) chief honcho K P S Gill.

Dear PM: As sports lovers, we suggest that sport be left alone for its lovers, without injection of politics—within and outside our country.

PCB chief thanks India

MID-DAY • March 22, 2004 • Lahore

Pakistan Cricket Board (PCB) chairman Shaharyar Khan is "pleasantly surprised" at the sporting behaviour of the home crowds in the current series.

PCB chief Shaharyar Khan

"It has really been beyond all expectations," the suave, articulate PCB head honcho told KHALIDOSCOPE yesterday.

Given that the Pakistani fans' behaviour was not particularly sporting on previous Indian tours of this country, how did this transformation come about?

"In the last three months President Pervez Musharraf, the Governors of the various provinces, Information Minister Shaikh Rashid and I have been constantly urging crowds not to be chauvinistic and ultranationalistic.

"We have been dinning in their heads through the media and other means that, after all, we are only playing a game and that it is the crowds' responsibility to ensure that it is played in true traditions of the game and in a sporting spirit that would reflect the true personality of the people of Pakistan.

"And we are surprised and delighted that the fans have taken on the role required of them with such genuineness, spontaneity and, most importantly, a sense of responsibility."

Replying to our question as to whether the series was an idea whose time had come, Shaharyar agreed that the crowd's conduct has demonstrated the Pakistani people's genuine desire to live with India in "peace, goodwill and good neighbourliness".

"On the other hand, your fans also demonstrated these sentiments marvellously in Chennai, Kolkata and Mohali, in particular, where the reception given to our team was fabulous."

Complimenting the Board of Control for Cricket in India (BCCI) for its "positive" approach, Shaharyar said, "BCCI has always been in favour of regular cricketing contacts between the two countries."

And, where do we go from here?

"Both Boards have agreed to play a yearly series. The resumption of cricketing contacts after 14 years has proved that cricket between the two countries is extra-special, it has a different meaning and atmosphere.

"In fact, as far as we are concerned, we were ready to resume cricketing ties with India even when tension between us was high.

"A new climate was created on January 12 this year when Prime Minister Atal Behari Vajpayee met with president Musharraf during the SAARC summit in Islamabad. Let us hope our politicians on both sides will continue to let us play each other.

"Unfortunately, their track record shows that they normally take one step forward and two backwards."

Shaharyar has a message for Mid-Day readers and all Indian cricket fans: "Throughout South Asia, cricket has become an obsession. Its appeal is no longer limited to people from the upper and middle classes.

"The game is a tremendous binding factor between countries. It should be allowed to remain a continuous process in terms of creating ties and PR.

"Enjoyment of the game by the public must remain the commitment of those who administer the game.

"Building of bridges should remain our constant endeavour.

"Thank you, India, for helping us prove that cricket between our two countries makes sense."

Team India fulfils all wishes

MID-DAY • March 25, 2004 • Lahore

"Your wish is our command"

VVS Laxman

This could well be Team India's refrain at the end of the one-day international (ODI) series against Pakistan for fulfilling Prime Minister Atal Behari Vajpayee's desire that they should win both series and hearts on this tour.

Whether or not this victory will help the PM and his party in the forthcoming elections is not the subject of this piece.

Cricket wise, in the end it was India's greater resilience and mental fortitude that enabled them to fight back from a one-match deficit to score the deserving, historic win in the mentally and physically draining series.

Yesterday's stirring victory—the first-ever in this country—at Lahore's Gaddafi Stadium was the result of superb team-work, but to VVS Laxman and Irfan Pathan (the latter was unlucky not to be named man of the match) must go the lion's share of credit for seeing India shine.

Pakistan skipper Inzamam-ul-Haq's decision to put India in to bat was obviously dictated largely by the fact that his team prefers to chase a target.

To that extent, it suited India just fine, thank you, given their oft-demonstrated preference to bat first, put up a match-winning total and either bowl out the opposition or restrict their score to less than their own.

Another reason could have been the Dew Factor. In the previous match here on Sunday, the late evening dew was not to the liking of the Pakistani pace bowlers, who found the moist ball difficult to grip.

Be that as it may, trenchant criticism by Imran Khan and others levelled against the home side's vaunted pace attack for its indiscipline in bowling an unconscionable number of wides and no-balls seemingly had the desired effect.

Imran had gone to the extent of suggesting that a bowling coach be appointed to cure what appeared to be a galloping cancer. Shoaib Akhtar, who likes to live only by his own rules and those of physical trainer and mentor Tauseef Razzaq, told me in no uncertain terms on the night before the match that he had taken offence at the proposal.

Nevertheless, the upshot was that Akhtar and Shabbir Ahmed, prime culprits in this respect, bowled with extreme caution, in the process sacrificing speed in favour of legitimate deliveries.

For once, the Pakistan miscellaneous column read just 16 (2 b, 4 lb, 5w, 5 nb), which was a dramatic improvement from the earlier extras average of 30-plus.

The proceedings got off to a sedate start in the manner of sparring pugilists:

Pakistan's fast men gently eased into their rhythm and India's opening pair of Sachin Tendulkar and Virender Sehwag eschewed unnecessary risk.

Sehwag's exit was the result of a failure to get in line to an incoming Shabbir delivery. On the other hand, Tendulkar, who was showing encouraging evidence of quickness of eye and sharpness of reflexes, succumbed to what is becoming an Achilles' heel - a failure to get his front foot across far enough.

Sourav Ganguly's palpable annoyance with himself upon getting out, caught at the wicket off Shoaib, after he and Man of the Match VVS Laxman had put on 92 off 111 balls, was understandable, given the fact that he was middling the ball unfailingly and timing his strokes mellifluously.

Before the start of this match, Ganguly and VVS Laxman were the only Indian top-order batsmen not to score a 50 in the series. With the Hyderabad stalwart notching his sixth ODI hundred yesterday, the captain remains the only specialist batsman in the side to have missed out on a half-century.

With Pakistan President Pervez Musharraf witnessing proceedings, the run-rate, which had been constant at a promising 5-plus until Yuvraj Singh fell at 227 in the 43rd over, was given a late kick restart thanks to the wondrous wristy stroke-play of Laxman, the fleet-footedness of Mohammed Kaif and the swashbuckling abandon of Laxmipathy Balaji, the last-named hitting a cavalier six off Shoaib and breaking his bat in repeating the stroke.

'Ballaji' would be an apt surname for Laxmipathy, given the 23-year old Tamil Nadu youngster's belligerence with the balla (bat). He has an aggressive streak which his introvert personality belies and which is in refreshing contrast to Indian tail-enders of recent vintage.

Balaji has won the hearts of cricket fans in this series with his lusty hitting, which has fetched him scores of 14 (off 10 balls), 21 (off 12) and 10 (off six) at the 'death' in the three matches in which he has batted.

With India scoring 293—identical to Pakistan's total in the previous ODI here last Sunday, which India overhauled to win—the question on everyone's lips was whether history would repeat itself.

Three lethal blows in rat-a-tat succession by Iran Pathan after Balaji sent back the in-form Astir Hammed for two, consigned Pakistan to the ropes.

And, when Inzamam was consumed by Karthik, caught by Tendulkar inches inside the long-on "skirting", Pakistan were looking down the barrel.

Shoaib Malik and Moin Khan's gallant fight-back, while setting a new Pakistan record partnership of 99 for the seventh wicket enabled the home side to cause jitters among some

Indian fielders, who were disturbed by the legion of moths on the field and the moist ball that made both bowling and fielding a nightmare.

Moin had a lucky reprieve when Sehwag struck him on the pads but umpire David Shepherd could not adjudicate since his view was blocked by the bowler on his follow-through. Television replays showed the ball would have struck the stumps.

Pakistan needed 99 from 55 balls when Shoaib Malik perished caught by the reliable Mohammed Kaif, who has taken exceptionally good catches in the series, off Sehwag.

Moin strove valiantly and was engaged in a 52-run partnership with Mohammed Sami but it was too little too late.

The Indians kept their nerve. Inspired wicket-to-wicket bowling by Zaheer and Balaji made sure of victory, which was greeted by fireworks organized by the authorities.

But the bowling hero for the Indian team was 19-year- old Irfan Pathan, who bowled magnificently to scalp Yousuf Yohanna, Taufiq Umar and Younis Khan to break the back of the Pakistan batting. He finished with three for just 32 in 10 overs.

'Friendship series' mere political charade

MID-DAY* • *April 19, 2004

Now that the dust has settled on Team India's historic achievements across the border, one can attempt an assessment of the positives of the epochal Friendship Series realistically and dispassionately.

In my view, rushing to knee-jerk conclusions on the basis of superficial parameters can lead only to erroneous, illogical conclusions.

To begin with, it is important to scrupulously differentiate achievements on the cricket field from political ones.

There is no gainsaying the fact that the heartwarming series victories in the one-day and Test series were truly well-deserved and have done a world of good to our peoples' self-esteem.

But, without meaning to sound churlish, it must be conceded that the present Pakistan side is perhaps the weakest in its illustrious history that has thrown up some great, even legendary, cricketers.

Moreover, there has never been any doubt about the genuine desire on the part of the common man (as distinct from politicians) on both sides of the border for peace and good neighbourliness.

Sportsmen and media persons like yours truly—who have visited Pakistan over the years—have always found nothing but warmth and cordiality, oftentimes seemingly exaggerated, but nevertheless sincere, among people across the border.

That being the case, reports in the Indian media emanating from Pakistan about the overwhelming gestures of friendship shown by the average Pakistani towards fans who went across to watch the cricket is nothing new.

The Friendship Series did not bring it about between people. The common man on both sides understands friendship only too well, despite the machinations of politicians.

The desire for peace and friendship has always been there, albeit latent, for want of sporting contact between the two countries, thanks to the propaganda games indulged in by politicians and bellicose chauvinists.

The resumption of cricketing ties after 14 long years was undeniably long overdue.

Thanks to our political masters' munificence, the Friendship Series has helped the Pakistan Cricket Board (PCB) make a neat profit of a reported US $20 million from the series and will encourage other cricket playing countries to tour that country, that has been considered unsafe after its notorious law and order problems, notably in Karachi and Peshawar.

But the fact of the matter is that cricketing relations should never have been snapped by politicians in the first place.

Therefore, by facilitating, nay steamrolling, the cricket series they have done no great favour to cricket lovers.

The Indian players and their families were strongly opposed to the series for reasons of security. They also resented the arm-twisting by the Indian government and cricket Board, who were both perceived as indulging in political expediency of the cheapest kind.

Fortunately, the matches were played *sans* incident and in exemplary spirit of sportsmanship concerning players and spectators alike.

The fact that their defeat has not gone down well in the higher echelons of Pakistan cricket and governance is none of our concern.

What does matter is the political fallout of the Friendship Series in Musharraf-land.

Amidst all the bonhomie and exaggerated posturing of friendship during the tour, Musharraf has thought nothing of blowing hot and cold on the political front, even threatening dire consequences if a solution to the vexed Kashmir problem is not found expeditiously.

In simple, if not simplistic terms, India's heady success on the field of play hardly guarantees any improvement on the political front.

I, for one, will be convinced that the Friendship Series has been a success in its avowed objectives only when, among other things, tangible progress on the Kashmir issue is made, when the awesome potential for trade between the two countries is adequately tapped and when people from either side are allowed to cross the border freely.

Until then, for me the Friendship Series will remain a charade, mere window-dressing for our political and military masters.

Feel Good Factor? Sure, I feel great!

But only because of the cricketing aspects.

England sport thru English eyes!

MID-DAY* • *June 30, 2004

Michael Vaughan

Call me biased if you like.

But, before rushing to judgment, pause awhile—and, carefully, consider the factual evidence:

To start with cricket, crazy cricket: Yesterday, England's cock-a-hoop team, captained by the can-do-no-wrong Michael Vaughan, were hammered by seven wickets by New Zealand in the triangular cricket series.

That too, woe betide, after England's high-and-mighty cricket team had been "shockingly" humbled in the tournament by the eccentric West Indians, described, hitherto, by the English media as "living on a different planet".

For a number of years now, KHALIDOSCOPE has been expressing good-natured amusement at the infinite capacity of the English media for deluding their ardent sports fans into believing that they will scale Olympian heights – at every international event.

My own so-called 'bias' apart, for many of my fair-minded Englishmen friends (as a race, they are second to none in self-deprecating humour), who take their country's sporting accomplishments with a pinch of salt, English sport is a bit of a joke.

In this context, a comment by London Times columnist Mary Ann Sieghart may interest readers.

"Tim Henman and the England football team are spookily similar," Sieghart writes in a recent article (June 24).

"Each time they get through to the last eight or four, with some incredibly hairy moments on the way - such as Henman almost being beaten in the first round by a novice who had barely played on a grass court before.

"And each time they lose.

"On the way, the country manages to work itself into the most absurd emotional contortions. The anticipation of ultimate victory is as overblown as the crushing disappointment when it fails to materialise.

"Wouldn't it be easier if we simply chanted the following mantra each morning? 'English players don't win Wimbledon. English football teams don't win the championships."

Intimidation or legitimate?

SPORTSWEEK* • *May 2, 1976

The question on the lips of even those remotely concerned with the game of cricket is: did the bowling of Michael Holding, the toast of the Caribbean, in the final Test about which Bishan Bedi has said "it was not so much a match as a war," amount to intimidation?

Mike Holding

To answer the question fairly and correctly it is necessary to examine Law 46 which states; "The persistent bowling of fast, short-pitched balls at the batsman is unfair if, in the opinion of an umpire at the bowler's end, it constitutes a systematic attempt at intimidation. In such an event if it continues, the bowler's end umpire must first caution the bowler, then inform the fielding captain and the other umpire and if it continues, call dead ball, instruct the captain to take the bowler off, the bowler being not able to bowl again in the innings," If we are to accept Lloyd's version, the Indian batsmen were themselves to be blamed for injuries insofar as they were frightened and technically not equipped to face the thunderbolts of local hero Holding who should now rank among the fastest in the world.

This point of view is supported by John Arlott who says, "Indeed, by the standard of modern Test cricket they (the West Indians) have been temperate in not employing that weapon (bouncers) to any great extent until now."

Says he, "The persistent use of the bouncer is virtually confined to Test cricket where careers are made and broken, publicity, standing and high income created. Indian batsmen of the modern period are invariably at a disadvantage against high pace because none exists in their domestic cricket and they encounter it only in other countries at Test level."

But Arlott also feels that the alternative is to prepare pitches of such pace, life or sympathy to spin that bowlers could beat batsmen by the traditional skill and, therefore, did not need to resort to intimidation.

On the other hand we have the opinions of Tony Cozier and the cricket correspondent of the *Jamaica Daily Gleaner*, both of whom maintain that Holding overused the bouncer, at times upto four times in an over. They maintain that umpire Gosein at Holding's end would have been justified in cautioning Holding on this score.

The subject of intimidatory bowling has been a vexed one for quite some time now. The problem stems from the vague definition of a bouncer vis-a-vis a fast short-pitched delivery, when a bouncer, a fast bowler's legitimate weapon may be termed intimidatory bowling and the vast discretionary powers which vest in the umpires in the matter of interpretation. But while the arbiters, and lawmakers at cricket's headquarters have been seemingly more concerned with the semantics of the problem, a young cricketer (Martin Bedkober) has lost his life in Australia and another, Ewan Chatfield, of New Zealand came close to losing his, as did our own Nari Contractor in the West Indies in 1962.

In our opinion the essence of intimidation is danger to life and limb. Chauvinism and fierce nationalistic pride put a premium on winning at all cost but intimidation should be viewed in relation to the ability of the batsman to handle bouncers safely. This is precisely why, traditionally, bouncers have been frowned upon when bowled at tailenders.

We submit, therefore, that ridge or no ridge (Bedi denies there was one) the 90 m.p.h, potentially lethal and persistent bouncers of Holding, delivered with a high arm action, around the wicket, were intimidatory to the technically ill-equipped Indian batsmen, who are slow to get in line or move away from the ball, although, they may not have been so against the Australians or even West Indian batsmen who have the requisite technical ability to face bouncers.

Holding can hardly be blamed for the shortcomings of the Indian batsmen but then surely human life is more precious than the winning of a cricket Test by any means.

It's hardly our intention to squeal, over our defeat but the facts, as reported by our correspondents must be viewed in proper perspective. It is during situations of the type that obtained at Sabina Park that the arguments of the advocates of neutral umpires even for a 'gentleman's game' which cricket is supposed to be, gain added weight.

Board President Ram Prakash Mehra has eloquently denounced the 'atom bombs' and 'nuclear-weapons' employed by the West Indies. It is significant that these were resorted to when the match seemed to be slipping out of the hands of Lloyd who was already under great pressure after West Indies' unexpected reversal at Port of Spain.

Having reportedly prepared an extra fast track on a side strip and having packed the side with four pace bowlers, the events which took place with India in the driver's seat at 191 for one were hardly surprising. Can we expect the Board president to take up the sorry episode as vehemently and eloquently with the International Cricket Conference when it meets at Lord's in a few months from now?

And more importantly, will the Cricket Board at last wake up and do something in the matter of producing effective pace bowlers of our own not only for their own sake but also to provide invaluable practice to our batsmen—a plea which finds more detailed expression in the latest issue of SPORTSWEEK's World of Cricket.

Bedi's much-debated decision to 'declare' or 'close' the second innings notwithstanding, our lads have emerged with much credit from the arduous twin tours. The future of Indian cricket appears bright once again. So rally round, ye cricket aficionados and roll out the red carpet for your heroes. Bedi and his gallant lads return home from the fray bruised and confused but strong in spirit. They have done India proud.

"African sportsmen want dialogue and understanding with white sportsmen," says Schume. They realise that white sportsmen would like to see an end of all racial barriers in sport. But they realise, too, that both black and white sportsmen are faced with a rigid Government policy. Also, the fact that traditions die hard obviates overnight changes in the South African sports situation as far as the white electorate (which makes the laws) is concerned.

"African sportsmen," according to Sehume, "state that affiliation to white sporting organisations fosters good relations and creates an atmosphere of co-operation, which can only lead to progress for black sportsmen coupled with the vital financial assistance necessary for existence."

Food for thought, this, for the "hawks" in our sport.

Windies deservedly win an absorbing series

SPORTSWEEK • February 02, 1975

The deserving side has won. A most absorbing series has ended. As the popular band of talented cricketers from the Caribbean leave our shores, we bid them a fond farewell. And we're sure we echo the sentiments of millions of cricket lovers in this country when we say "It's been great having you here. We shall miss you".

Clive Lloyd

In the ultimate analysis, the visitors had an edge over us in all departments of the game except spin. In the matter of fitness the West Indians were head and shoulders above our team. Most importantly, they brought to bear on their performances at Bangalore, Delhi and Bombay a thoroughly professional approach.

On balance, the nature of the Wankhede Stadium wicket, (about which so much rubbish was spouted), the spin of the coin, Bedi's indisposition on the first day and the atrocious Indian fielding determined the outcome of the final Test. One is tempted to conjecture as to what the result might have been, had India won the toss for the fifth consecutive time and accepted the catches that came her way.

That there is no substitute for class, was amply demonstrated by Lance Gibbs in the first innings and Vanburn Holder in the second innings, both of whom turned in superb bowling performances on an unhelpful wicket which remained chock full of runs until the very end and which made a laughingstock of the so-called 'experts'.

While it is no doubt true that our pathetic catching aided the West Indian batsmen, there can be no denying the fact that Lloyd, Fredericks, Kallicharran and Murray cashed in on their chances in thoroughly professional style.

From India's point of view, the series has thrown up two talented cricketers namely Gaekwad and Ghavri, but the former will have to learn that it is not much use scoring runs and gifting them away in the field and, more importantly, flooring catches which prove expensive.

The return to form of 'Mr. Reliable' Solkar was long overdue. Gavaskar was greatly missed in the series.

He demonstrated all the qualities of a good captain: shrewdness, sound strategy, an understanding of the strengths and weaknesses of the opposition, an intelligent deployment of the resources at hand and the capacity to inspire his team to play positively, to fight back from a losing situation against tough professional opposition. Most of all he set a fine example with his batting. His innings at Lord's was a true captain's knock and one learns he played an innings of real beauty at the Oval.

We are grateful

SPORTSWEEK CRICKET QUARTERLY

Our worst fears were confirmed when the charity match planned by SPORTSWEEK, in conjunction with the ROTARY CLUB OF BOMBAY MID-TOWN, did not come off last March.

We should like to place on record our sincere appreciation of the spontaneous response to our request for participation, by Barry Richards, Mike Procter, Younis Ahmed, Anura Tennekoon and David Heyn, all of whom agreed to play in the proposed match for the Prime Minister's Relief Fund *gratis* (barring actuals).

We are particularly grateful to Richards and Procter who went to the extent of offering to forego participation in a single-wicket tournament in South Africa, from which they stood to gain considerably financially.

We are also indebted to the Sri Lanka Cricket Board for agreeing to release Tennekoon and Heyn in the midst of the Sri Lanka team's tour of Pakistan, as also to the Pakistan Board for altering the itinerary of this tour to enable the Sri Lankan players to participate.

Barry Richards

By agreeing to raise funds for a humane cause, these cricketers demonstrated unequivocally that sport knows no barriers, that it can indeed build bridges between people, surmount all manner of artificial man-made differences. We salute them.

Hard-liners on the apartheid issue who advocate South Africa's isolation from international sport until such time as she plays non-racial sport at club level have an antagonist in Leslie Sehume, Sports Editor of the South African newspaper "The World".

According to Sehume, a black South African, "the majority of the 16 million blacks of African descent (who are almost three times as many as all other races put together) in my country are disillusioned and disenchanted with those overseas countries which have maintained vigorous campaigns to keep South Africa out of international sport."

Asks Sehume in an article in "Sportsword", "Who are these sworn enemies of South Africa trying to help? Certainly not black South African sportsmen . . . now we know that it is not only white South Africa which has become the polecat of the world. We, too, come into the unpleasant category. . .

Africans in South Africa are not racists, according to Sehume, who maintains that the agencies recognised abroad as representative of African sport in the Republic do not represent the present feelings of African sportsmen in the land of the Veldt.

I maintain it was team spirit in England MORE THAN IN THE WEST INDIES which brought us victory. Look at the records and you will find that it was only a few who performed with any degree of consistency in the West Indies.

In fact most of the burden of our batting in the Windies had to be borne by Sardesai, Gavaskar and Solkar while the brunt of the bowling fell on the able shoulders of Bedi, Prasanna and Venkatraghavan. That was indeed a case of so many owing so much to so few.

In the series against England, on the other hand, there were NO tall scores, in fact not a single century from our batsmen, OR a really stand-out performance with the ball, with the exception of Chandrasekhar's deadly spell at the Oval.

This I maintain was team spirit.

One wonders why the people who parrot-like repeated the expression 'team spirit' in the context of our victory over the West Indies are today fighting shy of using it.

Ajit Wadekar's 100% series win record is indeed enviable by any standard. To have welded his unit into a cohesive fighting, one that could humble the redoubtable West Indies and England for the first time in their own countries in the short space of seven months is a staggering achievement, one which will take a lot of beating.

Most importantly, under Wadekar's leadership our players have demonstrated an admirable capacity to fight back when the chips were down as at that historic Oval Test.

No more, thank heavens, the sorry spectacle of throwing in the towel when the pressure was on.

FIGHTING CRICKET

Our victory in the last Test is a glorious example of fighting cricket. The manner in which our team struck back after being in arrears in the first innings and in the closing stages of the match blunted the stratagem of Illingworth, that master tactician, was proof of an abundance of guts and spine in our players.

Ajit Wadekar

Right through the series our boys have demonstrated a positive attitude, the will to win.

It is perhaps a tribute to the influence of Col. Adhikari that with the exception of the second Test when the chips were really down and we had no option but to try and play out time, our team always played for a win.

It was refreshing to see our batsmen, in most cases, stand up to the bouncers of the fiery English pace attack courageously, and without flinching, hook them to the boundary.

Yes that is how cricket should be played. And it was this positive approach which helped decide the fate of the series to a very large extent.

For it instilled in our batsmen the confidence that they could knock the much-feared English pace attack at will if they set their minds to it and at the same time also made it crystal clear to the opposition that our team really means business.

This coupled with the manner in which our spinners had awed the English batsmen in the first innings as in the earlier part of the tour against the counties, went a long way towards rattling the confidence of the England team.

PSYCHOLOGICAL ADVANTAGE

For as we all know, a psychological advantage of this kind can play a big part in swinging a series either way when the teams are more or less evenly matched.

I really must make a mention of the tremendous goodwill that our team has created wherever it has played. Other problems apart, the players have at all times conducted themselves with decorum.

Not once have they been guilty, as far as I know, of any unsportsmanlike behaviour.

The umpires' decisions, no matter how unpalatable, have always been accepted with good grace. There have been no tantrums or display of emotion on the field of play.

And the manner in which our team and Col. Adhikari, in particular, conducted themselves in that unfortunate "shoulder charge" episode has won for them, I am happy to say, tremendous respect and esteem all over England.

Col. Adhikari

Could we have won the first Test if rain hadn't intervened. "Yes, we could have, but I don't think we would have"

It was a matter of so near yet so far. And one must admit some of our senior batsmen let the side down by throwing caution to the winds in their quest for quick runs.

A MASTER STROKE

The promotion of Farokh Engineer in the batting order at that juncture was truly a master stroke. And the decision to go for quick runs deserves commendation, but one could not help feeling that some of our senior batsmen were somewhat irresponsible in the execution of the plan.

The ultimate result of the first Test was a just one. For on the run of play both teams had deserved to win.

It is said that in the second Test we were lucky in that bad captaincy of England was to some extent responsible for our finishing second best.

In my humble opinion, one has to reorient ones definition of "luck" in the English context, what is generally termed luck by our standards is an integral part of cricket in England due to the weather and the consequent conditions that obtain there.

Ajit Wadekar's performance as captain in the two Tests that I witnessed was of an exceptionally high order on the whole.

Gavaskar unhappy

***SPORTSWEEK* • February 01, 1981**

Indian captain Sunil Gavaskar is most dissatisfied with the umpiring in the second India-Australia Test which ended in a nerve-wracking draw at the Adelaide Oval on Tuesday.

Sunil Gavaskar

He told SPORTSWEEK after the match that he had expressed his feelings to Mel Griffin, the chairman of the umpiring sub-committee of the Australian Cricket Board, but clarified that no official protest had been lodged.

Gavaskar did not lambast South Australia's Tony Crafter and Victoria's Rex Whitehead, who umpired the Adelaide Test in so many words, but said the Indian captain at a press conference on Tuesday, "When cricketers from all over the world come to India and say things about our umpiring, all I can say is that they are moaners and grumblers".

The Australian journalists were amused at Gavaskar's choice of expletives but seemed to take it in their stride.

"I've said it before and I'll say it again", continued Gavaskar, "Australian umpiring is as good as Indian umpiring", but he would not give his opinion of the standard of Indian umpiring.

Australian captain Greg Chappell did not, however, agree with Gavaskar's assessment. "They're welcome to their opinion," said he "There were a few mistakes," said he. "I do not know of any Test in which there are not some debatable decisions. You have to expect the mistakes and the batsmen to be given the benefit of the doubt—as they were given."

Gavaskar told SPORTSWEEK, "It's a good feeling to go to Melbourne with a chance to square the series. India would put up an improved performance on the slow Melbourne wicket which assists spin bowling and fight back strongly."

Gavaskar told newsmen that India deserved to draw the Test.

Question: Does that mean that Australia did not deserve to win?

Gavaskar: Yes.

Question: Were there anxious moments in the Indian dressing room?

Gavaskar: Naturally.

Question: Doshi didn't look nervoūs after his brilliant cover drive in the first innings?

Gavaskar (Smilingly): He may not have been but we were.

Question: Any comments on the Indian batting?

Gavaskar: Our specialist batsmen—and that includes me—let the situation get out of hand. They succumbed to the pressure after Chetan and I had got out before lunch. Our senior batsmen—Vishy, Dilip and I have been struggling for runs and this has imposed a great burden on the lower order. In fact it was they who saved this match for us. What we are lacking in is application.

Question: Have your early dismissals been responsible for your batting collapses?

Gavaskar: Not really. There have been many occasions in the past when I have got out early but the other batsmen have carried the team.

Question: How do you feel now about your decision to put Australia in to bat after winning the toss?

Gavaskar: As I've said before it was a team decision. The feeling was that it would be better to have to chase 450-runs plus. We expected Australia to get at least that many on this wicket—than to be 80 for 5 as we were at Sydney and then have to fight back. Besides we didn't want to give Australia the advantage of bowling first on a fresh wicket.

Question: Faced with a similar situation would you take a similar decision.

Gavaskar: You bet.

Australian skipper Greg Chappell told pressmen he was not disappointed with the result when you take into account the nature of this wicket and the weather. Chappell stated that Hogg was tired after his first innings stint so he gave Lennie Pascoe a go because he had a disappointing first innings and he bowled magnificently to put Australia in sight of victory by sending back the first three Indian batsmen.

The Aussie skipper was all praise for Dennis Lillee whom he described as the only bowler in his team who can cut the ball. He added that Dennis was a tremendous team man with a lot of personal and team pride.

Yashpal and Vengsarkar told SPORTSWEEK that they were most dissatisfied with the decisions responsible for their dismissals. Yashpal thought the ball from Yardley which he missed while playing forward would have gone outside the leg stump.

Vengsarkar said it was the first time that he had been given out wrongly. "The ball that Chappell caught clearly went off my boot as everybody saw on the television replay. And the ball to which I was out leg before in the first innings—from Liliee—would have gone over the stumps. It struck me high on the thigh."

Be that as it may, the Indians lived to fight another day and the organisers are assured of sizeable gate-money at the Melbourne Test commencing on February 7. The Melbourne fans are the most enthusiastic supporters of traditional cricket in all Australia.

The Benson and Hedges award of Rs. 10,000 (approximately.)—this writer was one of the judges—went to Kim Hughes who on Tuesday failed in his bid to enter the hall of greats of those who have scored a double century and a century in a Test.

"I haven't come across one touring team which was happy with the Australian umpires and the Australian players, approach to them," Bedi added.

"But I am not squealing. I am not saying this because we are in a mess at the moment.",

Bedi said he was not complaining as much about the Australian players as the Australian umpires.

"The umpires haven't been terribly competent in this game. And they're the best we have had so far in Australia. We came into this Test happy with anyone they gave us. We left the selection to the good judgment of the Australian Board.

"Other umpires on this tour have committed a lot more blunders., We've had the rough side of it—and not only in this Test."

The opinions of Bedi's teammates and Indian correspondents covering this tour are similar to those of Bedi. Australian umpires are known to invariably give the batsmen the benefit of the doubt for appeals for leg before when the batsman has played off the front foot. But it does appear as though right through the series starting from the Brisbane Test, Australian players, particularly Simpson, have benefited more by comparison from doubtful decisions

Bedi was right when he stated he was not squealing. The feelings of the Indian players' about what they consider "incompetent" if not "unfair" umpiring has been pent up for a long time and Bedi was merely giving vent to his and his teammates' emotions.

The timing of the complaint is unfortunate and may give the impression of being in bad taste or of poor sportsmanship.

But facts are incontrovertible and they have been corroborated by other visiting teams to this country. Rohan Kanhai, who is presently in Australia, and former Pakistan captain Mushtaq Mohammad too have been very bitter in their criticism of the standard of Australian umpiring.

India, Pak to sponsor World Cup?

MID-DAY • February 18, 1980

A World Cup, jointly sponsored by the cricket boards of India and Pakistan, is among the proposals informally proposed by Pakistan as part of a move to strengthen sporting relations between the two countries.

MID-DAY understands from reliable sources that Air Marshal (Retd.) Nur Khan who recently took over as president of the Board of Control for Cricket in Pakistan (BCCP) is keen on "reaching out" to India with the objective of breaking barriers and building bridges between the people of the two countries.

He is of the opinion that more frequent sporting encounters between India and Pakistan are "absolutely essential" to raise the overall standard of sport in the two countries.

It will be recalled Nur Khan offered India the use of Karachi's astro-turf stadium for preparation for the Moscow Olympics.

Eminent cricket commentator Omar Qureishi, who is director of operations, Pakistan International Airways, and former Test spinner Haseeb Ahsan were in Bombay over the weekend for exploratory talks with Indian sports officials and are understood to have sent out feelers to cricket officials for closer sporting ties between the two countries and the response is said to have been "encouraging".

They also met government officials, office-bearers of the Indian Olympic Association; organising committee members of the next hockey World Cup scheduled to be held in Bombay in 1982 and officials of the Indian universities and railways sports control boards.

The proposal for the hosting of the cricket World Cup is still in the embryonic stage. It envisages cosponsorship by India and Pakistan with Bombay and Karachi as venues.

Other avenues suggested by Pakistan are regular exchange of club, school and college teams.

It is futile to argue that the outcome of the series would have been any different. It is also arguable as to whether India could have reduced the margin of defeat had she adopted bold, aggressive methods, gone for runs at the end of the fourth day of the Bombay Test and declared after about an hour's batting on the fifth morning when the tourists' over-rate fell to a pathetic 11 in the first hour. It would not be incorrect to state that the tourists' bowling and scoring rates were largely responsible for making the series such a huge Y-A-W-N.

If the attempts of the British journalists touring with the team at defending and denying, playing down the Vaseline episode were laughable in the extreme, the partial, prejudiced reporting of some of them (at least one of them reported through 'instinct' and 'rumour') was highly unethical and, therefore, contemptible. So were the constant appeals, indecent, vulgar gestures and 'chatting up' tactics of Tony Greig which hardly brought honour to the cap he was wearing.

The British press was quick to rush to print and damn 'Sunny' Gavaskar for running down the Wankhede Stadium wicket, totally forgetting the fact that Lever and Greig had done likewise right through the series and for which Lever was warned.

Willis broke the stumps in protest against a leg-before decision. Greig stamped on the ball to supposedly bring it back to shape after an appeal to the umpires on the crucial last day of the Bombay Test was turned down.

Vice-captain Brearley waved his bat in anger at the crowd when given out caught in the second innings of the last Test and Randall whose boorish antics and juvenile attempt at humour wouldn't amuse even his own six year old son if he had one, made it a point of stressing to the press, as he returned to the pavilion in Bangalore, the fact that he had been given wrongly out.

In his attempts at raising cheap laughs, Randall thought nothing of bodily lifting up a Test umpire, of grabbing a constable's cap to don it on his own head. People in India respect their police and umpires. Would this clown ever dream of doing the same to a London bobby or to umpire Frank Chester? Or any other English umpire for that matter.

We salute England on her victory. But for many cricket-lovers here, the regard for the country which taught the world a gentleman's game called cricket, has diminished. considerably. In this fiercely competitive age, many hallowed traditions have gone by the board, as has the precept that "winning is not the important thing". But, need it be the ONLY thing?

And, what of the gentlemen of the British press? Should reporting be based on 'instincts' and 'rumours'? What of the venerable member of the Fourth Estate who publicly rebuked and insulted a hapless Bombay photographer whose only 'sin' was to request payment from a foreign correspondent for a long-overdue four-year old bill for camera repairs? What of the insolent scorer who kept gate-crashing into press boxes, demanding the best seats, picking up arguments with Indian journalists, making an absolute nuisance of himself? This worthy had his comeuppance in the Garware Pavilion of the Wankhede Stadium when he was reprimanded for walking on seat cushions and, made to clean the cushions in full public view.

Traditional Indian hospitality is well-known. Visitors to this land are always considered 'honoured' guests. But, as Mr. S. K. Wankhede stated at a function organised by the Bangalore Sports Journalists Association, Indian hospitality should not be mistaken for weakness.

Bedi blasts the umpires

SPORTSWEEK • February 05, 1978

India's captain Bishan Singh Bedi blasted Australian umpires at the end of the third day of the final Test at the Adelaide Oval.

Bishan Singh Bedi

"India has had the rough edge of umpiring decisions," he said.

He also accused umpires Max O'Connell of Adelaide and Dick French of Sydney of being "not very competent."

"Toohey was out caught behind. Simpson was lbw, both to me, but that's not important," Bedi said.

Both appeals were turned down by O'Connell who also had declared Amarnath (Ghavri was given out by French) out to a controversial catch in India's first innings when he gave French the all-clear from square-leg although he was unsighted by Cosier who held the catch.

"The scene with Simpson in the last over of the day was not about that however. Wicket-keepter Kirmani wasn't ready. It was my fault."

Simpson explained that "there was a lot of noise coming from Vengsarkar fielding close at point." (Vengsarkar later said he was drawing the attention of Kirmani, who was not ready, to the fact that Bedi was coming in to bowl).

"Vengsarkar obviously was shouting at the wicket-keeper, so I pulled away."

Bedi said Simpson and some of the Indian players had exchanged words. "I just wanted to cool everyone down. No one wanted to get excited," Bedi said. "It should have been the one day there shouldn't have been any fuss over.

"A lot of unpleasantness can be avoided in such cases. But we didn't start it. We couldn't help it.

"It was a terrible pity it happened after having gone through such a tour. We don't swear on the field but how can you hide your emotions? We are human after all.

"Australia play hard and we accept that. We play hard ourselves but we play fair," he said.

Bedi said Australian cricketers always waited for the umpire's verdict when they were obviously out and had the habit of appealing for catches from half volleys.

Of Vaseline, gamesmanship, clowns and insolent scribes

***SPORTSWEEK* • March 1977**

John Lever

England's well-deserved 3-1 win over India in what was often a remarkably painful, dull, agonising series between two mediocre, lack luster sides was largely the result of excellent teamwork.

And, of course, the most admirable elements of dyed-in-the-wool professionalism characterised by a remarkable ability to adjust, adapt, improvise. Also to outwit, outmaneuver, 'psyche out', 'con' the opposition. A capacity to apply all the ruses, devices, gambits of gamesmanship and one-upmanship. Of 'psychological warfare', to win-Machiavelli-like at all cost, by means most often fair and within the framework of the rules but, alas, not always so.

Looking back—not in anger—after the dust of the 'battle' has settled, the conclusion is inescapable that the scales of the balance were tilted by the technical ability, dynamism, qualities of leadership and the do-or-die, win-at-all-cost determination of one individual—Tony Greig, the 'man of the series', who on arrival in India had rated his team's chances of victory "50:50".

It was Greig who through sheer personal example with bat and ball (is he really a bowler of Test calibre?) and the ability to command and inspire, rallied his side time and again (how often did the specialist batsmen lose their wickets early!), boosted its morale and in the end lead it to a most creditable victory on wickets which were presumably prepared to assist spin, a strategy which not only boomeranged thanks to the presence of 'Deadly' Underwood in the opposition but also demonstrated the sad fact that the so-called groundsmen are incapable of producing even wickets to assist spinners.

Verily can it be said that the 1976-77 India-England series marked a watershed in the modern history of English cricket. For it was here that an England captain about whose credentials there still prevail grave misgivings in his own country, transformed the mood of a nation which, after her dismal performances against Australia and the West Indies, had plummeted to abysmal depths of dejection and despair, to dizzying heights of euphoric ecstasy.

Many of the cognoscenti in this country still find it difficult to believe that the same side which they, only in moments of 'charitable' expansiveness, termed 'mediocre', could have come so close to defeating Australia (admittedly a depleted side) in Australia in the memorable Centenary Test. But then such has been the transformation in English cricket.

There have been post mortems galore. A great deal has been spouted and written about the reasons for India's defeat, the fact that the margin of England's victory was not a true index of the relative strengths and weaknesses of the two teams, that the Indian players were tired, stale, jaded, about the faulty itinerary which pitted the visitors against weak sides in the early part of the tour enabling them to strike form and boost their morale.

Enough verbiage has also been expressed about India's timid mental approach, the inability to take the fight to the enemy camp, about the lack of application, patience, determination, about gutless, spineless, technically inept batting especially against the moving ball, about faulty footwork and even more faulty selection. Also about atrocious fielding and the need for pace bowlers who can move the ball (the one effective pace bowler available—Ghavri—was treated scurvily).

By contrast, England were perhaps the best-ever fielding side to visit India. The only silver lining in the home team's performance in the fielding department were Yajurvindra Singh's seven catches on his debut in the Bangalore Test to equal two world records. On the whole, however, the spin trio strove manfully but was let down—yet again—by the batsmen and fielders.

The umpiring, too, for the greater part of the series, left a great deal to be desired. True, umpires today officiate under tremendous pressure, both from players and spectators, the more so from the huge crowds at Test matches in India. It would be most unfair to impute motives or to accuse the umpires of dishonesty.

But the fact remains that although quite a few doubtful decisions did go against the visitors, all in all, the home side suffered considerably more by comparison, with Gaekwad, Patel and Viswanath being the worst sufferers.

On balance, it would appear that some of the umpires are technically and physically incompetent. And the old 'hang-up', being sympathetic towards 'phoren' guests (the brown-man's burden?) persists. It is interesting to note that whereas one umpire ensured that the prefix 'Mister' was always used when addressing the England players, it was just "Bedi" or "Gavaskar" or plain "batsman" for the Indians.

No essay on the series can be complete without a reference to the obnoxious 'Vaseline' episode. Both Greig and Barrington have acknowledged that vaseline was used in the Madras Test, a fact confirmed by the chemical analysis. In an article in the London *Daily Mirror*, former England captain Ray Illingworth and fast bowler John Snow have admitted in so many words that 'greasy substances' such as vaseline and lip-ice have been used by past England sides. They have mentioned Geoff Arnold, Basil D'Oliveira and Tony Greig as those responsible for what they term 'cheating' on this score.

What is most surprising is the hurry with which the MCC treated the matter as closed, exonerating Greig and his team even before the report of the technical committee of the Board of Control for Cricket in India had been received by it. We now learn that the committee did not recommend action against the team and decided merely to refer the matter to the MCC because Bishan Singh Bedi did not wish to press the issue.

According to the India skipper, the use of vaseline by the England side started in the very first Test in Delhi. Bedi is said to have brought this to the attention of a high Board official who promised to get the ball chemically analysed. Instead, the 'rogue' ball was given as a souvenir to John Lever for his 'outstanding performance'.

met when Pakistan thwarted India's determined late bid to draw the Test yesterday in a snail-biting finish with only 6 overs to spare.

Although local hero Anil Kumble put up stout resistance in association with tail-enders Irfan Pathan, Harbhajan Singh and Laxmipathy Balaji in the heart-stopping final moments (as predicted in this column yesterday, if one might add) it was, alas, all futile.

Whatever hopes India might have entertained overnight to force a bold win evaporated when a gross error of judgment by Gautam Gambhir resulted in Virender Sehwag being run-out as a result of a brilliant piece of fielding and bulls-eye throw-in by Abdul Razzaq from a difficult angle.

Whereas the Pakistanis were infinitely more resolute in their quest for victory, India's celebrated batsmen revealed a negative, almost beleaguered, mindset once the dashing opener had departed.

The ultra-negative approach on a wicket that assisted spin but was fairly true even on the last day, was self-defeating, for which India paid the price.

Rahul Dravid and Harbhajan Singh fell to brilliant catches by man-of-the-match Younis Khan, the Pathan from Mardan, who is estimated to have been on the ground in the match as acting captain, batsman and fielder for over 25 hours.

Sachin Tendulkar achieved the distinction of becoming the highest Indian Test run scorer and the third highest in history after Allan Border and Steve Waugh.

As long as Tendulkar (his ultra defensive innings of 16, played with a pronounced short back lift, took him 98 balls and 140 minutes) was at the wicket, India had a fighting chance of salvaging the Test.

His capitulation to Shahid Afridi for the third time in two Tests with 35 overs remaining signalled the beginning of the end.

Being the ultimate team-man that he is, Tendulkar's achievement will surely be bittersweet, since he could not save India from defeat.

To Shahid Afridi, the other Pathan in the Pakistan team, must go major credit for his team's victory on the last day after his ballistic 58 on Sunday.

He claimed the valuable wickets of Tendulkar, VVS Laxman and Ganguly.

Afridi had the Indian batsmen bewitched, bothered and bewildered with his brilliant, varied repertoire of leg-breaks, googlies and flippers, delivered at speeds ranging from 86 to 139 km p h.

He finished with the amazing figures of 17-7-13-3, but one cannot help feeling that all's not well with his action, especially when bowling his faster ones.

Inzamam handled his bowlers with uncanny judgment, alternating pace and spin at the two ends.

The tall Arshad Khan failed to get much lift from the wicket despite bowling into the rough outside the off-stump, but Mohammad Sami and Abdul Razzaq both obtained impressive reverse swing, whereas Danish Kaneria was the perfect foil for Afridi.

The typically laid-back Pakistani skipper showed impressive urgency on the day and his fielding, for once, was excellent.

Inzamam's unconcealed exuberance after the finish was understandable, this being his 100th Test.

On the other hand, Sourav Ganguly's woeful form continues.

The skipper was all at sea in India's moment of need which called for a "cometh the moment, cometh the man" heroic performance. When I met him on Monday night, he looked clearly jaded. A rest will surely do him good.

So on to the one-day series. Aficionados can look forward to another humdinger of a series. After their impressive showing in the Tests the Pakistanis, having got their act together, can be counted on to enter the fray with their tails up.

Team India can underestimate them only at their own peril.

We save Bhajji

MID-DAY* • *April 13, 2005* • *Sydney

Mid Day has good news for Harbhajan Singh and his legion of fans.

Harbhajan Singh

I have it on good authority that, following the pleas by your paper (March 25 and April 5) to former Board of Control for Cricket in India (BCCI) president Jagmohan Dalmiya to intercede in the matter concerning the legality of the Turbanator's 'doosra', the game's supreme governing body has declared a moratorium on the issue.

Which means that following our efforts, for the time being at least, the off-spinner's 'doosra' is not being called in question.

Upon being asked to do so by the BCCI president and secretary, Dalmiya took up the matter with the ICC, which has decreed that Harbhajan will not be required to undergo any further tests until a prima facie case can be made against the off-spinner.

Videotapes of Harbhajan's bowling action in the last series against Bangladesh and the current one against Pakistan have been reportedly called for by the ICC.

This is precisely why Harbhajan has been left well alone by the dreaded, controversial Chris Broad who continues to terrorise players in the present India-Pak series with his perverse born-again morality.

KHALIDOSCOPE (April 5) had stated, "Now that the International Cricket Council (ICC) has dug itself in an unholy quagmire of confusion and controversy in l'affaire Harbhajan Singh, it becomes incumbent upon the Board of Control for Cricket in India (BCCI) to stand steadfastly by its worthy son.

"The ICC's action (after the off-spinner had been reported by controversial umpires Steve Bucknor and Darrel Hair upon the report of match referee Chris Broad, the self-appointed upholder of ethics of the game is extremely unjust and high-handed.

"The decision is bizarre in light of the fact that Harbhajan's 'doosra' had been cleared by the ICC's own physiotherapy gurus in Perth Australia, barely a few weeks earlier.

“In other words, not only is the ‘Turbanator’ being sentenced by the ICC repeatedly for the same ‘crime’ (his action was considered suspect three times earlier and cleared subsequently), the game’s supreme body is also astonishingly implying that the naked eye is to be trusted more than its own latest scientific technology.

“It is extraordinary that Asian bowlers, in particular (barring Afridi), are being singled out by the ICC for allegedly bending their arms to break its rules.”

This writer went on to say, “It is hoped the BCCI - and especially its former president Jagmohan Dalmiya, who was largely instrumental in Shoaib Akhtar’s clearance (in Australia) - will forcefully take up Harbhajan’s case, as he so successfully did when Sourav Ganguly’s Team India got the wrong end of the stick from ICC match referee Mike Denness in South Africa in 2001.

“Too often in the past has the BCCI been guilty of spineless capitulation to the authoritarian, eccentric, if not inequitable, powers-that-be in the portals of the august ICC.

“It’s time it stood up for justice,” we concluded.

Shabash, Jagmohan Dalmiya. Well done, BCCI.

Miscellaneous

Cricket humour-stories I

How can I ever forget the incident concerning the gentleman, who was sent abroad for the first time in his life as commentator in Hindi with Bishen Singh Bedi's touring team to Australia in 1977-78?

Readers will recall that at the end of the first day in the second Test at Perth, India were in a position of strength, having reduced the home side to 33 for two after scoring 402 in the first innings and bowling Australia out for 394, for a lead of eight. Left-arm spinner Tony Mann was sent out as night watchman, and to the chagrin of the Indian side, not only deprived them of an expected win, but went on to steer Australia to a two-wicket victory.

The Test had been preceded by a pre-series smear campaign (which seems to be a regular practice Down Under) by the local media alleging that Bhagwat Chandrasekhar, he with the freak bowling arm, was a chucker.

Imagine the scenario of the last morning: India, with their tails up, sniffing victory; Australia fighting for dear life. In the first session Chandra raps Mann on the pads. The bowler and fielders go up for a confident leg-before appeal. "No out," says the umpire. Much aggro on the part of the Indians. Next ball: ditto-ditto. "Not out," says the umpire, to shock and amazement of almost the entire India team. More aggro, plenty more tearing of hair.

Some time later, with Australia looking like saving the Test, a repeat of the leg-before appeal. This time, the Indians have no doubt, whatsoever that bogey man Mann is plumb out. There is no daylight at all in a straight line from the ump's vision between pad and stumps "Not out," rules the gentleman in white coat. More tearing of hair, gnashing of teeth among the Indian fielders.

Chandra snatches his cap from the umpire and walks to his customary fine-leg fielding position to jeers of "Chandra chucker, Chandra chucker" from the partisan crowd.

This prompts the normally genial, but now agitated, Chandra to give the crowd the famous two-finger Aussie salute. At which stage, the commentator, poor innocent abroad, describes the incident to his listeners back home thus: *"Ab Chandra fielding karne jaa rahe hain. Log cheekh ranen hain* 'Chandra chucker, Chandra chucker.' " ('Chandra is now going to his fielding position and the crowd is chanting 'Chandra chucker, Chandra chucker')

Raising his two fingers, a la Chandra, our commentator friend explains: *"Aura Chandra unse keh rahay hain 'Woh ek hee bar nahin, do bar out they' "* ("And Chandra is explaining to them (the crowd), 'He was out not merely once, but twice."

Cricket humour-stories II

There's the story which former Indian Test skipper Nari Contractor repeated at my urg ing (I never tire of hearing Nari recount it) about Mansur Ali Khan Pataudi's ghost mask, at a recent felicitation function for Dicky

Rutnagar, hosted by CCI president Raj Singh Dungarpur, which had both of us in splits, in tears and near to collapse with laughter. Nari would have us know that 'Tiger' Pataudi, then a past master in the art of practical jokes, acquired this frightful mask in Port of Spain, Trinidad.

After dinner one evening, Pataudi, Nari, Ghulam Ahmed, manager of the team, and perhaps M.L. Jaisimha or Dicky Rutnagar (his recollection is rather vague) decided to visit K N Prabhu, sports editor of the *Times of India,* who was touring with the team and staying at the Queen's Park Hotel across the road.

"Tiger" wore the mask and donned a white sheet around him as they crossed the road to the hotel. A passing motorist saw the apparition, screeched his car to a halt and fled for his life with his tail between his legs! The group entered Prabhu's hotel, roaring with laughter at the poor motorist's plight. Ghulam (may his soul rest in peace), who was in hysterics, was so consumed with laughter that he failed to see the swimming pool in the compound in the dark and found himself in the drink - suit and all! The pranksters then made their way to Prabhu's room. The venerable TOI correspondent, dressed in his pyjamas, was reading a book.

He answered the knock at the door only to run smack into "Tiger" who, mask, sheet and all, let out an eerie shriek. You really ought to hear Nari describe the incident, but it seems Prabhu's pyjama cord was rather loose. You can imagine the scene as Prabhu recoiled in horror and fled to the back of the room exclaiming "Hoo, hoo, hoo," even as he tried desperately to prevent his pyjamas from falling off!

Cricket humour-stories III

Then, there was Dicky Rutnagur's prank at the expense of Hindi commentator Jasdev Singh at the Oberoi Hotel in Melbourne during the 1980-81 tour, where both the Indian and Australian teams were staying.

On four successive nights, Dicky would fill out the room service breakfast card, from top to bottom, asking for a huge variety of juices, cereals, eggs, savouries, ham, bacon, sausage, an assortment of bread and toast, tea, coffee—the lot, and hang it outside Jasdev's room after he had retired for the night.

For four consecutive days, Jasdev told me the next morning, "Khalid, *pata nahin yeh hotel ki room service kaisi hai. Who roz mujhe subah savare chaar baje utha dete hain, sab qism ka ajeeb non-veg. nashta la kar. Tum to jaante ho main strict vegetarian hoon.* ("Khalid, this hotel's room service is rather strange. They wake me up at four every morning with a strange kind of non-veg breakfast. As you know, I'm a strict vegetarian.")

You can be sure Jasdev Singh was not amused in the least when he discovered he had been at the receiving end of Dicky's puckish humour.

Our plan for refugees

SPORTSWEEK • 1971

SPORSTWEEK has a plan in to help the Bengal refugees.

Since we first hit the stands we have always Steered clear of politics, within and without—In fact we have always tried to fight the scourge which have ever been bane of Indian sport

PROBLEM

To our way of thinking, the Bengal refugee problem is a HUMAN problem even though it is political in nature. And we would like to do our bit to help.

Seems to us that sport can do a great deal to help alleviate the misery and suffering of the unfortunate victism of the barbarous occupation of West Pakistan.

To this end we suggest to the government the staging of a series of sports encounters in different parts of the country, starting with cricket. Sportsmen have always been willing to help a good cause and there is no reason why they cannot be counted on for help during one of the greatest tragedies of all times.

At the time of writing it seems as though the M.C.C. will not come to India this winter despite the insistence of our Cricket-Control Board. The impression that I have got talking to various journalists and cricket administrators in England is that the M.C.C. are not keen on coming.

SUGGEST

In the event of the M.C.C. not coming, SPORTSWEEK would like to suggest to the Government and the Board of Control for Cricket in India to organise a short tour of India by a cricket team comprising of players from different countries, which would play possibly three matches against a representative India XI at different centers.

BENEFIT

Obviously the Board of Control for Cricket in India will have to be involved in this venture, proceeds of which will go entirely for the benefit of the Bengal refugees.

A committee of prominent citizens would be set up to organise the series, to supervise arrangements, the financial end etc.

The matches would be of three-day duration on a limited-over basis to ensure bright cricket and a result.

We would like to express our cooperation in every possible manner. We are absolutely willing to devote as much time and effort that we are capable of for the project. We expect no financial reward—only the satisfaction of helping a good cause. In fact we would even go to the extent of offering that we will go to England at our expense if need be to help organise the tour.

We have worked out a tentative blue print and would be more than happy to discuss the project with Government and cricket officials, anytime, anywhere.

We must ensure our glory is not short lived

SPORTSWEEK* • *April 25, 1971

Despite the inconvenicnt hour, Wadekar and his boys are in for a tumultous heroes' welcome when they arrive at Santa Cruz airport on Sunday. They have unquestionably brought glory to the country by their performance on the field, and their conduct off it.

Ajit Wadekar

On balance, the series verily marked a watershed for Indian cricket. A series characterised by rare wisdom on the part our selectors. A series which witnessed the blosoming of 'Little Master'

On his debut at a very tender age, Sunil Gavaskar has already staked his claim to greatness. It was a series which has dealt a resounding slap on the face of Dilip Sardesai's detractors, a series in which so many owed so much to so few, a series, which from our point of view was notable for team-spirit, fighting-spirit. It was fiercely-fought, historic series.

But our success must not be allowed to go to our head, to cloud our judgment and perspective. Let us not forget that the present West Indies side is only a shadow of what West Indies teams have been in the not-too-distant past. And that it has also been beaten by England and Australia, even New Zealand.

Just ahead lies the tour of England. It is imperative that we take dispassionate stock of the situation and plan pragmatically if we are to ensure that our glory is not short-lived.

England are an extremely difficult side to beat at home, due largely to the peculiar cricketing and climatic conditions that obtain there.

Their morale is now at a peak, after the Ashes victory. In fact, quiet predictions are already being made in England that she will win 5 of the 6 Tests in the forthcoming series against India and Pakistan.

Onerous indeed will be the task of our selectors. They will be faced with the, dilemma of disturbing a victorious combination that has evolved an admirable team-spirit as a result of playing together for three months, and replacing those members of the side that did not measure up to expectations.

Sagacity demands the learning of lessons from past mistakes: to wit, the disastrous consequences that stemmed out of indiscriminately disturbing the successful side that toured New Zealand in 1907, that had got going as a team only in the second half of the tour of Australia and New Zealand.

Confronting the selectors will also be the contentious doctrine of "giving youth a chance" demands, not altogether unreasonable, that a touring side must be a blend of youth and experience. To add to their woes will be the fact that at least two "experienced" members of the side, namely Salim Durrani and ML Jaisimha were hardly the success they were expected to be.

Then there will be the indefinable consideration of "class." If it is agreed that Vishwanath and Durrani are sufficiently endowed with this attribute, should their none-too-happy showing in the West Indies necessarily spell 'finis' to their careers, as should the fact of lack of opportunities in the case of Govindraj and Jeejeebhoy?

These factors allied with the serious limitations that have been exposed in the side in the Caribbean, namely the absence of a penetrative pace attack (so vital a requirement in England) and lack of solidity in the middle-order batting must weigh heavily with the selectors in their deliberations. Also, our none-too-impressive showing in the field that has often brought to nought the good work of our tireless bowlers.

We were pleasantly surprised at the selectors' retort to our question, "Reason was the selectors' lodestar when the side for the West Indies was selected. Can we expect the same this time as well?

And will reason ever dawn on the Cricket Control Board in the interest of Indian cricket, or is the unprecedented, ill-conceived "policy-decision (which seems to have become a matter of prestige for the pooh-bahs in the Board) to deprive the country of the services of Farokh Engineer and Rusi Surti?

Its never too late to mend one's ways. The Board can still win the trust and respect of the cricket-loving public.

If your eyes were moist

SPORTSWEEK • August 29, 1971

If your eyes were moist, your voice choked with emotion as you heard Brian Johnston over the B.B.C. on that memorable 24th of August describe Abid Ali square-cut Luckhurst deliriously for four you may be sure you had this writer and countless others in this country and abroad for company.

Ajit Wadekar

Historic day for India, Ganesh Chaturthi 1971. A proud never-to-be-forgotten day. A day for rejoicing—twice-over.

Everybody's doing it. The obvious is anathema to us. But we'd be failing in our duty. So congratulations to Ajit Wadekar, his gallant men, to Hemu Adhikari, a much-maligned Vijay Merchant, members of the selection committee who now stand vindicated, to the board of Control for Cricket in India (of course!!).

Three cheers to Ray Illingworth and the English team. They fought hard, played in the right spirit, were darling losers.

EXHILARATION

Exhilaration. Only recently, a first-ever series victory for the West Indies in the West Indies. Now, a first ever rubber win over unofficial world champions England in England after 39 years of trying.

The rule-of-three cannot be applied in this context, and this victory does put us among the foremost cricket playing countries in the world, apart from promoting us "from the little league to the big league" as Keith Miller later said to me at Lord's (SPORTSWEEK Aug. 8th).

A well-deserved, hard-fought victory. Unexpected. Not many could have reasonably forecast the sudden turn of events at the Oval after India had finished in arrears on the first innings. We achieved here what we came so close to achieving at Lord's. True the weather-gods were kind to us at Old Trafford but then that's cricket in Blighty.

IN RETROSPECT

In retrospect, both teams were fairly evenly-matched. India decidedly superior in the spin department, England in her pace attack. The peculiar, unpredictable English conditions played their usual role to make the series a cliff-hanger.

What tilted the scales ultimately were the repeated and inexplicable failure of England's much-vaunted batting stalwarts, India's spin, particularly Chandrasekhar in the last Test and yes—team spirit. It was combined effort—in England more than in the West Indies—that saw India through until the final Test and won the day for her at the Oval.

Shabash boys, yours has been a magnificent performance. The nation is proud of you. May this spur you on to even greater achievements.

Many a lesson has to be learnt from the series. But we will take dispassionate stock later. For the present the nation exults in your glory. You may be sure a heroes, welcome awaits you.

And finally, if readers will please forgive a spot of trumpet-blowing. Recall that issue of SPORTSWEEK (dated July 18) in which this writer first suggested India could surprise England? Care to discuss this issue now, ye gloomy prophets of doom?

In search of quickies...
It's all talk but no action!

SPORTSWEEK* • *November 18 - 1973

"The latter half of his commonwealth" complained Antonio in Shakespeare's *The Tempest* (act: 2, scene: 1), "forgets the former".

Karsan Ghavri

Antonio's grouse could very well have been directed at the pooh-bahs of Indian cricket who never tire of making grandiose plans for producing fast bowlers etc., but whose speech is seldom translated into action.

Time and again has this vexed question cropped up. Diverse remedies, some worse than the disease itself, have been prescribed. But if there is one root-cause of the malady, it is the absence of lively wickets that assist and encourage pace bowlers.

Sad to say, the organisers of the Irani Cup match played at Bangalore over the weekend also failed to come up with a sporting wicket which could have given some assistance to the youngsters on trial. It would be unfair to attribute sinister motives for this shortcoming, but the fact remains that justice was not done to Amitava Roy, Karsan Ghavri, Mohinder Amarnath and Abdul Ismail.

In an interview with this writer in the SPORTSWEEK Annual '73, Ajit Wadekar has stated in no uncertain terms that the going will not be easy for us on the tour of England next year.

It is imperative that the touring party consist of new ball bowlers who will be able to exploit the humid conditions and the quick wickets in the first half of the English summer, since it is doubtful if our renowned spinners will succeed in getting much assistance from the wickets, witness the fact that both Bedi and Venkatraghavan really got going during the last county season only after June.

The writing on the wall is clear. We can ignore it only at our peril.

This can spell disaster

SPORTSWEEK* • *January-March 1974

AS we go to press for this inaugural issue of the Sportsweek Cricket Quarterly, comes the disturbing news regarding the unhappy Kallicharran run-out episode in the first England-West Indies Test at Port of Spain.

Alvin Kallicharran

Even the most partisan among those who were on the spot have admitted that Kallicharran was out technically insofar as he was out of the crease at the non-striker's end when Tony Greig's shy at the stumps found bull's eye and 'time' had not been called. To that extent umpire Sang Hue's verdict was correct, although there is no denying the fact that the manner of 'dismissal' of the West Indies idol was extremely sad, the more so if one accepts Greig's explanation that his action was 'impulsive'.

What is shocking by our reckoning is the fact that the decision of the umpire (unfortunately this is not the first time that he has been at the centre of a controversy) should have been reversed in what has been termed, "the interest of cricket in general ... and the tour in particular."

I say the decision to overrule the umpire's decision, was contrary to the interest of the game and vitiates the cardinal principle that the umpire's decision, right or wrong, is absolute and irreversible, although instances of batsmen who have been given "wrongly" out being recalled at the instance of the fielding side are not altogether rare in these days of win-at-all-cost cricket.

To those of us, who have been brought up to respect the decisions of umpires and referees as final in all games at all times, what transpired in the committee room at Port of Spain is outrageous.

England were certainly gracious in allowing 'Kalli' to continue his innings the following day but there is no escaping the fact that the action amounted to pandering to the dictates of unruly elements in the stands.

One recalls the commendable sporting manner in which skipper Tony Lewis handled Greig and Alan Knott when they indulged in contemptible gamesmanship during the Madras Test last year and wonders as to how Mike Denness reacted on and off the field during the episode under discussion. One is also tempted to speculate as to whether the same MCC side would have agreed to a reversal of the decision had the incident occurred later in the tour or, for that matter, taken place elsewhere in the world, perhaps India.

It goes against one's grain to start off a new publication on a sour note, but in our opinion so compelling is this issue, that there is just no way out of commenting on it.

We sincerely hope that realisation will dawn soon enough that undue regard for the mob's wishes can only spell disaster for the game.

Lacklustre — this series

***SPORTSWEEK* • October-December 1976**

That in one word was the mini three-test series against New Zealand which India predictably won by a 2-0 margin. With a little bit of luck it would well have been a clean sweep but the tourists deserve fulsome praise for fighting back from the edge of the precipice to save the Kanpur Test.

It is hardly surprising that the series failed to generate much public enthusiasm. All in all, the cricket played during the 16 days was rather undistinguished, what with the New Zealanders being unfortunately not fully representative of the countries current cricketing strength.

To add to the tourist' woes, skipper Turner lost all three tosses on pitches where batting first was decidedly advantageous. And the cramped itinerary which called upon them to—breathlessly, so to say—play five consecutive Tests in Pakistan and India could not have helped matters any. Most of their players had far too much Test cricket on the twin-tour, with no three-day matches between tests to relieve pressure, to provide opportunities for experiment, to play anyone into form.

TEAM-SPIRIT

Viewed from India's point of view, the series should certainly have helped considerably in building team-spirit on the eve of the series against England. Inspired by Bishen Bedi's flair to command through personal example, the players came closer together after the twin-tour of New Zealand and the West Indies. It is a truism that to captain a winning side is an easy task. Still, Bedi had the boys fully with him and he made them give of their best.

Albeit against a none-too-impressive bowling lineup, the frontline batsmen struck form sometime or other, with Gavaskar, Viswanath, not surprisingly, standing head and shoulders above the rest. But one could not escape the conclusion that the middle-order was lacking in solidity, unable to build on good starts, accelerate the rate of scoring. In all three Tests, the lower batting, with Syed Kirmani in particularly good touch, had to step in to give the total a look of respectability which was a refreshing change indeed for in recent times Indian 'nine, ten and jack' have been somewhat of a joke.

As in the past, our bowling depended largely, and at times disproportionately, on three spinners. Bedi and Chandrasekhar proved to be match-winners with able support from Venkatraghavan. Ghavri, who came back in the side for the last two Tests, bowled very well at Madras. But then, all this is not saying very much in the context of a mediocre opposition. Most of the chinks in our armour persist and prevent the Test side from being rated particularly high.

The series, as a whole, taught us nothing new. Events panned out as per expectations and the revelation that our close-in catching was well below the high standards set in recent years was again underscored. The Solkars and Abid Alis were sorely missed for their close-to-the-wicket catching proficiency alone, if nothing else. But then they, too, as is well known, are no longer quite as razor-sharp in their reflexes.

Ill-equipped in the extreme in the matter of tackling India's world-class spin, most of Turner's batsmen were out in trying to hit their way out of trouble on wickets which were, by and large, slow turners. Moreover, they proved to be a surly lot with atrocious manners, showed scant respect for the umpires with some of them betraying signs of positive immaturity.

There were incidents galore during the series in which the Kiwis tarnished their image of being a 'sporting side'—witness their protests, gestures and actions on the field of play and their refusal to join the Indian team at lunch during the Kanpur Test.

Despite the rather poor fare dished out in terms cricketing, the Board of Control for Cricket in India and the three associations who hosted the Tests raked in substantial profits. The coffers of the Board are overflowing. But what is being done to promote the game, to unearth fresh talent (in a situation where the Test side shows woeful weaknesses), to produce more coaches, to provide adequate coaching facilities in our large country? Precious little!

Finally, whatever happened to the grandiose schemes to produce fast bowlers? Vanished into oblivion—fast!

The Indian pace bowler: As elusive as the Yeti, the Loch Ness Monster, the Scarlet Pimpernel

MID-DAY* • *March 27, 1977

Now that matters of historic moment concerning vox populi and Parliament—the repository of the people's will—have been settled, can it be reasonably hoped that the Board of Control for Cricket in India—the fountainhead of Indian cricket—will address itself in all earnestness to the pressing problems on hand?

Too often in the past have some lotus-eaters in the Board basked in our glory, exulted in our euphoria only to be rudely awakened, brought crashing down to earth.

If the apparent languor of the powers-that-be is any criterion at all, the Board is presently blissfully unconcerned about the problems that confront our cricket which led to so much national mourning, heart-burning and breast-beating only recently when we were soundly thrashed by a mediocre England side.

Many a head of hair has turned grey, many a youthful face wizened while a loadful of gibberish has been spouted by all and sundry about preparing fast bowlers, quick wickets etc. The pace bowlers that we do have we treat shabbily. And one is sick to the stomach reading and hearing of ambitious plans in this regard. The net result? An 'impressive' cipher, very much in the mould of the runs of our classic batsmen! The search for Indian pace bowlers continues to be as futile as the search for the elusive Yeti, the Loch Ness Monster, the Scarlet Pimpernel.

Earlier, in these columns SPORTSWEEK has expressed the opinion that our cricketers are today a jaded lot which has been the result of too much continuous cricket over the past seven months. The summer is about to set in and the Ranji Trophy is yet to be concluded and this will be followed by a limited overs cricket tournament sponsored by India Tobacco Co. Ltd. which, although an eminently commendable undertaking, has been scheduled faultily. All these is nothing if not erroneous planning.

From time to time we have also drawn attention to the fact that the entire Ranji Trophy setup needs to be overhauled, not only from the point of view of scheduling but also in order to provide greater opportunities to players of the weaker Ranji Trophy teams and Duleep Trophy zones for displaying their ability. There has been no valid opposition to this point of view but the Board remains characteristically insouciant.

The last two series at home namely those against the West Indies and England have spotlighted the fact that effective pace bowlers who can move the ball, can succeed even on the most heartbreaking slow wickets tailor-made for spinners. The veracity of this argument has been lent credence to in the West Indies in recent times as well.

There can be no doubt in the minds of right-thinking people that among the prime needs of Indian cricket today is effective pace bowling, not to mention reliable batsmen of whom there has been an awful paucity as also of substitutes for our famed spinners.

In short, there is room at the top in Indian cricket in every department. One need not dwell upon the errors of omission and commission of the past. Can we not look ahead right away to the coming season during which we are scheduled to take on Australia on their bouncy wickets for which pace bowlers who can move the ball are a decided asset if not a 'must'? Can we not, really, gentlemen of the Board of Control for Cricket in India?

Pak Tour Diary

SPORTSWEEK • November 19, 1978 Pakistan

Rumours are afloat here once again that six of the Indian cricketers are signing up with Kerry Packer. But tour officials deny knowledge of any further developments and at least two of the players said to be involved have categorically denied the rumour as "absolutely without foundation."

Bishan Bedi with manager Fatehsinhrao Gaekwad

"We will go all out for a win," Pakistan captain Mushtaq told me before the start of the Karachi Test. "You can expect a lot of runs to be scored. There isn't much in the match for the bowlers as it looks now but don't surprised if it assists spin in the later stages".

"Even though a draw here will suffice for us, we will try our very best to make it 2-0. Let's hope it's a good match and may the better side win."

India skipper Bishan Bedi, on the other hand, was less positive in his utterance. "*Dekhiye kya hota hai*" (let's see what happens), said he. There's a bit of grass on the wicket and I expect the bounce to be uneven. Yes, there should be something in it for our spinners later in the game.

India manager Fatehsinhrao Gaekwad told me: "It looks a draw all the way. I do not see either side getting out twice on that track. It looks chockful of runs to me, unless of course the batsmen bat dreadfully."

Zaheer Abbas said he was looking forward to the Test. " Let's hope my luck with the bat lasts". He expressed the opinion the Test would see a lot of runs scored.

Karachi students who are known for their assertiveness and tendency to disrupt Tests made no secret of their displeasure with arrangements at the National Stadium. They demanded comfortable covered seating in the new students stand on the east side and had to be pacified by the organisers who promised them over the public address system that their grievances would be looked into and appealed to their patriotism "in the name of God" requesting them to maintain discipline.

A few enthusiastic ones rushed on to the field when Gavaskar completed his 50 and veteran Pakistani scribes who have been witness to abandonments of many Test matches in Karachi were prepared for the worst.

But sanity soon prevailed. Twenty-five minutes of playing time was lost when the students encroached upon the field and threw bottles and fruits on the ground. Some students in the north stand shone mirrors in the eyes of Gavaskar and Vengsarkar causing the latter to object to umpire Shujauddin.

Official circles in Pakistan are puzzled—and disappointed—at the fact that Indian Board officials Chinnaswamy, Chidambaram and Ghulam Ahmed have not arrived here for the match.

Board of Control for Cricket in Pakistan president, Gen. K. M. Azhar and secretary Lt. Col. (retd.) Rafi Nasim, who had gone to the airport on Monday night, were surprised the Indian officials were not on the PLA flight by which I arrived alongwith "Tiger" Pataudi and his wife Sharmila.

Board treasurer Chidambaram is reportedly in London for medical treatment. But it is hoped here that Chinnaswamy (who was complaining of eye trouble) and Ghulam Ahmed can come later not only to witness this Test but also to finalise plans for future series between India and Pakistan and the under-19 tour of India by Pakistan.

The reason for the non-arrival of Chinnaswamy and Ghulam Ahmed is said to be "non-clearance by the Indian Government and nonreceipt of permission for foreign exchange". But Ministry of Education officials in New Delhi state that the necessary clearance was granted as long as two months ago. If that be the case, wires have apparently been crossed somewhere along the line.

It is also understood that the visa granted to the two officials was for a duration of seven days.

Give the players a fair deal

SPORSTWEEK* • *January-March 1979

Kerry Packer

The reported statement of Peter Lush, assistant secretary of the Test and County Cricket Board (TCCB) that his Board "will not influence the decisions of the Indian authorities to include Packer signatories in the squad which tours England this summer in view of the High Court ruling of 1977 which specifically restrains the International Cricket Conference (ICC) and its members from omitting any individual from Test or from first-class cricket on grounds of association with Kerry Packer" must have made the holier-than-thou, the more traditional than the most dyed in the wool traditionalists, among those who stalk the corridors of cricket power in our land hit the roof, take a double somersault.

For, it is these sanctimonious prudes, who in the name of "tradition" and "beauty of the game" refuse to accept reality and stubbornly resist change. They have arrogated to themselves the mantle of preventing the miasma of WSC from "polluting" the "purity" of cricket. Their refined sensibilities have been so offended that they sing wishful elegies for the death of WSC in tones stentorian from the Olympian heights upon which they have foisted themselves.

TAMPERING

Undoubtedly, the right-thinking cricket lover does find a great deal wrong with the brouhaha and razzmatazz of World Series Cricket (WSC). The orthodox are repelled—and quite rightly so—by the rainbow-hued gear, by the blatant reliance on sex and glamour in promotional campaigns, by the unabashed tampering with the laws of the game.

Be that as it may—and this is not an apology for any of the foregoing—one thing is certain: every cricketer, as indeed every sportsman has, and should have, in the matter of employment, the right to take his very own decision, of his own volition, sans pressure and influence. The fact that the argument of a sportsman's 'life' being limited has been repeated ad nauseam in no way reduces the weight of its logic. If, for better or worse, a cricketer decides on a certain course of action job-wise, he should be free to do so without let or hindrance by the self-styled keepers of the cricketers' conscience.

No amount of sophistry, prevarication or equivocation can detract from the basic truth: every individual has the fundamental right, in India at any rate at this point in time, to determine his livelihood. To deny him this, and the opportunity to play for his country if he makes himself available, is to travest justice.

The Board of Control for Cricket in India is a model of efficient administration. It is fortunate to have at the helm of its affairs some dedicated men of sagacity, acumen, sapience and unimpeachable integrity, men beyond reproach who, through prudent management of its affairs have made the Board's financial condition enviably sound and robust.

But there are, unfortunately, around them lesser men, satellites, schemers, devious people who are inordinately articulate, excessively garrulous and totally lacking in wisdom and foresight. These men, alas, are the bane of Indian cricket.

The sooner the hawks and the diehards, who are screaming for the blood of our cricketers contemplating signing up with WSC realise this harsh reality, the less traumatic will the process of crashing down to earth be for them. It's time they realised that at the root of the unnecessary—and unsavoury—impasse at the top level of international cricket is a domestic quarrel over television rights which should have been confined to Australia, the country of its origin. All the more, since as a UNI report would have us believe "there comes the news from Australia that the Cricket Board there has now abandoned its intransigent stand against awarding exclusive television rights—the very matter which gave rise to Packer's entry into cricket in the first place."

The West Indies, Pakistan (and New Zealand to a lesser degree) have had the good sense and pragmatic outlook to view the problem in its correct perspective. They have granted their cricketers the right to seek employment with the WSC while keeping the door open for them to play for their country which, in the words of more than one cricketer under contract to WSC, is the supreme honour.

It's time we broke free from our colonial shackles. The Brown Sahebs who still converge at the Gateway of India with high-powered binoculars should have realised by now that there isn't a chance in Heaven of the Fleet returning.

A World Cup Comedy

***SPORTSWEEK* • April-June 1979**

The place: Bombay.

The occasion: The special general meeting of the Board of Control for Cricket in India.

Scenario (in a nutshell): Hothead: "Let all those who wish to desert the Board realise that they are traitors to the country. Let them be ungrateful if they wish, after all that this benevolent Board has done for them."

The floor: Hear, Hear! Down with the traitors. Up with the Board.

Rabble rouser: Nobody is indispensable. We can do without the deserters. The Board is strong enough to find replacements.

Voice of Reason: Nobody is indispensable but there should be freedom . . . (the voice is shouted down).

The floor: Hear, Hear! Long live the Board. The Board is strong. Down with the deserters.

Fire breather: We shall not be cowed down by threats. The Board has the strength and the resources to produce twenty Gavaskars.

Voice of Reason: Let's not get emotional . . . (the voice is barely audible).

The floor: Hear, Hear! May the Board go from strength to strength.

Angry young man: It's time they realised that this Board has the ability to produce not only 20 Gavaskars but also as many Kapil Devs and Karsan Ghavris. After all who discovered them?

Voice of Reason: We must be sensible, balanced. Let's not get carried away . . . (the voice is drowned in the cacophony).

The floor: The Board, the Board. Long live the Board. Down with the traitors, the deserters.

Consensus at meeting: The Packer affair is a non-issue. We have not received anything in writing from the players.

The place: Bangalore.

The occasion: Meeting of selection committee of Board of Control for Cricket in India.

Consensus: Gavaskar replaced as captain because he had reportedly said to newspapers that he does not enjoy Test captaincy. (Nothing given by Gavaskar in writing. Experienced wicketkeeper Kirmani, veteran of 29 Tests who had made no secret of his intention to join

Packer's WSC replaced "because he was off form." Instead, two totally inexperienced wicketkeepers who had never played in Tests are included in side for Prudential Cup and tour of England. Former skipper Bishan Singh Bedi, who had thrown his full (not inconsiderable) weight behind the Board of Control for Cricket in India in l'affair. Packer is also included despite strong criticism all around).

THE ACTION

The place: Madras.

The occasion: Felicitation function on eve of departure of Indian team for England.

Scenario: Captain Venkatraghavan: "I have a fine bunch of boys. We will do very well."

The place: London.

The occasion: Press conference on team's arrival in England.

Scenario: Venkatraghavan: "We will win everything. The only thing we fear is the weather. Give us good weather and we will give you great cricket."

The place: Edgbaston, Birmingham.

The occasion: Press conference after India's nine-wicket defeat at the hands of West Indies.

Scenario: Venkatraghavan: "The umpiring was bad. They (the umpires) did not enforce the short-pitched rule strictly and fairly."

The place: Old Trafford, Manchester.

The occasion: Press conference after India's eight-wicket defeat at the hands of New Zealand.

Scenario: Venkatraghavan: "Our batting let us down."

THE EPILOGUE

SPORTSWEEK tries to contact Hothead and Rabble Rouser. Both are not available despite frantic and repeated efforts.

Angry young man available but refuses to comment except to say: "So what if we did not win. We do not have enough experience of one-day cricket despite the best efforts of the Board of Control for Cricket in India to give the players practice of limited-overs cricket. Besides, the weather was bad, the umpiring atrocious and the spin of the coin wretched from our point of view. Don't forget, you do need luck in any game."

He continues: "I have no doubt that if we had had even a little luck we would have won the World Cup. Don't forget the Board is doing so much for our cricket and our cricketers. It is self-sufficient and robust in financial health. Even the president of the Indian Hockey Federation envies us our financial stability."

The hothead goes on: "The Board is strong, united. It does not bother about press criticism. As our Prime Minister says, the press is biased and prejudiced. It never presents the true picture. Not one reporter has even mentioned the fact that we could have won the World Cup and that we were unlucky. Nor has any paper made any mention of the tremendous contribution that the Board is making to Indian cricket."

Choice abuse on TV

***SPORTSWEEK* • October 29, 1979**

An incident of scandalous proportions took place over Calcutta television yesterday during the cricket Test.

Following a discussion during the tea break on the Eden Gardens wicket in which Australian team manager Bob Merriman, "Tiger" Pataudi and others took part, viewers were horrified when the choicest of expletives, came over.

It appears the Hindi commentator and expert were engaged in a private discussion regarding the groundsman without realising that their microphones were "open" for transmission.

Embarrassed Doordarshan officials from elsewhere in the stadium rushed to set things right but only after viewers had heard almost two minutes of character assassination in choicest terminology.

A bomb scare

SPORTSWEEK • February 15, 1981

A bomb scare in the room of team manager Wing Commander Shahid Durrani sent Indian journalists scurrying for cover on the eve of the Melbourne Test.

An anonymous telephone caller informed the (Oberoi) Windsor Hotel where the Indian team is staying that a bomb had been planted in the manager's room. Police were summoned but the call proved to be a hoax.

After considering circumstantial evidence and by a process of elimination, the Sherlock Holmes among the scribes pointed a finger of suspicion at India skipper Gavaskar as the perpetrator of the prank.

Back to square one

SPORSTWEEK • January 17, 1982

Not many tears will be shed here at the return home of England opening batsman Geoffrey Boycott.

Geoff Boycott

Those who know the Yorkshireman and his magnificent obsession with Mr. Boycott himself are not surprised that the world aggregate record holder has decided to return home—now that that distinction has been achieved.

From the point of view of Indian cricket aficionados in Bombay, Bangalore and Delhi it has been an experience indeed watching the single-minded Yorkshireman in action. And cricket lovers in Madras, that well-known cricket centre, and Kanpur will indeed be sad that they were denied the pleasure of watching the exploits of the great batsman.

At the time of going to press, mystery surrounds the circumstances which prompted the "sending back" of Boycott by the tour management as initial reports indicate.

On balance, however, right thinking people in this country may be forgiven for now believing that they could have been spared the inclusion of Mr. Boycott in the touring side.

What with the other Geoffrey, namely Cook, being a mere passenger on the tour, the Indian prime minister, government and Board of Control for Cricket in India could have been spared the embarrassment of having to fight for the tour which hinged over the inclusion in the England party of the opinionated and self-centred Geoff Boycott.

In any event, Boycott has gone on record as saying in Bombay that he has no regrets whatsoever over his sporting contacts with South Africa and that given a chance he would resume them.

So it's back to square one, really isn't it?

The Gulf Extravaganza

SPORTSWEEK* • *April 11, 1982* • *Sharjah

Seven thousand wildly cheering spectators saw Indian Test stars Dilip Doshi and Madan Lal bowl Sunil Gavasker's Indian XI to victory over Intikhab Alam's Pakistanis at the Sharjah cricket stadium.

Brought in as last-minute replacement for deported Dilip Vengsarkar, left-arm spinner Doshi who is here on a private business trip and Madan Lal shared eight wickets between themselves to frustrate Intikhab Alam's victory effort in the first of two limited overs internationals being played in this haven for immigrants from the Indian subcontinent.

The matches are being organised by local business tycoon Abdul Rehman Bukhatir, a cricket fanatic, to promote the game of cricket in the Gulf. Proceeds from the one-week long annual extravaganza costing over half a million US dollars will this year go to Sunil Gavaskar and former Test spinner Subhash Gupte from India and former Pakistan Test skipper Intikhab Alam and opener Nazar Mohamed, father of Mudassar Nazar.

Last year the beneficiaries were former Test stumper Madhav Mantri and Pakistan skippers Hanif Mohamad and Asif Iqbal who is on a five year contract with the Bukhatir group of companies. Those slated for benefits in the years ahead include Viswanath, Vengsarkar, Kapil, Kirmani, Bedi, Chandrasekhar, Prasanna and Mansur Khan Pataudi who like his Pakistani counterpart Asif Iqbal is coordinator for the organising group in India.

INVITEES

Pataudi is here along with his film star wife Sharmila Tagore. Bapu Nadkarni, some players' wives and prominent cricket correspondents and photographers from India, Pakistan and England, including Henry Blofeld and Patrick Eagar Board of Control for Cricket in India president S.K. Wankhede and secretary A.W. Kanmadikar were expected, but have not made the trip.

Apart from the two one-day internationals between the full Indian and Pakistan sides, a double wicket tournament has been slated. The teams are Clive Lloyd and Malcolm Marshall from the West Indies, lan Botham and Graham Stevenson from England, Kapil Dev and Sandeep Patil from India and Imran Khan and Javed Miandad from Pakistan apart from two local pairs comprising of Mohamed Munir and Humayun Sumar as also Saleem Iqbal and Sahid Hussain. The winners of each double-wicket tournament will receive 20,000 US dollars put up by Mr. Vashu Chainani of International Watch Co, Sharjah.

Other sponsors include Rothmans International, Bukhatir Investments Ltd. Gulf Air, Novotel Hotels, Bank of Baroda, Galadari Brothers, *Khaleej Times*, and *Gulf News*. The prize money for the two one-day internationals is 20,000 US dollars each. The Man of the Match award is 20,000 Dirhams (approximately Rs. 50,000). The winner of the award of the first match was Dilip Doshi who bagged the prize wickets of Pakistani superstars Zaheer Abbas, Wasim Raja, Imran Khan and Haroon Rashid.

Viv Richards who was to have partnered Clive Lloyd in the double wicket tournament has not been able to come because of a clash of dates with his country's national tournament (the Shell Shield) in which he captains the Windward Islands. Graham Gooch was dropped following his participation in the rebel series in South Africa. His place has been taken by former England player Graham Stevenson, who is a close friend of Ian Botham.

The deportation of Dilip Vengsarkar is unfortunate in so far as it was the result of misunderstanding on the part of the Sharjah immigration authorities. Indian players who were then with Vengsarkar confirm that no rude or abusive language was used by the Bombay batsman. The consensus of opinion is that the action against him is harsh and unwarranted.

At one stage the Indian players contemplated returning home in protest, but it was felt that such a course of action would most certainly scuttle the series, embarrass the organizers, the Cricketers Benefit Fund Series (CBFS), and deprive the beneficiaries and participating cricketers of well-deserved earnings. Moreover the organisers could not be held responsible for the action of the immigration authorities. It is learnt that the organisers suggested that Vengsarkar land in the neighbouring sheikhdom of Dubai by a later flight from Thiruvananthapuram, but the suggestion was understandably turned down.

*****

The beautiful 10,000 capacity Sharjah cricket stadium is spankingly new. Built at a cost of Rs. 1.3 crores, it has a synthetic blue-coloured matting-like surface and a lush grass outfield which is a sight for sore eyes, an oasis in this desert Emirate.

The efforts of Bukhatir and the Cricketers Benefit Fund Series are indeed commendable. It is heartwarming to see the utilisation of petrodollars by a cricket-minded patron for the promotion of the game and by way of appreciation of the services of Test cricketers.

Already, Abdul Rehman Bukhatir is being referred to as the Kerry Packer of the Gulf. But whereas Packer's WSC series had a short though highly successful innings, Bukhatir bids to be more durable, which is all to the good of the game and the players.

At present there are in Dubai 20 internationally renowned *Shairs* (Urdu poets) from Pakistan and a large contingent of film stars from India including Dilip Kumar, Saira Banu, Sanjeev Kumar, the Kapoor brothers (Randhir and Rishi), Neetu Singh, Pran, Shatrughan Sinha, Vinod Mehra and Rajendra Kumar. A 'variety entertainment' programme and a cricket match played last Friday in Dubai, however, were colossal flops.

When David Frith ate his Words

SPORTSWEEK* • *November 16, 1983

The sports-loving Rajmata Gayatri Devi of Jaipur has sent us a "delicious" clipping of a letter from the September 1983 issue of Wisden Cricket Monthly.

In his letter to the editor, Mr. Man Singh, the erstwhile prince of Jaipur who is now resident in the U.S.A., ' writes, "living in a country where cricket is almost unknown, I try to keep up with all the cricket news and scores by reading British journals and papers. I used to subscribe to another leading journal but since its writers were too biased, I decided to change to Wisdem. I find now your journal is guilty of the same sin. I like to read about cricket from a writer who is fair in his reporting, not one-sided".

Continues Mr. Man Singh, "I refer to David Frith's World Cup preview in the Juna WCM. He really berates the Indian team and suggests that they should withdraw from this tournament. I don't know how far back goes, but I go back quite a way and back in 1948, when Bradman's Australians, with Lindwall and Miller, were demolishing England with scores as low as 52 in Tests, no one suggested England should withdraw from Test cricket. Mr. Frith does not take into consideration that this one-day cricket, an English invention, took time to take root in India. I saw this year's semi-final against England, and what a demolishing England got from India, the same team he wants to withdraw from the tourney".

Mr. Man Singh goes on to write, "I will give him a sporting chance to eat his words now that the team he wrote off has won the World Cup, defeating en route West Indies, Australia and England. I am enclosing the cutting from my copy of WCM with the remarks that have so inflamed me. In all fairness to good journalism and sportsmanship, Mr. Frith should eat this...so be a good sport and swallow the lousy paragraph you wrote".

And what did Mr. Frith do?

Ate his offending words "on behalf of thousands who nurtured similar views on India's World Cup chances".

While hoping that the unpalatable truth went down well enough him and the "thousands", we compliment Mr. Frith for upholling the highest traditions of journalisum and fair play.

The letters column in the clipping kindly sent by Rajmata Saheb contains another letter from a Perrie Deighton-Lonsdale of Rea Berkshire, which will be of interest to readers. The con writes, just how many genuine lady cricket crazy fans really do appreciate current craze for cricket glamouras, ups'?

"I have long had a soft spot for, old Imran Khan but having sea hotograprsd every which way, his usual dignified self. and head renouncing on various cricketing on-cricketing subjects with a startling degree of pomposity. begin to doubt it.

"Last summer's bombardment the Test series left me reeling afraid to open a newspaper-would say it filled seats at Test matches, I suppose. "Well. I preferred a bit of Eastern promise and the rest left to the imagination. Now I see David Gower's started with red-striped underpants. and details of his domestic arrangements".

Readers' views, especially from belonging to the distaff side welcome. We would be particular interested how women readers about "Eastern imagination" and "leaving the rest to the imagination.

Make cricket selectors accountable

MID-DAY • January 9, 1997

Javagal Srinath

"Sack the jokers who masquerade as our national cricket selectors."

" Tar and feather them ".

"Parade them in sackcloth and ashes".

Such is the anger being expressed by aficionados towards the cricket selection committee following India's humiliating defeats in the first two Tests in the current series in South Africa.

When the team for the twin tours of South Africa and the West Indies was announced, impartial writers had described the selection process as nothing short of scandalous.

The spineless performance in the first and second Tests in which the team was routed by 328 and 282 runs respectively has resulted in investing the selection with attributes of a scandal.

One need not harp upon the many chinks in the armour of the touring team, namely lack of international experience in general, the woeful imbalance as regards penetration in the attack, the glaring lack of back-up support for Javagal Srinath and Venkatesh Prasad (the manner in which they are having to be bowled into the ground, they will be physical wrecks by the time this leg of the tour is over), the inexplicable absence of reliable opening batsmen and the overall shoddy fielding and catching standard in terms of modern cricket.

But for those who have followed the dismal fortunes of Indian cricket over the years, all this is par for the course.

For as long as one can remember, the I-scratch-your-back-you-scratch-mine syndrome in the working of the Board of Control for Cricket in India (BCCI) regarding the sharing of loaves and fishes of office has been the bane, nay curse.

No wonder, then, that Indian cricket history should be replete with instances of injustice and favouritism.

Under the pernicious and perfidious zonal representation (more correctly, quota) system, the high-and-mighty inquisitors rather than selectors have learnt how to omit players of real merit and talent from zones other than their own to placate their masters in their state associations, to whom they owe their selection on the national selection committee.

The cricket selectors have been a law unto themselves, with nobody to answer to except the powers-that-be in the cricket board. Witness the high-handed manner in which Chandrakant Pandit has been stripped of his Central Zone captaincy. A contemptible travesty of justice, this, if ever there was one.

Given the craze for the game of cricket in our country and national pride (if not chauvinism and jingoism) which modern sport engenders the world over, it is time the selection committees of all sports disciplines in the country were made answerable to the people of the country.

A handful of individuals, for whatever reason, should not be allowed to let down the hopes and aspirations of an entire nation.

The legal ramifications of sports associations and federations of the kind which obtain in India by virtue of their being 'autonomous' should not mean licence to abuse authority, to bring the image of Indian sport into disrepute, to make it a laughing-stock internationally.

Moreover, there is no reason why the captain of the national cricket team should not have a vote in the selection process.

A former Pakistan captain was known to have not only the final, but the only say in matters of team selection stemming out of his conviction that if he is to risk being blamed for his team's unsatisfactory performance, he must have a major hand in its composition to ensure the best results.

Even after due allowance is made for the differences in style of functioning of the cricket boards in India and Pakistan, one wishes Indian captains would demonstrate similar assertiveness in the national and, indeed, in their own interest.

To give them their due, the South Africans have been deserving winners in both Tests having outplayed India in every department of the game. At the same time it has been proved yet again that the myopic policy of preparing easy-paced wickets at home in India to suit our players has boomeranged. Cocks of the walk at home, they are today considered 'poor travellers', worse than even England.

Moreover, the pigeons have come home to roost, what with the surfeit of limited-overs cricket at the expense of the five-day variety for which our cricket board has gone hellbent-for-leather, in its frenzied pursuit of gate-money at home and abroad.

One's heart goes out to Javagal Srinath and Venkatesh Prasad who have toiled manfully against an opposition thirsting for revenge, without much back-up support and with poor support from their fielders.

Whereas Sachin Tendulkar and Mohammed Azharuddin more than lived up to their formidable reputations as belonging to the numero uno category of batsmen of the world in the first innings of the Cape Town Test, they must be held culpable of irresponsibility in the second innings, when they threw away their wickets in a manner unbecoming of their seniority in a young side and their standing in world cricket.

Of the much-hyped 'new' Azharuddin. the less said the better. This writer is no admirer of the new found cavalier, devil-may-care approach of the former captain.

His swashbuckling antics at Cape Town as, indeed at Calcutta and Kanpur in the last (home) series against South Africa, may have been considered orgasmic by the uninitiated brought up to gourmandise on the fast-food of one-day pyjama cricket. In my view, they were abdication of responsibility to his team.

"Azhar's enjoying himself and that's the way he should be allowed to play hereafter" exult his admirers.

Enjoying himself he may be, but should that be at the expense of the team's—and the interest? If one were to go by the criteria of undeserved selection in the first place, injury, unsatisfactory form thus far on tour and lack of commitment and motivation, at least five if not more members of the squad in South Africa need to be replaced.

There is still time before the third Test, commencing on January 16, and the one-dayers to follow, to recall them and send out in their place the likes of Ajay Jadeja, Abey Kuruvilla, Salil Ankola and in the absence of any other experienced players, Robin Singh and Vinod Kambli (the last three have demonstrated good form in the ongoing Deodhar Trophy League tie at Mohali).

Their undeniable talent and experience may yet help resurrect a battle-scared unit and inject into it an element of *jazbah* (spirit) or chutzpah if you will while enabling the team to retrieve prestige lost because of a curious selection process.

POSTSCRIPT: Will the pooh-bahs of the BCCI please explain the logic of making the team fly back home all the way from Bermuda and soon thereafter back to the Caribbean for the West Indies tour? It seems there is a travel agent genius in the august ranks of the Board.

High time MCA & CCI kiss and make up

***MID-DAY* • December 9, 2004**

Listening to the evergreen Jagjit Singh render his intoxicating ghazals in inimitable dulcet voice on the salubrious floodlit lawns of the Cricket Club of India last Tuesday night made me ruminate on the tragedy of the Brabourne Stadium.

I use the word 'tragedy' advisedly because that is precisely the sad tale of what is, arguably, among the most beautiful stadiums in the world and the venue of some of cricket's most stirring historic and memorable exploits in days gone by.

History emanates from, tradition abounds, in every nook and cranny of the Brabourne, and the continuing acquisition, restoration and display of cricket photographs, paintings and memorabilia make the old stadium, now renovated, a truly historic, well-maintained edifice comparable with Lord's and the Melbourne Cricket Ground (MCG).

It was, therefore, logical for the parent bodies of the three afore-mentioned stadia - the Marylebone Cricket Club, the Melbourne Cricket Club and the Cricket Club of India - to enter into an informal fraternal association, which saw the CCI host the first triangular inter-club tournament last year. Ask any international cricketer, who has played at the Brabourne, what he thinks of the stadium and chances are, a 'chinaman' to a 'doosra', he will lapse into ecstasy.

With all due respect to the late Mr Seshrao Wankhede, who was a very close friend of mine, the stadium he built almost a cricket ball's throw away to prove a point in the face of arrogant obduracy of the powers-that-be, that then ruled the roost at the CCI, over the issue of allocation of seats to affiliated members of the Bombay Cricket Association (as it was then called), is not a patch on the world-renowned Brabourne.

If a cricket match at the Brabourne Stadium is a joy to behold, any encounter at the Wankhede can be a painful experience, starting with cramped, uncomfortable seats and lack of basic facilities, stinking toilets included. Entry and exit are nightmarish, the narrow approaches a veritable disaster waiting to happen.

The Wankhede does not have a Clubhouse en suite like the Brabourne. Theresidential accommodation at the two stadia are like chalk is to cheese, the improved facilities at the latter now comparable to the best internationally.

Similarly, the dressing rooms at the Wankhede suffer by comparison, although it must be admitted that those at the Brabourne could have been better designed in keeping with modern-day requirements of the game. That said, the Wankhede Stadium has proximity to train and bus facilities and world-class floodlights (which the CCI does not, at present), and the compact design of the amphitheatre enables the spectator to be seated almost cheek-by-jowl to the action than at the Brabourne.

Kevin Pietersen walks back to the pavillion after being bowled by Munish Ansari for 26 runs against CCI President's XI in a three-day warm-up match at Brabourne Stadium on February 15,2006

A lot of water has flowed in the adjacent Arabian Sea since Mr Wankhede's stadium was inaugurated with understandable - and well-deserved - pride and fanfare for Mansur Ali Khan Pataudi's Test team against Clive Lloyd's West Indians in 1974-75.

Meanwhile, the managements of the two stadia have converted them, for the most part, into hallowed monuments, sacrosanct tourist attractions, and places of pilgrimage for cricket's devotees.

Meanwhile, the city's cricketing fraternity has had to make do with sub-standard playing facilities for matches at the junior, inter-school, inter-collegiate and inter-club (like the Mid Day Kanga league) tournaments in the few crowded maidans available - that is when our netas do not hijack them for their tamashas.

* It's time the two stadia were put to better use for the game of cricket, for which they were originally intended. Ideally, they should be the nursery from which a thousand flowers must bloom, to borrow an expression from Mao Tse Tung.

* It's time, perhaps, for equitable time-sharing of resources in a metropolis, bursting at the seams, in the larger interest of the game.

* It's time for the interests of the city's cricketers to prevail over the narrow, sectarian concerns of administrators.

* However, the good news is that sanity seems to have prevailed between the Mumbai Cricket Association (MCA) and the CCI, one instance being the allotting of the Australian team's opening tour fixture recently to the Brabourne Stadium.

* From all accounts, the Australians were bowled over, if triteness be forgiven, with the facilities at the discarded venue.

* One also has reason to believe that, now that the passage of time has settled the dust on a senseless, ego-driven controversy, the time is opportune for the MCA and CCI to let bygones be bygones and talk turkey in the larger interest of game and city.

KHALIDOSCOPE entreats the warring factions to eschew sectarian and egoistic considerations, turn the clock back, if necessary, respond to imperatives and act in the best interests of the game and its devotees in Mumbai.

Given a spirit of give-and-take as regards the justified demand of MCA, the parent body, for a larger allotment of seats for any international fixture in Mumbai and the international perception stakes for our decaying metropolis, it's time the two protagonists came to terms keeping in mind the adage "When an irresistible object meets and immovable force, something's gotta give ..."

Surely, seasoned, action-oriented Maharashtrian politician Sharad Pawar, who presides over the destines of the MCA, and CCI president Raj Singh Dungarpur, known for his passion for the game and the admirable care and efficiency with which he runs his club, can sit across the table and sort out their differences.

All that it calls for is foresight, sweet reasonableness and an uncompromising concern for the game of cricket.

The moment is here at hand. History beckons. Will they be equal to the occasion?

Is BCCI prepared for a Langer-like situation?

MID-DAY* • *April 7, 2006* • *Sydney

Justin Langer

Australian opening Test batsman Justin Langer may well have played his last cricket match last week if neurosurgeons find long-term damage to his head.Doctors admit that the daredevil 35-year old could have been killed had he gone ahead with his courageous (foolhardy?) resolve to go out to bat (KHALIDOSCOPE, April 6) if Brett Lee and Michael Kasprowicz had not knocked up the runs required for victory.From an Indian perspective, the incident has highlighted the responsibility of the Board of Control for Cricket in India (BCCI), and the multitudinous legal ramifications it throws up, should an Indian player be in a similar situation.

Batsmen are increasingly being struck on their helmets these days: Sachin Tendulkar, Virender Sehwag and Akash Chopra on the last tour of Australia and Anil Kumble on the 2001-02 West Indies tour are only a few cases in point.One wonders if the BCCI has a contingency plan in place to deal with similar situations that would ensure the safety and well-being of our cricketers some of who, given the craze for the game in India, are national treasures, no less.The West Australian veteran of 100 Tests returned home to Perth yesterday afternoon after being forced to pull out of the Australians' present tour of Bangladesh, following a nasty blow to the head incurred when he ducked into a vicious rising delivery from Makhaya Ntini.

The world champions won the Test by two wickets in a nail biting finish last Tuesday to complete a 3-0 whitewash.Skipper Ricky Ponting said after the match that, with his team having wrapped up the rubber 2-0 and seeing Langer's stubborn resolve, although still suffering from concussion, he would have considered declaring the innings closed, thereby forfeiting the match.Langer, who admitted yesterday to being "scared after the neurosurgeons' diagnosis", joked later he would not have spoken to Ponting ("a good mate") had the captain declared."Every cricketer wants to be a hero," he said at his Perth home yesterday, as he hugged youngest daughter Amy in his arms.Langer's wife, Sue, mother of their four daughters, had reinforced his own decision to bat (he had even donned pads, chest pad and helmet in readiness when his team was struggling to attain the target) saying she could not live with him if he didn't bat if needed.However, his father had advised him to put the "interests of his wife and daughters ahead of his cricket aspirations".

Langer is arguably the most battered batsman in history. He has twice spent time in hospital in the course of his 17-year first class career. Statisticians who keep a record of such matters aver that he has been hit on the helmet seven times — in Tests, ODIs, domestic matches, and at nets. This includes the number of times he has been hit while fielding in the suicidal short leg position, where Raman Lamba was fatally hit during a game in Dhaka some years ago. No longer permitted to stand in that position, Langer has taken to fielding in the slips.The Australian opener's injury has brought to the fore the important issue of team doctors and captains having a legal responsibility to protect players in such circumstances.

A spokesman of Cricket Australia is quoted as being non-committal: "The safety and welfare of payers is always of paramount importance. Cricket Australia continues to take this issue very seriously."While admitting there was no Australian doctor with the team in South Africa, the spokesman said that a local doctor and other specialists had advised Langer to take no further part in the match. He stated that team doctors would be considered negligent if they allowed an obviously concussed batsman like Langer to go to the crease.

TVS Victor
TVS Victor
TVS Victor